Penguin

BELOW THE PEACOCK FAN
First Ladies of the Raj

Marian Fowler was born and grew up near Toronto. She received a Ph.D. in English literature from the University of Toronto and has taught at York University. She is the author of the widely acclaimed books *The Embroidered Tent: Five Gentlewomen in Early Canada* and *Redney: A Life of Sara Jeannette Duncan,* and was the recipient of the Canadian Biography Award. Marian Fowler divides her time between a flat in London and a country house near Shelburne, Ontario.

BELOW THE PEACOCK FAN

—•—

FIRST LADIES OF THE RAJ

Marian Fowler

Penguin Books

PENGUIN BOOKS

Published by the Penguin Group
Penguin Books Canada Ltd., 2801 John Street, Markham, Ontario, Canada L3R 1B4
Penguin Books, 27 Wrights Lane, London W8 5TZ, England
Viking Penguin Inc., 40 West 23rd Street, New York, New York 10010, USA
Penguin Books Australia Ltd., Ringwood, Victoria, Australia
Penguin Books (NZ) Ltd., 182-190 Wairau Road, Auckland 10, New Zealand
Penguin Books Ltd., Registered Offices: Harmondsworth, Middlesex, England

First published in Viking by Penguin Books Canada Limited, 1987
Published in Penguin Books, 1988

Copyright © Marian Fowler, 1987

Manufactured in Canada

Canadian Cataloguing in Publication Data

Fowler, Marian, 1929-
Below the peacock fan: first ladies of the raj

ISBN 0-14-008233-6

1. Women—India—History—Biography.
2. British—India—History—Biography.
3. India—History—British occupation, 1765-1947.
I. Title.

HQ1742.F68 1987   305.4′821054   C86-093723-2

The map of India on page 11 is from *The Great Mutiny India 1857* by
Christopher Hibbert, © Christopher Hibbert, 1978. Reprinted
by permission of Penguin Books Ltd., Viking Penguin Inc., and
David Higham Associates Limited.

THIS BOOK IS DEDICATED

TO THE MEMORY OF

MY GREAT GRANDFATHER ROBERT MACONACHIE,

WHO SERVED IN THE PUNJAB

AS AN INDIAN CIVIL SERVICE OFFICER

FROM 1871 TO 1896

ACKNOWLEDGEMENTS

I am indebted, first of all, to the late Professor Sydney Checkland, Professor Emeritus, University of Glasgow, who suggested to me in the spring of 1984 that a book on India's Vicereines would be an interesting project. To my deep regret, he did not live to see the finished product.

My research was carried on mainly at the London Library and at the India Office Library in London, England. In both places, the staffs were courteous, efficient and extremely helpful, especially Dr R.J. Bingle; Director, Mr D.M. Blake, European Manuscripts division; and Miss Jill Spanner, Prints and Drawings, at the India Office Library. I spent a fascinating week in the Leeds District Archives working on Charlotte Canning's papers. Mr W.J. Connor and his staff made my time there pleasant and profitable. I am grateful to the Earl of Harewood, and to Mr Gerald Long of the Estate Office, Harewood House, Leeds, who arranged for me to peruse at my leisure the folio volumes of Charlotte Canning's watercolours, now in the Old Library of Harewood House. It is a charming setting for them, one that I feel sure the fastidious Countess Canning, always so concerned with matters of interior decoration, would heartily approve. Some of my research was done in the Metropolitan Library, Toronto, and I am grateful to the staff there, and also to its architect, Mr Raymond Moriyama, who designed such a truly beautiful setting in which to work.

I would like to thank those individuals and institutions who granted me permission to quote from unpublished manuscript material. These include: the Earl of Harewood, for permission to quote

from the Canning papers; the Hon. David Lytton Cobbold of Knebworth House for permission to quote from Lytton family papers
and Edith, Countess of Lytton's privately printed Indian journal;
the India Office Library and Mr J.C. Lyall for permission to quote
from the Lyall papers; the India Office Library, Lord Scarsdale and
the Trustees of the Kedleston Estate for permission to quote from
the Curzon papers; the India Office Library and the Strachey Trust
for permission to quote from the Strachey collection; the India
Office Library, who own the Canning scrapbook and Fanny Eden's
journals; Lady Alexandra Metcalfe, for permission to quote from
Mary Curzon's letters published in *Lady Curzon's India*, edited by
John Bradley; the Department of Palæography and Diplomatic,
University of Durham, for permission to quote from Emily Eden's
letters to Elizabeth Copley and to Maria, Countess of Grey. I am
particularly grateful to Dr J.M. Fewster, Senior Assistant Keeper
of the Department of Palæography and Diplomatic, University of
Durham, who was kind enough to inform me of the existence in
the Grey collection of the letters to the Countess of Grey.

Mr Andrew Drummond allowed me to reproduce his portraits
of Fanny and Emily Eden, and became a valued friend as well. The
Earl of Harewood, the Hon. David Lytton Cobbold, Miss Mary
Lutyens, Lord Scarsdale and Major William A. Spowers graciously
gave me permission to reproduce photographs or portraits in their
private collections. The institutions who granted me permission to
reproduce illustrative material are listed in the picture credits at the
end of the book.

My editors, Catherine Yolles and Mary Adachi, were hard-
working and patient, and I am grateful to them both for greatly
improving the manuscript as it went through revisions. Cynthia
Good, Editorial Director at Penguin Books, Canada, also read part
of the manuscript and made extremely useful suggestions. My mother,
as always, read each chapter as it came from the typewriter and
offered the kind of unqualified approval only mothers can give. My
son, Tim, not only read parts of the book at various stages but also

had me as a short-tempered and preoccupied flat-mate when I was working on revisions. His unfailing good humour, vast fund of general knowledge and willingness to take on domestic chores were all very much appreciated.

In the Acknowledgements of male authors, the final paragraph almost always expresses their heartfelt gratitude to the willing wife who did all the really tedious chores, such as typing, proof-reading and footnoting. I therefore wish to state with modest pride that I did these tasks all by myself.

One final note: The spelling of Indian place names, particularly in the early days of the Raj, was extremely idiosyncratic and wildly inconsistent. I have therefore modernized both spelling and punctuation in quoting from published and unpublished sources.

Elvaston Lodge, London.

CONTENTS

BELOW THE PEACOCK FAN

INTRODUCTION

This book traces the progress of four remarkable women embarked on the greatest adventure of their lives. There they were, settled snugly into the plush upholstery of their English days, when suddenly the call came: brother or husband had been appointed by the British Sovereign as Governor-General of India, and sister or wife was expected to accompany him to that distant, disturbing land. One moment, they were looking forward to afternoon tea under the elms if the mists cleared in time and the sun came out; the next, they were painfully uprooted, flung half-way round the world to a country where to venture outdoors when the sun struck straight down was to risk sudden death. None of them, even for an instant, thought of *not* going to India, of staying behind and sending their menfolk off without them. All of them went willingly, motivated by duty and love. They went to India not to govern, but to give, looking not for power and a place in history but for praise from their beloved, and a place in his heart.

Emily Eden went out to India in 1836, together with her sister Fanny, to look after their bachelor brother, Lord Auckland. Charlotte Canning arrived there with her husband in 1856. Edith Lytton went out with hers in 1876, and Mary Curzon landed with her "imperious Lordship" in 1898.

I have chosen to view each of these four women in the light of three particular historical backgrounds: their previous social and moral conditioning, the experiences of other British women living in India, and, thirdly, the changing aspects of the British Raj itself.

As a guide to the parameters of their conditioning I perused that genre of literature known as the female conduct books, which set forth the character traits and behaviour expected of young gentle-women. These books were required reading for young English women throughout the eighteenth and nineteenth centuries. They were often given to young ladies on their birthdays, their fly-leaves fondly inscribed by aunts or godmothers, and their lucky recipients were expected to learn the requisite conventions and follow them to the letter. Tensions and traumas within the female psyche began to occur when these rigidly programmed ladies found themselves in some radically different setting in which their regular patterns of conduct were either inappropriate or impossible. In other corners of Britain's Empire, not just India, British women in the nineteenth century were forced by frontier conditions to change their concepts of role and behaviour. In *The Embroidered Tent: Five Gentlewomen in Early Canada* I traced the progress through the intimidating wilderness of five British women, two of whom were Governor's ladies. In some ways, this present book can be seen as a sequel. For all five women in that book, and three in this, the challenge of a strange country represented a double bind, for married women had to adapt not only to an unfamiliar setting and role, but also to a husband in process of adapting to a new culture and career. Since the nineteenth century was the age of the dominant male and the dependent female, it was the wife who had to mould herself to the needs of her husband, never the other way round. He acted and she reacted.

Adapting to a familiar man and an unfamiliar land was a challenge not just for First Ladies, the Lady Sahibs, but for all the British women who, in increasing numbers, found themselves in India during the nineteenth century. How these women coped and how their reactions compare and contrast with those of First Ladies forms the second background context of this book. The Lady Sahibs were in India for only five or six years; the *memsahibs*, as they were called, went out with husbands who were soldiers or merchants or civil servants and stayed for the long, hard ordeal. "India is an ogre, eating us up body and soul," declares one, "ruining our health, our

4

tempers, our morals, our manners, our babies."[1] Far more than First Ladies, cosseted within the Viceregal court, the *memsahibs* had to meet the challenge of India head on. We catch sight of some who succeeded: Florentia, Lady Sale, Fanny Parkes and others. "Some beneath the further stars / Bear the greater burden / Set to serve the lands they rule" Kipling wrote, referring, as usual, to the men.[2] Surely the greater burden was the women's.

Thackeray, at least, understood. "What a strange pathos seems to me to accompany all our Indian story," exclaims Colonel Newcome in *The Newcomes*. "Besides that official history which fills Gazettes and embroiders banners with the name of victory ... besides the splendour and conquest, the wealth and glory, the crowned ambition, the conquered danger, the vast prize, and the blood freely shed in winning it – should not one remember the tears too? Besides the lives of myriads of British men ... think of the women."[3]

Yes, think of the women. Think of the fears, the fevers, the homesickness, the isolation. Think of the cost of Empire to the women. Most accounts of the British presence in India, both history books and memoirs, are masculine in their bias: tales of administration and annexation, boundaries and battlefields. I have tried to right the balance, to tell a small part of the women's story of India, the private view of heart and mind.

In addition to First Ladies and *memsahibs*, there is another important protagonist in this story: the British Raj itself. The term "Raj" is a Hindi word meaning rule or sovereignty, and I have used it to denote both the rule of London's East India Company in India, which ended in 1858, and the rule of the British Crown and Parliament, which ended in 1947. Our particular segment of Raj history begins in 1836, when the East India Company had already been in India for more than two hundred years, but since its plans and personnel were still rather modest, I have called this period Early Raj. Britain's trade with India had begun on the last day of 1600, when Queen Elizabeth I signed the charter granting the newly formed East India Company an eastern monopoly. In 1613, Britain received permission from the Great Moghul, Ruler of India, to found its first trading post or "factory" along the north-west coast. A year later the first cargo of Indian cotton and indigo reached London. After that, Britain never looked back, grabbing India's raw materials – sugar, cotton, silk, indigo – for her own industries, and shipping out to expanding Indian markets her manufactured goods. After the death of its Emperor Aurungzeb in 1707, the Moghul Empire grew more and more divided by internal warfare and eventually collapsed. The British, whose military and economic power outpaced that of France and Holland and Portugal, marched into the disarray and began to extend their sphere of influence and direct rule across the Indian subcontinent.

Our story continues through the blood-bath of the 1857 mutiny and the changeover from East India Company to Crown on November 1, 1858. I have designated this period the Middle Raj years. When the Imperial Assemblage proclamation declared Queen Victoria Empress of India on January 1, 1877, the High Raj period began in self-conscious solemnity. By 1905, when the fourth and last of our ladies left India, the Late Raj period had begun, marked by growing doubts and disillusionment on the part of the British, and growing demands for self-government on the part of the Indians. For India's First Ladies, the Raj was conduct book and conscience, a very formal presence, and a formidable one, casting a larger and larger shadow across the map of India.

As the years passed, the Raj went through four main changes of personality and mood, being by turns fanciful and greedy, sanctimonious and fearful, hypocritical and hidebound, arrogant and despondent – and doomed. India's Lady Sahibs had to adapt to that touchy and temperamental presence, the Raj itself, as well as to their own particular Governor-General.

The Governor-General, so called from 1774 on, was the Chief Executive of British India; after 1858, he was sometimes called Viceroy instead, a name unofficially acquired to designate the representative of the British Sovereign in the Indian subcontinent. There were in all thirty-three Governors-General of India, from Warren

Hastings, who took office in 1774, to Earl Mountbatten, who was at the helm until Independence Day in 1947. Through the years, the Governor-General surrounded himself with a steadily increasing amount of pomp and circumstance. On all state occasions, the Lord Sahib, with his Lady close by sometimes, sat on a throne surrounded by native attendants splendidly garbed, holding aloft those symbols of eminence traditionally used by Indian royalty. There were golden maces and silver sticks to signify high rank and authority. There were fly-whisks made of yaks' tails to keep not flies but evil spirits from settling on the august head. There were peacock-feather fans with long handles and peacock-feather brushes with short ones made of gold, the peacock being an Indian royal symbol whose plumage-eyes could outstare the Evil Eye and so keep the royal personage unharmed. The full pomp of maces, sticks, fly-whisks, fans and brushes was trotted out for all Viceregal Levees, Drawing-Rooms, Investitures and Durbars. On some occasions there was the golden umbrella, held over the heads of Viceroy and Vicereine for state processions via elephant or carriage. In Late Raj years, the panoply and parade of the British court in India certainly outshone Aurungzeb's earlier Moghul splendours at Delhi; and that was exactly the point: to impress on native minds the Might and Majesty of the British Lion in symbolic terms that they could understand.

The male halves of the Viceregal pairs had prestige and power, but they never felt the real India. They were much too busy super-imposing their Western grid of reason and regulations and rhetoric on the land. They spent their days fenced round with secretaries and officials and red dispatch boxes piled high as brick walls. Two of the Viceroys we shall meet were compulsive workers; the other two took a more cavalier approach to their duties. Because they were men, *their* conduct books had told them they were expected to be active, aggressive, rational creatures. So they commanded and inspected and went hunting and planned impressive Durbars. Their womenfolk, on the other hand, had been programmed to be passive, receptive and intuitive. The First Ladies of India, far more than the

Governors-General, thus had the proper training to send their imaginations soaring beyond the gates of Government House and to respond to India's unique pulse.

The women had the right frame of mind and plenty of time as well. The hot weather forced them to spend their days on sofas, behind closed shutters. They reclined like invalids, dreamy and languid, in darkened rooms. When they went abroad, they were often carried in palanquins (covered litters, each carried by four servants), which more than one Lady Sahib likened to coffins. Physically, India reduced them to almost total indolence; if they dropped a handkerchief a servant would pick it up. They perspired gently in their muslin dresses, thought about India, recorded their impressions in long journal-letters mailed off to family and friends. Two of them, Emily Eden and Charlotte Canning, spent long hours as well sketching and painting. India moved them, and they tried, with pen and brush, to capture it all, the diamonds and the dust, the real India.

But what *was* the "real" India? According to Jawaharlal Nehru, India is "a myth and an idea, a dream and a vision, and yet very real and present and pervasive."[4] When they arrived, the Lady Sahibs tended to see India with the myth of the exotic East firmly in place: jewelled rajahs and caparisoned elephants. And this vision materialized before their delighted eyes; one rajah whom the Eden sisters met wore pearls "as big as pigeons' eggs," and another's horse looked like "a living map of emeralds." How they viewed emeralds and elephants, however, is not nearly as interesting to chart in their journals as how they viewed what lay coiled underneath. For each of them, the real India flashed a different underbelly. They saw it, and were forever changed.

"India tests a woman's character to the uttermost," wrote Maud Diver, novelist and long-term resident. "For, with all its surface laughter and lightness, Indian life is real, and you live it desperately from start to finish."[5] Beneath the gold and glitter, the real India was mud and muddle: mud which Fanny Eden once saw being stuffed by friends into the mouth of a dying man on the bank of the Ganges,[6] and muddle everywhere one looked. The confusion resulted from the fact that India's contrasts were so violent and so irreconcilable that one could never find a mean, or any consistency. In the northern plains, where all four Lady Sahibs toured, the ground was dead flat, mile after mile after mile, and somehow, pounded into it was a power and a hunger terrifying as the ocean's. At Simla, in the Himalayas, where the Lady Sahibs spent the hottest months, there was, as Charlotte Canning noted, "a sea of hilltops" with "no straight lines, and not a spot of level ground. Here, if one sees ten yards level, one screams out, 'What a site for a house!' "[7] In the hot weather, it never, ever rained; in the monsoon season, it poured torrentially every day.

Nothing but extremes, even the colours were violent. No pencil-shaded landscapes, misty and gentle, like England's. Only splendour and squalor, opulence and offal, always together, cancelling each other out, leaving a void without values. The Viceroy's silver how-dah (seat for elephant's back) was polished with cow-dung; on the stone lions atop the entrance to Government House crouched rows of hideous scavenger birds called adjutants.[8]

No middle ground and no clear dividing line. Nature wouldn't stay outdoors; lizards darted up one's bedroom walls, snakes coiled on the bathroom tiles, huge insects scuttled across the damask at dinner. Mary Curzon once woke to find a stinking civet cat drinking the glass of milk beside her bed.

And nothing was permanent, everything decayed. Fish insects ate one's favourite books, and one's favourite relatives in their silver frames; dresses shredded into strips during the rains, mould obscured the outline of one's shoes and matting parted beneath one's feet.

Fears clustered in the mind as thickly as fruit-bats in the trees, flew, without warning, straight for the centre. Everything was so sudden in India: twilight, for instance, or death: brightness one minute, blackness the next, someone chatting pleasantly at break-fast, struck down by cholera at noon, dead by evening. Fear of disease, of dying, of the unexpected, and, the nastiest fear of all:

fear of falling into the darkest crevices of one's psyche, below the propriety of peacock fans. The Lady Sahibs were buttoned and gloved, but all around them were naked bodies, brown-skinned ones bathing in the Ganges, stone ones copulating on a frieze. India taunted, India tempted.

After five or six years of coping, it was time to go home. The Lord Sahibs returned to England virtually the same men who had gone out, picking up their English lives where they'd left off, elbowing their way forward with the same right-angled rectitude. Not so their women. One never returned to England at all: one died in her prime shortly after her return; all of them, to their last breath, felt the tremendous impact of India on their personalities and in their bones.

All I have had to guide me in plotting the poignant passage to India of Emily, Charlotte, Edith and Mary, are the tangible artefacts which mark their path: bundles of letters, bound journals, fading photographs, watercolour sketches. Occasionally, I have happened on bits of ribbon, pressed ferns, locks of hair; these brought the Lady Sahibs very close. One can still catch the colour of their feelings, but some of the finer shadings must ultimately remain a mystery, like India itself.

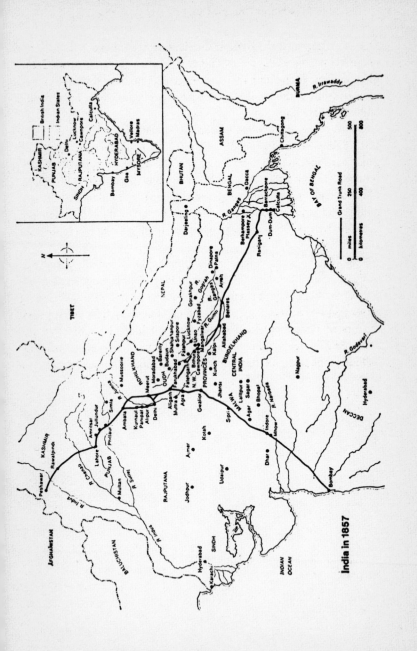

India in 1857

I

EMILY EDEN

Such jewelry as we saw yesterday morning! A native was sent by one of the gentlemen to show us some really good native jewelry. There is an ornament called a supêche, *which the rajahs wear in their turbans, but there is seldom such a handsome one as this man had for sale. It was a diamond peacock, holding in his beak a rope of enormous pearls, which passed through an emerald about the size of a dove's egg.*

EMILY EDEN
Up the Country

SHE HAD BEEN DREAMING again of Eden Farm; she almost always now, whenever she could get to sleep, found herself reliving her happy childhood days in Kent. In this particular dream, she and her favourite sister Mary had been walking down a lane between green hedgerows silvered by early morning mists. Emily cried a little when she woke and realized where she was, still in the *Jupiter*'s stuffy cabin, lurching ahead under a cruel copper sun towards India, every day taking her farther and farther away from her contented English life and her close circle of family and friends. She and George had already been at sea for four months, and she'd been "as sick as death the whole way" as she put it dramatically in a letter to a friend,[1] lying in her bunk, unable to move more than an eyelid, living on a little arrowroot and memories of Eden Farm.

Emily Eden's father, son of a Durham baronet, created first Baron Auckland by William Pitt after a distinguished diplomatic

career, had retired to Eden Farm near Beckenham, Kent, in 1801.
Emily's mother was a daughter of Sir Gilbert Elliot and sister to
the first Earl of Minto, who had become Governor-General of India
in 1806. Emily had been born at Old Palace Yard, Westminster,
on March 4, 1797, so that she was four when the family settled at
Eden Farm. In that year her sister Fanny was born, completing the
close family circle of eight girls and four boys (two more boys had
died in infancy). Emily was educated at home by governesses and
encouraged to read anything she wished. She once boasted to her
lifelong friend, Theresa Lister (née Villiers) that she knew Boswell's
Life of Johnson, Shakespeare and "a great part of the Bible almost
by heart before I was eleven years old."[2] Intellectually she wanted
to keep up with her brother George. Thirteen years her senior,
George was the star and stay of her life; the two of them were very
close, united by private jokes and prejudices against the rest of the
world. Emily felt most at home in the company of George and his
male friends, probably because she herself in personality and tastes
was more "masculine" than "feminine," according to her society's
understanding of those terms. When Emily was growing up, women
were expected to be physically delicate, shy and retiring, submissive
to male authority, passive and intuitive. Their powers of reasoning
were held to be inferior to men's. They were to stay quietly at
home doing their embroidery and dreaming their sentimental dreams.
This is the clear message of the conduct books. Two of the old
favourites when Emily was young were the Reverend James Fordyce's *Sermons to Young Women* (1766) and William Kenrick's *The
Whole Duty of Woman* (1753). Fordyce's *Sermons* had run to fourteen
editions by the time Emily was eighteen, Kenrick's *Whole Duty of
Woman* to seventeen. These two and all the others of the time follow
the Pauline prescription of the New Testament, stating, first of all,
that young ladies must be modest and timid. Kenrick's definition
of modesty includes "diffidence in voicing an opinion and a low,
gentle voice."[3] Proper young ladies were never to show any signs
of learning, nor of wit. "Men of the best sense have been usually
adverse to the thought of marrying a witty female," according to

Fordyce.⁴ Dr John Gregory agrees: "Wit is the most dangerous talent you can possess," he tells his female readers.⁵

Emily Eden, in her formative years, seems to have ignored all this conduct-book advice completely. Politics were not considered a fit subject for women; they were Emily's chief interest. She spent many hours with George and his Whig friends arguing in a carrying voice, showing off her learning and fine mind, making them all laugh with her witty sallies. She was brisk, bold and boisterous. If the conduct-book writers proved to be accurate in their prediction that such a young lady would never find a husband, Emily didn't seem to care.

When her mother died in 1818, Emily was quite content, along with her sister Fanny, also still unmarried, to set up housekeeping with bachelor George, who had become Lord Auckland four years before, upon the death of their father. Fanny was less intellectual than Emily, more feminine and frivolous. George and Emily made a couple; Fanny stood apart, slightly wistful and a little fey. George was "austere and almost forbidding in his manner, silent and reserved in society,"⁶ showing his inner warmth and affection only to Emily. "Today is the first of September," Emily wrote to Theresa in 1827, during an illness, and George "is sitting here with me nursing and coaxing me up, and the partridges are all flying about the world, and he not shooting them" (MEL, p. 140).

In 1829, when George was appointed Commissioner of Greenwich Hospital, he and his two sisters moved into Park Lodge, Greenwich. "I am always so happy here that it frightens me," Emily wrote to Theresa a year later (MEL, p. 205). Emily had George to laugh and gossip with and a delightful garden which he helped her to plant. They filled the house with their mutual friends, including Theresa's brother George Villiers, the future Lord Clarendon and Foreign Secretary. He was Emily's closest male friend, and a lifelong correspondent. "We have heard the chimes at midnight, Master Shallow," she wrote to him years later, recalling one hilarious evening at Greenwich when after dinner, the park having been locked up, "we let ourselves into it through the little garden gate, and had coffee. G. Tierney tied a shawl over his head and gave us imitations of Mrs. Siddons."[7]

In the summer of 1834, the first of Emily's painful uprootings took place, all of them caused by George's blossoming career. Their friend Lord Melbourne became Prime Minister for the first time, and offered George the post of First Lord of the Admiralty. They had to leave Park Lodge and moved into a cottage on Ham Common near Richmond, until Admiralty quarters were ready. "That giving up Greenwich was nearly the death of me," Emily wrote to her friend Pamela Campbell in July:

> Our glorious promotion was inflicted on us on a particular Thursday ... which George and I had set apart for a holiday, and a *tête-à-tête* dinner, and a whole afternoon in that good little garden.... There I sat under the verandah crying. What else could be done, with the roses all out, and the sweetpeas ... and the whole garden looking perfectly lovely (*MEL*, pp. 234 – 35).

All their friends agreed what a plum the Admiralty appointment was for George but "my personal luck," complained Emily, "consists in having entirely lost his society and Greenwich, the two charms of my life" (*MEL*, p. 240). George spent long hours at the Admiralty now; he rushed in and out of the Ham Common house looking stern and preoccupied, while Emily consoled herself by writing the first chapters of an amusing novel called *The Semi-Attached Couple*, and by acquiring a black King Charles spaniel puppy called Chance.

She still saw something of George on their frequent visits to England's most beautiful country houses: Woburn Abbey, Chatsworth, Longleat and Bowood. Emily beat the men at chess, tramped with them through the woods, argued politics round the fire, making the sparks fly. During an 1832 visit to the Cowpers at Panshanger, Lord Melbourne, four years a widower, grew very warm in his attentions to Miss Eden. Emily, however, wasn't looking for a husband: "I am more and more confirmed in the idea that a life of single blessedness is the wisest," she'd written to Theresa in 1826, when she was twenty-nine. So, at Panshanger, she threw cold water on Lord Melbourne's ardour, telling Theresa that "he frightens me and bewilders me and he swears too much," and concluding:

> I know that I am very happy now, and have been so for some years, and that I had rather not change.... I am quite contented with my position in life and only wish it may last. If I were younger, or less spoiled than I have been at home, I daresay I could put up with the difficulties of a new place; but not now. I cannot be blind to the faults of the few men I know well, and though I know many more faults in myself, yet I am used to those, you know, and George is used to them, and it all does beautifully (*MEL*, pp. 215 – 16).

Emily didn't want a mate because, in her eyes, she had one already. She loved her brother George deeply and devotedly and passionately. She thought of George and herself as a permanent couple, and she was quite as dutiful and caring in regard to his physical and mental well-being as any wife. It was Emily's love for George which would radically and permanently alter her life. But not quite yet.

She continued her snug existence, and her round of country-house visits, feeling sometimes a little bored, but most often content, particularly at Bowood, the home of Lord and Lady Lansdowne, where there was "always rather superior society in point of talk."[8] "Lord Auckland I like very much," wrote a fellow guest there in 1833. "He has a grave, gentle manner, with a good deal of dry fun about him. Emily Eden is undeniably clever and pleasant" (*MEL*, footnote to p. 230). In 1834, there was one visitor to Bowood who, had Emily but known, would reappear in her life seven years later in a horribly violent and disturbing way. As she told George Villiers,

There was a Mr. Burnes who has been to Delhi through the
Kabul and Bukhara to Ispahan by routes which no European
has followed before, and he gave us his history, backed up by
a map, in such a lively manner that I swallowed a small quantity
of instruction without much nausea.[9]

George and Emily's companionable times continued, with an
occasional trip abroad. In 1833 they'd gone to Germany, Holland
and Belgium, a journey with "lovely weather and not an accident
– not even a loose lynch pin." "George thought he had left his gold
pencil case at Brussels," Emily reported gaily to George Villiers,
"but he discovered it in the wrong pocket at Antwerp, and that
was our best attempt at a misfortune."[10]

The chill wind of a greater misfortune blew across the velvet
greensward of her life in October 1834. There were rumours of
another promotion for George, this one to Viceregal eminence.
"There was a great *sough* of India for about a fortnight," Emily
wrote to Theresa.

> but I always said it was too bad to be true, which is a dangerous
> assertion to make in most cases, it only hastens the catastrophe.
> But this was such an extreme case, such a horrible supposition,
> that there was nothing for it but to bully it; and the danger is
> over now. Botany Bay would be a joke to it. There is a decent
> climate to begin with, and the fun of a little felony first. But
> to be sent to Calcutta for no cause at all! At all events, I should
> hardly have got there before George got home again, for I
> should have walked across the country to join him, if I had
> gone at all. I think I see myself going into a ship for five months!
> I would not do it for £1000 per day (*MEL*, p. 245).

When the Whigs were returned to office in 1835, Lord Melbourne rewarded his good friend Lord Auckland with the most
prestigious post he had to give: Governor-General of India. In August, Princess Lieven, the Russian ambassador's wife, wrote of it

to Lady Palmerston: "Lord Auckland is to go to India, and his sisters with him. They are making a great sacrifice for ambition's sake. Miss Eden is especially unhappy. They discussed the matter for ages before making up their minds."[11]

Fanny was eager to go, feeling the pull of new adventures; Emily was fearful and reluctant, propelled only by her love for George. She poured out her heart to Pamela Campbell:

> Besides, what is there to say, except "God's will be done." It all comes to that. I certainly look at the climate with dread, and to the voyage with utter aversion. Then, we leave a very happy existence here, and then, worst of all, we leave my sisters and a great many friends.... One thing is quite certain, I could not have lived here without George (MEL, p. 252).

Emily was thirty-eight and felt herself permanently deep-rooted in England. "We shall be off in less than a month I believe, not that I believe anything somehow, – I feel too dreamy and bewildered," she confided to Pamela:

> And besides the deep-seated real Indian calamity, you cannot think what a whirl and entanglement buying and measuring and trying on makes in one's brain, and poor Goliath himself would have been obliged to lie down and rest if he had tried on 6 pairs of stays consecutively.... It is so irritating to want so many things and such cold articles. A cargo of *large fans*; a *silver busk*, because all steel busks become rusty and spoil the stay; night dresses with short sleeves, and net night-caps, because muslin is so hot (MEL, pp. 253 – 54).

In between the frantic shopping and packing, Emily alternated between "blank despair" and blind rage: "I feel as if I could cut somebody's throat quite through – a sort of savage relief" she wrote (LI, 1, 2).

A letter from King William was small consolation:

His Majesty is not surprised that Miss Eden and her Sister should have determined to accompany so affectionate a Brother even to so remote a destination, and He is sensible how much their Society must contribute to his comfort (MEL, p. 259).

William IV was friend and mentor to the sisters; he had once shown them all the paintings at Hampton Court, telling them an improper story about each one. Since Emily and Fanny had grown up in the relaxed moral atmosphere of the Regency, they were quite without prudery and not at all shocked.

"Very few events could be more painful to me than your going," wrote Lord Melbourne to Emily, having brought it all about. "As to health, let us hope for the best," he added, sending her "a Milton, which I have had for a long time" and promising to write. [12]

On Saturday, October 3, 1835, Lord Auckland and the Hon. Emily and Frances Eden set sail from Portsmouth on the *Jupiter*, a tall-masted frigate. Going out with them as George's Military Secretary was the Hon. William Godolphin Osborne, their lively nephew, whose duties in India would be social rather than military, arranging parties and receptions. He had been in India previously with his regiment, the 16th Lancers. Also accompanying the Edens were Dr Drummond, their personal physician; St Cloup, a French negro chef; Emily's maids Wright and Rosina, the latter a half-Portuguese, half-Indian *ayah*; Fanny's maid Jones; William's half-dozen greyhounds; and Emily's spaniel Chance. It would be a long voyage; no steam as yet to help, and no Suez Canal, so ships went round the Cape and could take as long as six months to reach India.

Day after day, Emily lay in her bunk, feeling, for the first time in her life, quite as fragile and timid and helpless as the conduct-book writers decreed a lady should feel. It annoyed her that both George and Fanny were particularly well; Fanny's cheeks grew pinker with the excitement and the brisk winds on deck, her soft brown hair escaping in tendrils round her face.

Keeping George from growing bored was always for Emily a worrisome preoccupation. Occasionally they had a day's calm, when the sea looked "like a plate of silver that has been cleaned by a remarkably good under-butler" who "has not left a spot on it" (*LI*, I, 70). When the ship was becalmed, George grew "fit to hang himself" (*LI*, I, 57), but at least Emily's stomach stopped heaving. Her fears, however, continued to oppress her:

> George is very kind, and he says it will be easy to make new interests. It will for him, who has more to learn and to do than the twenty-four hours can hold – and he has no *time* for regrets. But, at all events, it must be some time before I can care about Calcutta; and there, too, he will be so busy that I shall lose him again as a companion (*LI*, I, 66).

En route to India, however, while Fanny strode the deck with William, George was still Emily's and they had some good laughs together. As she wrote to her sister Mary:

> I had been very sick since Thursday and had not got up, but was so tired of the noise of my own cabin, that I put on my dressing-gown and rolled into George's cabin on Saturday afternoon, and, by a lucky combination of lurches, was pitched on to his sofa. He ... tucked himself up on the other side of the sofa by way of steadying us. Just then the ship took one of her deepest rolls.... George was thrown upon me, and we both laughed so that he could not get up again (*LI*, I, 33 – 34).

Emily's insouciant description of this accidental physical closeness to her brother is innocent enough, but suggests that, while she probably never acted on it, she did indeed feel some erotic attraction to George.

Humour helped, but the feeling of unreality never went away. "How little we thought in old Grosvenor Street days," she wrote to Pamela,

> that in the middle of February, when we ought to be shivering

in a thick yellow fog, George and I should be established on a pile of cushions in the stern window of his cabin, he without his coat and waistcoat and shoes, learning Hindustani by the sweat of his brow. I, with only one petticoat and a thin dressing-gown on, a large fan in one hand and a pen in the other (*MEL*, p. 261).

So the voyage continued, the monotonous days one long blur of molten seas and tedium and inner tremors.

Five months after they had left England, on March 4, 1836, Emily found herself moving slowly up the Hooghly River towards Calcutta. It was her thirty-ninth birthday, a fact which, as she recorded in a letter late that night, "nobody knows or cares about except myself."[13] The outskirts of Calcutta, at least, looked reassuring. Facing the river, along Garden Reach, were the white Palladian villas of the British merchants who had grown rich on East India Company trade. Their mansions were elegant and stately, rather like those skirting London's Green Park.

The Governor-General's party landed at Chandpal Ghat at ten P.M., two hours behind schedule, then drove to Government House, their new home. It, too, looked reassuringly British and dignified, gleaming white through the dark night, its windows ablaze with light. Copied from Robert Adam's design for Kedleston Hall in Derbyshire, Government House had been completed in 1803. At the time the East India Company directors had criticized Lord Wellesley's extravagance in building it, but later grudgingly admitted that it was a fit symbol of British power in the Indian subcontinent. There it stood, solid and symmetrical, with central portico and dome, imposing Ionic pillars and four extensive wings. Around it were six acres of garden.

Emily and George, Fanny and William, slowly mounted the immense flight of steps, and entered a room more than one hundred feet long. Beyond it was the huge marble banqueting hall with two impressive rows of Doric columns where Sir Charles Metcalfe, the

2 Public entrance, Government House, Calcutta

provisional Governor-General who had succeeded Lord William
Bentinck, was half-way through dinner with eighty guests. Lord
Auckland was promptly sworn in and the banquet resumed.[14]

The banquet proved an accurate foretaste of the formality, the
flatness of Government House routines. For the duration of her
residence there, Emily would feel cut off from real living, suffering
particularly from the superfluity of servants, who deprived her of
her privacy, and of many of her practical, day-to-day English activities. She described a typical day to Pamela Campbell. Emily
rose at eight, dressed with the help of Wright and two native maids,
then,

> I have all my rooms shut up and made dark before I leave them,
> and go out into my passage, where I find my two tailors sitting
> cross-legged, making my gowns; the two Dacca embroiderers
> whom I have taken into my private pay working at a frame
> of flowers that look like paintings; Chance, my little dog, under
> his own servant's arm; a *meter* with his broom to sweep the
> rooms, two bearers who pull the *punkahs* [ceiling fans]; a sentry
> to mind that none of these steal anything; and a *Jemadar* [chief

servant] and four *Hurkurus* [postal runners] who are my particular attendants and follow me about wherever I go – my tail (4 times shorter than George's). These people are all dressed in white muslin, with red and gold turbans and sashes, and are so picturesque that when I can find no other employment for them I make them sit for their pictures.

They all make their *salaam* [bow] and we proceed to breakfast which is in an immense marble hall, and is generally attended by the two Aides-de-Camp in waiting, the doctor, the private Secretary, and anybody who may be transacting business at the time (*MEL*, p. 269).

After breakfast, Emily read or sketched or sewed in her darkened room. After luncheon – called *tiffin* – at two, she could loosen her stays and doze for an hour or two. At six, shutters and doors were flung open, and she and Fanny went out for a ride on horseback or in the carriage, returning in time to dress for eight o'clock dinner. After dinner, on nights when there were no parties, they played whist or écarté, with much yawning, and went to bed at ten.

Like all British women in India, Emily was suffering severely from having "nothing to do." It was the piteous cry of the typical *memsahib*, who found herself with no domestic chores, "few companions of her own sex, no shop windows to look at, no new books to read, no theatres," as novelist Flora Annie Steel would later observe, living out her desolate twenty-two years in the Punjab's remote stations, while her husband dispensed justice to the natives.[15] British men in India found relief in action, but women rarely found "the same amount of interest and occupation for their lives as their fathers or husbands" and were consequently "wont to complain of its tedium and monotony.... It is only a really energetic character," declares one British visitor,

> that does not become demoralized into flabbiness and inertia under the combined influences of heat, laziness, and servants at command.

The first sign of deterioration is when a woman omits her corsets from her toilette, and begins lolling about in a sloppy and tumbled tea-gown.[16]

From the moment of her arrival, Emily felt this physical lethargy stealing over her, and tried to cure it by writing long journal-letters home. "It is the only real action of life that I contrive to perform by myself," she told her sister Eleanor (*LI*, II, 34). Many other *memsahibs* sought a similar remedy, and some of their letters were published in England, establishing the parameters of role and reaction for later British women in India. Two of the works contemporary with Emily's sojourn there were Mrs Postans's *Western India in 1838* and Julia Charlotte Maitland's *Letters from Madras During the Years 1836–1839*. Both women, like Emily, found writing and sketching valuable resources.

There was one other remedy for ennui which was common to all *memsahibs*, being a less voluntary choice. This was active socializing, and in this, too, Emily conformed. "Promiscuous sociability," writes the novelist Maud Diver, is in India "the distinguishing feature of the country." "Be she the bride of a senior subaltern … or be she the wife of the Viceroy's self, the same unwritten law holds good.... Whatever her natural inclination," the *memsahib* "must needs accept the fact that her house belongs, in a large measure, to her neighbour also."[17] Married women were expected to open their homes to all the bachelors in the vicinity, to house British travellers, some of whom stayed for months, and to keep up a strenuous schedule of tea-parties and dinners.

At Calcutta's Government House, there were usually guests for dinner, as many as fifty on Monday nights. On Tuesday evenings, the Edens held Open House; often it took the form of a ball, where Fanny and Emily, who considered themselves too old to dance, sat, like Patience on a monument, on a platform surrounded by silver sticks, peacock-feather fans and fly-whisks. On Thursday mornings, Emily and Fanny were "At Home" to anyone of the British community who cared to call; often more than a hundred availed themselves of the opportunity. It was all, according to Emily, "very formal and very tiresome." And, worst of all, very dull.

The Calcutta circle of British officers, company officials and merchants, together with their wives and daughters, in which Emily found herself was certainly no replacement for her witty Whig friends in England. "It is surprising how small a show of fellow-creatures tires me in this climate," she complained (*LI*, I, 136). She found the women particularly stupid; they cared nothing about British politics or culture. "It *is* a gossiping society," Emily sighed, "they sneer at each other's dress and looks, and pick out small stories against each other by means of the *Ayahs*" (*MEL*, p. 280). After dinner, at Government House parties, "all the ladies sit in a complete circle round the room, and the gentlemen stand at the farther end of it" (*LI*, I, 123). Emily, of course, had to sit with the ladies, who whispered trivialities to the person next them, and surreptiously scratched their mosquito bites. Emily eyed with envy the men clustered around George. She wasn't used to being confined to female society.

The daily drive in the first cool of the evening allowed Emily some escape from the stultifying atmosphere of Government House. Calcutta's public buildings presented a fine British façade. Britain's East India Company had been there since 1687, and was firmly imprinting its burgeoning imperial presence on what came to be known as "the City of Palaces." Included in that elegant aquatint world of squared white buildings of classical design were the Mint, the Asiatic Society Museum, the Town Hall, the Supreme Court and the huge Writers' Building where so many younger sons of British gentry toiled and sweated over Company ledgers. There were fine shops and private residences, smugly British, but over them all hung the stench of Calcutta's open drains and rotting corpses. On those first drives, Emily caught a glimpse of Calcutta's disturbing discrepancies:

Then, after passing a house that is much more like a palace

than anything we see in England, we come to a row of mud-thatched huts with wild, black-looking savages squatting in front of them, little black native children running up and down the cocoa-trees above the huts…. The next minute we may come to a palace again, or to a regiment of *Sepoys* [private soldiers in the infantry] in the highest state of discipline, or to a body burning on the river-shore, or another body float-ing down the river with vultures working away at it (*MEL*, pp. 264 – 65).

The poorer Hindus couldn't afford firewood to burn a corpse so they simply pushed their dead relative into the river. The owners of those Palladian villas which Emily had so admired along Garden Reach, had she but known, employed a servant to keep shoving the corpses that piled up on the bank back into the river.

Emily sat fanning herself in the Governor-General's fine car-riage with its outriders and postilions in scarlet and gold, and men-tally absented herself from the cripples and beggars jamming the streets; the young mothers with scrawny children in their arms, screaming for charity; the old men, blind and emaciated, squatting at the two ends of every bridge.[18] The only good road ran in a straight line from Government House to Chowringee, the main street. Running off it in all directions were fetid alleys and tortuous lanes. British residents swung by in palanquins, borne aloft by four native bearers, screened and protected from it all. But Emily saw the first terrifying twist of India's underbelly: sordid and sinister and snaking from those stinking alleys all the way to Government House. Her new home was still gleaming white and illuminated as she returned through the sudden dusk, but she could hear jackals howling in the shrubbery, as they smelled the food being carried across an open compound in great iron boxes from the kitchen, three hundred yards away from the main house.

On Thursday afternoons came a flurry of activity and a wel-come change of scene as the whole Government House entourage,

3 Native bazaar near Calcutta

including four hundred servants, moved up river on a barge to Barrackpore for the weekend. Barrackpore, the Governor-General's country seat, was sixteen miles away. Begun by Lord Wellesley and completed by Lord Hastings, it was an imposing mansion with colonnaded verandahs, and extensive grounds laid out to resemble an English country estate. "It feels something like home," Emily wrote to Theresa shortly after her arrival: "a beautiful fresh green park, a lovely flower-garden, a menagerie which has been neglected ... I take a drive or ride on the elephant alone with George regularly" (MEL, p. 266). There was "something dreamy and odd" in these rides Emily took with George – Fanny usually rode out

4 *Government House, Barrackpore, South front*

with William – when the evening grew dark so swiftly. "There is a mosque and a *ghat* [landing-place] at the end of our park," Emily wrote, "where they were burning a body to-night, and there were bats, as big as crows, flying over our heads. The river was covered with odd-looking boats, and a red copper-coloured sky bent over all" (*LI*, I, 157). Emily viewed it from a great distance, as if looking through the wrong end of binoculars, and at this early stage of her Indian stay, felt no emotional response.

George's company was the only blessing at Barrackpore, apart from the lovely green park. "It is a more fatiguing life than Calcutta," Emily decided, "because there we are alone all the daytime, except on Thursdays from ten to twelve ... whereas here the house is always full" (*LI*, I, 183). "It is all very magnificent," Emily told Theresa, "but I cannot endure our [Barrackpore] life" (*MEL*, p. 265).

Even at Barrackpore there was no relief from the stifling heat.

"Griffins" [newcomers] were advised by all the guide books to take passage from England in June or July so that they could become acclimatized to India in the comparative coolness of October and November.[19] The Edens had, on the contrary, arrived at exactly the wrong time, just as the hottest season began in earnest. "The thermometer stood at 94° the whole day" wrote Emily on May 2nd. "I never can read, nor breathe, nor do anything but lie and think what a detestable place it is" (*LI*, I, 152). By August she was gasping to Pamela: "It is so very HOT I do not know how to spell it large enough" (*MEL*, p. 268). "It is what is by courtesy called the 'cold weather' now," she wrote the following November. "I have not been able yet to live five minutes, night or day, without the *punkah*, and we keep our blinds all closed as long as there is a ray of sun" (*MEL*, p. 275). The *punkahs* were made of fabric ruffles stretched on wooden frames twenty or thirty feet wide and suspended from the ceiling; they looked rather like huge, dirty petticoats. The ever-silent *punkah-wallah* sat outside the room, moving his big toe back and forth; the toe was tied to a rope which passed through a hole in the wall and was joined to the *punkah*. Additional cooling devices were the grass mats called *tatties*, hung in doorways and sprinkled with water by a servant on the far side.

In mid-June the rains began; Emily's skin felt constantly clammy, and when she drove out she saw with foreboding that Calcutta's fine white lime-coated buildings were growing darker and uglier by the day. Large stains rose like veins from the bases of the pillars, and dark-green ones spread down from the points where water continually cascaded off the roofs. "My drawings are all blistered, my books all mildewed, my gowns all spotted," wrote Emily from Barrackpore in July. "The day before yesterday the rain came down very much as if the river had got up out of its bed, and was walking about the park" (*LI*, I, 186). The eminently rational Emily tried desperately to find logic and pattern in that threatening mutability:

The degree of destructiveness of this climate it is impossible to calculate, but there is something ingenious in the manner in which the climate and the insects contrive to divide the work. One cracks the bindings of the books, the other eats up the inside; the damp turns the satin gown itself yellow, and the cockroaches eat up the net that trims it; the heat splits the ivory of a miniature, and the white maggots eat the paint; and so they go on helping each other and never missing anything (*LI*, II, 101 – 2).

Crawling and flying everywhere were hordes of insects. Some of them arrived in sudden plagues, like the white ants which marched into Government House in such millions that Emily and the others had to flee up river to Barrackpore. "I am not exaggerating," reported Emily, "when I say that there was not a place … where we could step without crushing twenty of these creatures, which are much larger than common flies. They shake off their wings after they have been five minutes in the house, and all the white marble tables were quite brown and covered some depth with these discarded wings" (*LI*, I, 63). That was India: white marble tables, brown discarded wings.

The mosquitoes didn't come in sudden waves, they were always there:

By an unheard-of piece of tyranny, George is the only individual who is allowed to have his mosquitoes driven away by two men, who stand behind him with long fans of feathers. We are not allowed this luxury in his presence; and of course have, besides our own mosquitoes, his refuse troop to feed. Nobody can guess what those animals are till they have lived amongst them. Many people have been laid up for many weeks by their bites on their first arrival (*LI*, I, 85 – 86).

The worst thing of all for Emily, however, worse than the inactivity, the dull society, the heat, the insects, was that in Calcutta she never saw George "except in a crowd." She had lost sight of the bright light which had drawn her to this country in the first

5 Portrait of Fanny Eden (by F. Rochard, 1835)

place. "We live in complete darkness," wrote Emily, referring to the closed shutters which kept the rooms cool (*LI*, I, 149), but part of the darkness was inside her. Fanny was no substitute for George; Emily found her far too conventionally feminine in interests and outlook. Fanny and Emily were as different as Jane Austen's *Sense and Sensibility* sisters. Emily, like Elinor Dashwood, was firmly rooted in eighteenth-century ideals of emotional restraint and reason. Fanny, like Elinor's sister Marianne, was a nineteenth-century Romantic, a creature of impulse and intuition and wild imaginative flights. Emily and Fanny were always courteous to each other, but never close. In India they opened their hearts only to their English correspondents. Their rooms in Government House were in different wings, and in their reactions to India the sisters went their separate, and solitary, ways.

George was now far less accessible to Emily than in Admiralty days; he was surrounded by his aides, engrossed in his official duties. The Governor-General was responsible to the East India Company's Board of Directors in London and to the Board of Control which was set up by the home government at the end of the eighteenth century, when the British government realized that India was becoming far too important in the imperial scheme of things to leave in the hands of a trading company. The Board of Directors and the Board of Control, however, were a long way away and communication was slow. That left Lord Auckland free from the avalanche of memoranda and instructions that increased as Raj bureaucracy grew; it also left him to make most of the decisions on his own. To assist him in Calcutta, he had a Council of civil and military ministers, a Political Secretary and a Private Secretary. Lord Auckland didn't like making decisions; he preferred to let his Political Secretary, William Macnaghten, or his Private Secretary, John Colvin, take the initiative. George would sit back in the Council chamber, reserved and unflappable no matter what the crisis, listening to his wise assistants, his hands clasped at the back of his head.[20] Not until the latter part of his term in office would the responsibilities of his position oppress him. For the present, he was rested and relaxed. "I never saw George so well; and he is really in danger of growing too fat," reported Emily in December 1836 (*LI*, 1, 263).

He, like Emily, was often bored, particularly during the Durbars (Levees for royalty), where he received India's native princes and exchanged endless compliments and trays of presents. Emily and Fanny often watched these Durbars from behind a screen. George always felt a bit silly when, as part of the ritual, he had to pour attar of roses over the princely hands. Emily described one such occasion: "There were so many who came that he [George] said that Capt. —— whispered to him not to tilt the bottle of attar of

6 Lord Auckland receiving the Rajah of Nahun in Durbar (watercolour by Emily Eden)

roses quite so much, for fear it should not last. I think the East India Company must be charmed with such economy" (*LI*, 1, 96). Emily is making a joke here, but she has, with her usual clarity of vision, seen what later Britons would refuse to see: that the British Empire in India was founded on the ideal of commercial gain, and no other. At least one other British woman in India in that early period shared Emily's acuity. "Many of the members of our social community in India," observed Mrs Postans, "are in the habit of considering a residence in the East as a state of exile; their only imaginable compensation for this irksome position, being the anticipated harvest of these pecuniary advantages, which shall entitle them to the future enjoyment of all the luxuries of their native land."[21] "If we live to come home," wrote Emily to Theresa in December, "we shall be very much better off than we could ever have expected to be, for there is no doubt that the Governor-General's

36

place is well paid" (*MEL*, p. 277). With a little help from his friends, especially Lord Melbourne, Lord Auckland had come to India to do his duty and – like all his fellow countrymen in this Early Raj period – to line his purse.

George was merely following the example of his friend Thomas Babington Macaulay who had come out to India as a member of the Governor-General's Council in 1834 with *his* beloved spinster sister Hannah. Macaulay arrived almost penniless and "he knew exactly why he had come to India: It was in order to save sufficient money to enable him to return to England, financially independent, as soon as possible.²² When Macaulay returned to England in the summer of 1838 he took back £20,000 pounds and never had to worry about money again. (Lord Auckland received almost that much in annual salary.)

All through the eighteenth century, there had been a steady stream of young Englishmen feasting and fattening on India's material riches and then returning to England to buy themselves country estates with the proceeds. The richest one was Robert Clive who, by his own calculation, left India in 1760 with £401,102.²³ By the 1830s, when the Edens arrived with their own pecuniary bias, there were roughly 40,000 like-minded Europeans, mostly British, living and prospering among 150 million Indians. There were some 37,000 soldiers in Company employ, 1,000 East India Company civil servants and about 2,000 merchants, lawyers and adventurers. Most of them traded and speculated on the side, no matter what their regular job. The only Europeans then in India who weren't there to get rich were the missionaries, and there weren't many of those.

During the Middle Raj years, missionaries and the reforming zeal which characterized them would be in the ascendant, but not in this early stage of the Raj. George and Emily's attitude to religion and proselytizing was shared by their compatriots in India. The Edens agreed with their friend Lord Melbourne, who had once remarked that things were coming to a pretty pass when religion was allowed to invade private life. Emily found the morning service in Calcutta's cathedral "much too long for the climate" (*LI*, I, 173), and when a member of the clergy accosted her one Sunday morning at Barrackpore with the words: "Pray, Miss Eden, are you aware that your *motties* [the correct word is *malis*] are at work this morning?" Emily reported the incident with characteristic flippancy. " 'I am very much shocked,' said I, 'but who are my motties?' 'Why, the gardeners,' he said. I thought it safe to deny the fact, but unluckily they all began picking away with their pickaxes under the window, so that I said I would mention it to Lord Auckland when he came" (*LI*, I, 151). (One can almost hear future Lady Sahibs tut-tutting in pious disapproval of Emily's cavalier attitude.)

Emily had no wish at all to proselytize the Indians; but she certainly felt her own Western superiority, and had no interest in learning anything about Indian culture. "There was such a pretty festival on Tuesday," she wrote vaguely, "one of the eternal Hindu festivals; I do not know what about" (*LI*, I, 254). "It certainly is tiresome not being able to speak the language of the country one lives in," she declared,

> but as for attempting to learn their gibberish, I can't. I get such horrible fits at times (particularly when I am driving out) of thinking that we are gone back to an entirely savage state, and are at least 3000 years behind the rest of the world. I take all the naked black creatures squatting at the doors of their huts in such aversion.... I cannot abide India, and that is the truth (*LI*, I, 148).

Emily wrote those words in 1836, and they accurately sum up her feelings during that first year. She turned her back, lay down on her sofa, pulled down the blinds of her mind and retreated to green, pastoral England. "I do assure you it makes me quite '*sick at my stomach*' sometimes when the morning comes," she confessed, "and I think I have another day to do.... I find it not at all unwholesome to think of home. I never think of anything else" (*LI*, I, 121). "I am never half an hour without a vague fancy or dream of some

kind," she confessed (*LI*, I, 195). "I do live in England for hours
together, though you don't perceive me," she told her sister. "I
have recollected so many bits of our lives that I had not thought
of for years, and we have certainly had a great many hours of very
considerable enjoyment. Most of my best recollections are Eden
Farm days" (*LI*, I, 211 and 199).

Emily had collapsed now into total lethargy. "I should have
been ashamed to be carried upstairs in England," she admitted, and
"never hesitate about it here. There are always two men with a sort
of sedan [chair] at the bottom of my stairs in case they are wanted"
(*LI*, I, 108). It was a strange death-in-life existence. "The real *ca-
lamity* of the life is the separation from home and friends. It feels
like death," she told Pamela (*MEL*, p. 268). "Now that I am dead
and buried," she told her, with just the ghost of a smile, "I sit in
my hot grave and think over all the people I liked in the other
world" (*MEL*, p. 267).

The plain fact was, since her arrival in India, Emily had moved
a long way towards the "feminine" stereotype endorsed by English
conduct-book writers and society in general. Now she too was
passive, sentimental, dreamy, and, above all, physically frail. The
latter attribute was held to be at the very core of femininity right
up until the 1890s. William Alexander, for instance, approves of
women pursuing "a sedentary life, a low abstemious diet, and ex-
clusion from the fresh air" because their physical weakness is the
source of "many of the finer and more delicate feelings, for which
we value and admire them."[24] Dr Gregory feels that "we so naturally associate the idea of female softness with a correspondent
delicacy of constitution, that when a woman speaks of her great
strength, her extraordinary appetite, her ability to bear excessive
fatigue, we recoil."[25] In India, Emily reverted to the "delicate woman"
norm. She languished on her sofa, allowed herself to be carried
about, and generally leaned heavily on the comforting cushions of
English convention. In reaction to the disorienting strangeness of
India and to its excessive heat, many *memsahibs* became "delicate"
to the point of invalidism, attacked by that "insidious inertia of

body" which Maud Diver sees as one of India's main ills.[26] In her *Narrative of a Journey Overland from England to India* (1830), Mrs Elwood notes that most Englishwomen in India in Early Raj days had entirely given up walking.[27] They either rode on horseback or were carried about in palanquins. The tragedy, for Emily, was that this physical lethargy, even after her return to England, would prove to be permanent.

India's initial impact on the Eden sisters had moved them in opposite directions. In England, it had been Fanny, with her frequent headaches and coughs, who had clung to the negligee and slippers of the "delicate female." Now she had shed them just as Emily had put them on. In February 1837, Fanny eagerly went off with William Osborne, four British gentlemen and one intrepid *memsahib* called Mrs Cockerell, for a tiger-hunt in the Rajmahal hills. Emily decided not to go: "I could not leave George for a month," she told a friend, "and, moreover, I never feel up to any fatigue" (*LI*, 1, 275). For Fanny, the tiger-hunt proved to be the highlight of her Indian stay. She loved riding her elephant by day, sleeping in a tent by night, finding in that white-rose jungle where wild peacocks soared a new Fanny Eden who was brave, resourceful, strong and independent. In awe and wonder Emily reported to a friend on February 23rd that Fanny had written to her "in ecstasies" about the camp life; she had never felt so hungry nor slept so well. On March 13th, Fanny came face to face with her first tiger, exploding through white roses in sudden spume and snarl while rifles cracked and pungent male smells – musk and sweat and gunsmoke – filled the air. "I am rather proud of having seen a tiger killed because, except for Mrs. Cockerell, there is not another woman in India who has" boasted Fanny in her journal.[28] In the tiger's powerful spring Fanny had seen the real India, and long after her return to Government House, tigers still ranged across her mind. She had seen another magnificent vision in the Rajmahal hills: Frances Harriet Eden with room to spread her wings. "Fanny is in prodigious spirits, and quite *brushed up* by her expedition" wrote Emily on April 1st, still supine on her sofa (*LI*, 1, 344).

Delicate or daring: all British women in India tended to polarize at these two extremes of feminine or masculine behaviour. India was a forcing ground, and in this, as in so much else, India allowed no moderate course between. There were frail women whom India completely vanquished physically or mentally or both. The ships bound for England in the years to come would always be packed with *memsahibs* going home in an effort to recover their health. There were plenty of women like the clergyman's daughter "a lady by birth and education" at one remote Punjab station, whom Flora Annie Steel had to nurse through delirium tremens. Flora describes a woman at the same station, "pretty and young," who drank so continually that her baby was suffering from malnutrition and covered with flies.[29] And there were women like Mabel Davidson "aged $19\frac{1}{2}$, assistant mistress of the Byculla Schools, Bombay" who "committed suicide after the G.I.P. Volunteers ball at Igatpuri on Wednesday by throwing herself into a well."[30]

There were strong women like Mrs Cockerell, or Barbara Baker, who was left alone in the middle of the jungle with six children. Her soldier-husband died of cholera in a matter of hours and servants and palanquin-bearers fled. She kept the home-fires burning each night with a huge blaze to ward off wild animals and was rescued by a missionary days later.[31]

Emily Eden had come to India with some of these masculine strengths of character, but soon retreated, under the shock of Calcutta's disorienting environment, to the feminine extreme. Whenever she was forced to stop dreaming of England and go abroad, Emily floated into a second dream-world. "I believe this whole country and our being here, and everything about it is a dream," she wrote (*LI*, I, 100) a dream or "a constant theatrical representation going on." In either case, it was unreal, and consequently there was no need to come to terms with it, to accept and attempt to understand. She described a visit to the Calcutta bazaar: "Out of their dirty-looking thatched tenements they produced such shawls, gold brocades, that were thicker than the doors of their transparent houses, and the men that sold them looked as if they were cut out

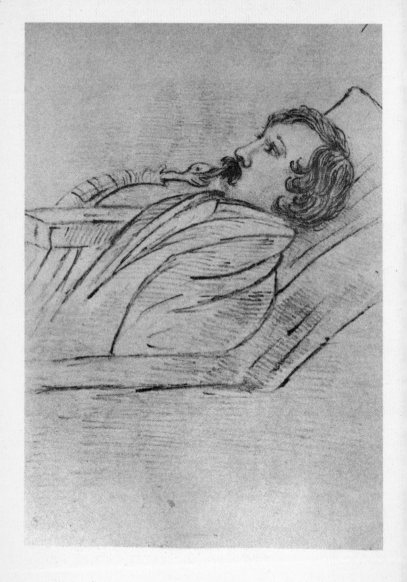

7 *William Osborne smoking his hookah (sketch by Fanny Eden)*

8 View from inside her tent, Rajmahal (sketch by Fanny Eden)

of the 'Arabian Nights' " (LI, 1, 319). The *Arabian Nights* had been translated into occidental languages during the first two decades of the eighteenth century, and formed the silken warp on which Westerners wove their myth of the "exotic East." That ideal was reinforced by the actual trading cargoes spilling out their luxuries on English shores: silks and spices, incense and ivory, all of it strange, sensuous, sybaritic. At the time Emily went to India, there was little factual information to counter the myth: James Mill's weighty tome *The History of British India* had appeared in 1817, but there was little else, and Mill was heavy-going for ladies dozing on their sofas. They much preferred the Arabian Nights view of India, reinforced later by the work of the Romantic poets, who were writing when Emily and Fanny were growing up. The Romantics rhapsodized about stately pleasure domes and "gardens bright with sinuous rills / Where blossomed many an incense-bearing tree." Not just Coleridge, but Southey, Scott, Byron and Shelley also painted the picture of an East full of sensuous splendours.[32] It was Tom Moore, however, whom Emily met at a country-house party in 1826 (MEL, p. 110), who really fired the imaginations of her generation. His poem *Lalla Rookh* appeared in 1817, the same year as Mill's *History of British India*, but *Lalla Rookh* was far more pleasing and popular. It was an instant success all over Europe, was translated, imitated and turned into an opera. It tells the story of Lalla Rookh, daughter of the Moghul Emperor Aurungzeb, who marries a Prince of Kashmir and lives happily ever after in that perfumed vale. Moore wrote of caged birds "Sleeping in light like the green birds that dwell / In Eden's radiant fields of asphodel." As Moore and his fellow poets conceived it, the East was all languor and lilies, a lovely East without disease or dirt. Journalizing *memsahibs* continued the myth, particularly those who didn't stay in India for the long haul. In *Western India in 1838*, Mrs Postans describes such delights as one rajah's courtyards completely covered with crimson cloth. Emily Eden, in 1866, would herself add fresh substance to the myth by publishing in England her journal-letters to her sister Mary Drummond, under the title *Up the Country*.

"These details," wrote Emily in the preface, "of a journey that was picturesque in its motley processions, in its splendid crowds, and in its 'barbaric gold and pearl', may be thought amusing."

To view India as picturesque was to retreat yet again to the conventional, for all British gentlewomen, in India and elsewhere, had been viewing nature that way for a hundred years. To see nature as "picturesque" was to see it as a series of more or less well-composed paintings – a vogue which reached its peak among art critics and painters in the 1790s but which persisted among the public well into Victorian times. The high priest of the cult was a country rector, the Rev. William Gilpin, who, beginning in 1782, brought out a series of travel books whose titles all began with the words: "Observations, chiefly relative to picturesque beauty ... ," each of which described one particular scenic region of England. Gilpin saw the artistic traveller as one who started out with ideal scenes derived from actual paintings in his mind – those of Claude Lorrain and Salvator Rosa were favourites – and then tried to find comparable scenes in nature. A Herefordshire squire called Sir Uvedale Price, in *Essays on the Picturesque* (1794), defined it as embodying roughness, sudden variation and irregularity of form, colour and lighting. Thus temple ruins were preferred to ordinary buildings, tangled jungle growth to manicured lawns. Genteel English ladies arriving in India, all of whom had learned to paint as one of their "polite accomplishments," were delighted to find, wherever they looked, pictorial scenes in abundance. They whipped out their sketch pads and went happily, and smugly, to work. Concentrating on the picturesque allowed them to ignore the human community in India – far too difficult to relate to – and concentrate on the drape of a turban, the folds of a shawl. Natives became objects in the landscape, nothing more. If classical art made one think, and romantic art made one feel, picturesque art, conveniently enough, merely made one see. For British women in India, it was a godsend. "I saw a very good-looking woman at a cottage door, in a very picturesque dress" wrote Fanny Parkes in her Indian travel-book *Wanderings of a Pilgrim in Search of the Picturesque.*[33] When Mrs Colin

Mackenzie, wife of a British army officer, drove through Calcutta's native quarter in November 1846, she wrote: "So picturesque are the people, so beautiful their forms ... that it was like seeing a succession of pictures."[34]

For the majority of *memsahibs*, the picturesque mode was a convenience and a comfort. For a few of the more sensitive and self-aware, however, it was proof of their imaginative failure to see India whole. After five years in India, the novelist Sara Jeannette Duncan told a journalist interviewing her that "one sees oneself projected like a shadow against the strenuous mass of the real people, a shadow with a pair of eyes. There is such intensity and colour and mystery to see, that life is hardly more than looking on."[35] E.M. Forster was another novelist who saw the typical *memsahib* as cool spectator. When Adela Quested in *A Passage to India* contemplates her future stagnation there, going out to dinner parties with "the Turtons and the Burtons ... while the true India slid by unnoticed," she realizes that:

> Colour would remain – the pageant of birds in the early morning, brown bodies, white turbans, idols whose flesh was scarlet or blue – and movement would remain as long as there were crowds in the bazaar and bathers in the tanks. Perched up on the seat of a dogcart, she would see them. But the force that lies behind colour and movement would escape her even more effectually than it did now. She would see India always as a frieze, never as a spirit ... [36]

During her first year in India, when Emily Eden found herself viewing the East at close range, she, too, veiled herself in the protective folds of literary myth or the "picturesque" mode. And she had one other distancing device during that initial phase: her humour. At this early stage of her stay, Emily used her humour as shield and defence: later, its character changed. If she could ridicule and belittle, turning India's natives and its British residents alike into figures of fun, it would all remain unreal – just some hilarious stage farce, or Punch-and-Judy show. And if, to the modern reader, Emily seems insensitive and even cruel in her remarks, we must remember that she was very much, in attitude and ideals, a product of the Regency (1812 – 20) whose moral obtuseness stemmed directly from the Prince Regent himself (later George IV) and whose flippancy and irreverence were fuelled by men like Beau Brummel and *Don Juan*'s creator, Lord Byron. Transported from this pre-Victorian society to India, it is not surprising that no aspect of Indian life is beyond Emily's ribaldry. The aspects which frightened her most – death, for instance – became her most frequent objects of mirth.

"One of our servants dropped down dead in the verandah," Emily reported casually. "He was talking and laughing with some of the others, squatting on the ground in their usual fashion, and he just laid his head back and died" (*UC*, p. 325). There were cholera, plague, smallpox, dysentery and malaria to carry one off. Emily sharpened her wit and took aim: "We drove to the Military Burial Ground," she wrote from Barrackpore. "We could not find one instance of a death later than twenty-five. We are much too old to die in India evidently, so do not be alarmed about us" (*LL*, 1, 119).

"We went to see the Alipore Jail," she reported in August, getting her first close-up look at India's violence and disregard for the value of a human life,

> where prisoners, who would be hanged in England, are shut up for life. They are … a most desperate set, and about two years ago murdered a Mr. Richardson, the magistrate who had the charge of Alipore Jail. They are all fettered, of course, but they threw him down when he was visiting them, and murdered him with the little brass jars which all natives carry about them to drink out of. His poor wife was sitting in the carriage at the door, and never knew what was going on till the body

was found. Mr. Patten, his successor, wished George to see the jail, and so we all went together that we might be all brass-potted at once, if it was to be done – and there was an army of soldiers – Dr. Drummond to bring us to life – and the Chief Justice to try the murderers (*LI*, I, 211 – 12).

Natives were a particular butt for her wit. Some of the servants at Government House had, on her instructions, built "a sort of altar" in the middle of her new flower garden:

My altar was built, and covered with all sorts of pretty ornaments; the three stark-naked savages who had put it up were admiring their work and putting a finishing touch here and there, when there came on one of those storms of rain which last ten minutes, and flood the whole place. The water filled the chinks of the new brickwork, and the altar fell quietly down like a card-house, and was all single bricks again. George was looking out of the window, and had the fun of seeing it. I have given general directions to be called when such a catastrophe is likely to occur, as no fun must be wasted here (*LI*, I, 206 – 7).

She also laughed at her maid Rosina's bungling and parodied her speech:

Rosina is an excellent old creature, yet she is sometimes ten minutes trying to put the eye into the hook instead of the hook into the eye; and in the morning, when I say I will wear my blue muslin, she brings out my pink satin with short sleeves, and says, "Dees blue gown the Lady Sahib mean?" … The only amusing thing I have here is their broken English (*LI*, I, 210).

Natives were slightly sub-human, and there to amuse. Attending a ball at Government House in June 1836 were "several very oddly dressed native princes. One enormous man," a nephew of the King of Oudh's, had his "immense expanse of person ... dressed in a thick gold brocade. He would have made a handsome piece of furniture in a large house" (LI, 1, 174).

When there were no natives to laugh at, Emily settled for her spaniel Chance, quite as black and silent as the "savages" but much more to her taste. Chance had his own servant, a gentle, adoring man called Jimmund. "That little black angel," Emily wrote indulgently of Chance,

> has the audacity to dote on India, and never enjoyed better spirits, or a more imperious temper ... . He swims so far out into the Ganges that his own attached servant screams with fright. He has learnt from the natives to eat mangoes, and is very much suspected of smoking his hookah whenever he can get comfortably alone with my tailors (LI, 1, 178 – 79).

William Osborne was teaching Chance a great variety of tricks "which he displayed at dessert, and which not only make conversation in a country where that article does not abound, but which really do surprise some people not used to the highly educated modern dog"(LI, 1, 241). "I found out the other day," reported Emily, "that Chance, without telling me, had hired another valet ... so I was obliged to represent to him that he never would make his fortune in five years if he went on in that kind of way" (LI, 1, 150 – 51).

Emily had Chance to amuse her, and Fanny adopted and dressed a lemur called Rolla who, together with various parrots and a gazelle, became her constant companions. Most British women in India surrounded themselves with pets – it was the thing to do, like sketching the picturesque. In his satirical portrait of the magistrate's wife in *Curry and Rice*, G.F. Atkinson describes how she enlivens her "wearied hour" with squirrels and Persian cats, cockatoos and canaries, minahs and mongooses, pigeons and poodles. Mrs Colin Mackenzie, stationed at Ludhiana, had "divers pets," including a "pretty little tiny red calf," two "handsome Punjabi black goats," and a white Afghan sheep which ate from her hand and followed her into the house. When the weather turned cold, she had coats made for her two dogs, and for the cow. She also had three parrots, one of whom perched on her shoulder, or sat on her chest while she slept.[37]

Why this craze for pets among the good *memsahibs* of India? Many of them feared that jungle violence just beyond their neat compounds and English-style gardens. They tamed and domesticated, and sometimes even dressed, India's animals because they couldn't tame and domesticate the rest of the country. Subconsciously, they wished that the whole alarming tangle – ash-covered madmen, naked beggars, cobras, alligators – could somehow acquire waistcoats and good manners and sit up straight at table and behave themselves.

For her part, Emily often elevated her black spaniel Chance to human status and demoted the black "savages" to objects, pieces of furniture. Emily wanted only to be amused, not horrified or disturbed. She therefore made herself laugh by creating with her caustic pen her own cosy little world of ridicule and hyperbole, of distortions and deceptions. Surely, if she were persistent, it would counter that mad world beyond, which was anything but a laughing matter.

Her satiric stance eased her into her second year and almost in spite of herself, helped her to grow reconciled to her Indian life, if only by jagged fits and starts. She found comfort in her *jemadar*, "that jewel of a man." Major Byrne was threatening to re-locate him elsewhere in the household, and Emily objected strongly. He was "her stay and support – matches my gowns and sashes, washes up my painting box, and takes care of everything I have, money included" (*LI*, II, 31). She enjoyed June gardening at Barrackpore: "It was great fun giving a poke at the bottom of a flower-pot and turning out a nice little plant – like Greenwich days, even though the poor little flower was received by twelve black gardeners very lightly dressed" (*LI*, II, 52). And when she found herself slipping into a daydream of "Eden Farm, and youth and home and that sweet time," she resisted it:

> All this was floating about me, and I had a considerable mind to cry about it, but then two little paroquets began screaming in a tamarind-tree, and there was a strong perfume of exotic flowers – Indian white blossoms that were dropping on the grass – and then I saw eleven of those white eastern figures whom I had told to sit down, all squatting cross-legged most obediently, but with their black eyes fixed on me, and I scorned to waste any English tears on such an eastern scene. So I looked at Chance, who was jumping about in the tank, trying to catch a gold-coloured frog, and I thought that he and ourselves were much alike. We are living in a marsh catching *gold* frogs (*LI*, II, 56 – 7).

By mid-June 1837, Emily was able to write: "I am more reconciled to India than I was, inasmuch as it is no use kicking against the pricks; and then the days are so monotonous that they go by quicker than they did when everything was new ... and the pain of being indolent is no longer very irksome, I am ashamed to say." "And, last of all," Emily ended her letter on a complacent note:

> I really feel every day that I would not be away from George – and think of him alone in this country – for any earthly consideration. If it were in the slightest degree possible to repay him any part of the obligation I owe him all through life, this is, I think, the only opportunity (*LI*, II, 41).

In October 1837, Lord Auckland and his sisters would start their great progress up the country to what were then called the Upper Provinces. Preparations for the trip had begun as far back as June, when Fanny and Emily had practised riding their elephants using "some new *howdahs* [seats for elephants' backs] for the march," but "the very best *howdah*," Emily continued despondently, will "reduce anybody to a shapeless and boneless lump in about six miles of travelling. I expect to walk my march. A palanquin looks like a coffin, the elephant shakes, and I am grown afraid of my horse. The carriages go with us, but there are few roads on which they can be used" (*LI*, II, 59). By September 11th, Emily reported that Byrne and his staff "have gradually removed many of the comforts" from Government House, "and in two days the band and the horses and most of the servants depart, and, as William Osborne observes with real consternation, we shall not have above eight servants apiece left to wait on us" (*MEL*, pp. 288 – 89). The packing and pressing accelerated. "Our first and best energies," Emily wrote, "are devoted towards making a *clinquant* [tinsel] figure of His Excellency, in order that he may shine in the eyes of the native princes" (*LI*, II, 81). His Excellency's purpose in going up country was partly to familiarize himself with East India Company territory between Calcutta in the east and the Sutlej river in the north-west, and partly to consolidate the treaty of perpetual friend-ship which had been signed in 1831 by Governor-General Lord William Bentinck and the Lion of the Punjab, Maharaja Ranjit Singh, Britain's most crucial ally in India. His Sikh Empire stood between British India and Afghanistan with its shifting allegiances. But mainly, Lord Auckland was going up the country to impress on native rulers the need for continued *salaams* (respectful compliments) and co-operation with the British. All along his route, he would hold stately Durbars where compliments and costly gifts would be exchanged.

It was an old Company rule that the Governor-General could not keep any of the sumptuous gifts presented to him. Some of them the Lord Sahib would hand out to other native princes along his route; some he would buy back at a fair price for himself or his sisters; the rest would end up in Calcutta's auction rooms and the proceeds would go into Company coffers. Lord Auckland's prog-ress up the country would be, for the Company, a most lucrative trip indeed, since many of the native princes had immense wealth, and generosity to match.

As the day of their departure drew near, Emily felt rather more sprightly than usual: her death-in-life existence was over. As so often, she centered her delight on Chance:

His servant informs me that he wants two new coats; he has one of Chinese brocade, with a gold breast-plate, which was presented to him last year; but that he can only wear when he goes to visit the King of Oudh's or the King of Lucknow's dogs. For his days of common Pariah audiences I should think a coloured muslin must be correct (*LI*, II, 94 – 95).

At last, everything was ready and on the morning of October 21st the great adventure began. "When we came down for some coffee," wrote Emily, "the great hall was full of gentlemen who had come to accompany his lordship to the *ghat* – even Mr. Macaulay had turned out for it" (*UC*, p. 2). George was eager to be off: "The instant he arrived at the *ghat*, he gave a general good-bye, offered me his arm, and we walked off to the boats as fast as we could. The guns fired, the gentlemen waved their hats, and so we left Calcutta" (*UC*, p. 2).

*T*HEY WOULD be gone for two and a half years. The first three and a half weeks would be spent going seven hundred miles up the Hooghly and the Ganges on long barges called flats, pulled by steamers. After that it would be a long, slow march across the plains and up to Simla in the Himalayas. Then they would leave the British sphere to meet Ranjit Singh in the Punjab, eventually arriving back in Calcutta in March 1840. Emily would be writing and sketching all the way in a fine, sustained creative flourish.

Two flats were towed up the Hooghly: the first one, fitted up into bedrooms and sitting-room, contained George and Emily, Fanny and William, Dr Drummond and a suitable complement of servants. The second flat held John Colvin, the Private Secretary, William Macnaghten, the Political Secretary, their wives and various other

9 Bathing in the Hooghly, Calcutta

officials. Macnaghten, destined to play a key role in Lord Auckland's reign, had come out to India in 1809 as a cavalry cadet, learned Hindustani, Persian and Tamil, entered the Bengal Civil Service in 1814 and become a Judge and Magistrate highly knowledgeable in Oriental law. Emily thought him "clever and pleasant" (*UC*, p. 3).

The two steamers and flats soon entered the Sunderbunds, an area of "low stunted trees, marsh, tigers and snakes" where "occasionally there is a bamboo stuck up with a bush tied to it, which is to recall the cheerful fact that there a tiger has carried off a man"

(*UC*, p. 3). The party had left Calcutta on a Saturday and by Wednesday George was "already bored to death with having nothing to do" (*UC*, p. 4). Emily turned her back on famished tigers and a fidgety brother and returned to her beloved Kentish countryside: she was reading of Mr Pickwick's exploits there, and laughing on every page. Before she left India, Emily would read Dickens's *Pickwick Papers* ten times – "the only bit of fun in India" (*MEL*, p. 298) – as well as *Nicholas Nickleby* and *Oliver Twist*. In addition to day-dreams and letters, she had found another route back to England, and another source of amusement.

News of William IV's death and Queen Victoria's succession had reached Emily before she left Calcutta, but it was not until they had anchored at Rajmahal that she received any details. Then she saw "a great fat Baboo standing at the *ghat* with two bearers behind him carrying the post-office packet" and having devoured her letters, pronounced the young queen "a charming invention." Emily could "fancy the degree of enthusiasm she must excite. Even here we feel it" (*UC*, p. 8).

On November 6th, they landed at Patna, amid boats "with gilded sterns and painted peacocks at the prow" (*UC*, p. 12), belonging to rich natives, so that George could hold a Durbar and distribute gifts. The next day, the rajahs sent George *his* presents – "shawls, kincobs [gold- or silver-weave brocades], etc., three very fine elephants, and two horses." Already, Emily is assessing the loot with a clearly commercial eye: "There was nothing very pretty in the presents, except an ivory arm-chair and an ivory *tonjaun* [chair carried by four bearers] inlaid with silver" (*UC*, p. 14). Throughout her journal, Emily carefully listed all the presents received and gave detailed descriptions of many of the magnificent jewels spilling out before her dazzled eyes from the rajahs' bottomless treasure chests. At Dinapore, on November 10th, she gasped at the splendour of "a diamond peacock holding in his beak a rope of enormous pearls, which passed through an emerald about the size of a dove's egg" (*UC*, p. 17).

The next day, passing Ballia, there was a fair in progress.
Hoping for some bargains, Emily and Fanny

persuaded G. [George] to go on shore just "to go to the fair",
as we should have done at home, only we sent all the servants
with silver sticks, and took our own *tonjauns* and two of the
body-guard, and went in the State barge and with all the aides-
de-camp. In short, we did our little best to be imposing, considering that we have only the steamboat apparatus to work
with (*UC*, pp. 17 – 18).

Mr Macnaghten afterwards declared "that the Governor-General
should never appear publicly without a regiment, and that there
was no precedent for his going to Ballia fair." Emily was more
than a match for Mr Macnaghten. "I told him we had made a
precedent, and that it would be his duty to take the next Governor-
General, be he ever so lame or infirm, to this identical fair" (*UC*,
p. 18). Emily had had more than enough stuffy formality in Calcutta; going up country she is quick to ridicule and remonstrate
and undercut the pomp with her irreverent wit.

At Benares, the holiest and richest city in India, famous for its
minarets and mosques, its silks and brocades, the Governor-General's party left the river and piled into carriages for the journey to
their camp site, four miles beyond the city. "Everybody kept saying
'What a magnificent camp!' reported Emily dourly, "and I thought
I never had seen such squalid, melancholy discomfort" (*UC*, p. 22).
She and Fanny and George each had a tent with a fourth to serve
as sitting-room, with "great covered passages, leading from one
tent to the other"(*UC*, p. 22). Around the four tents, placed in a
square, was "a wall of red cloth, eight feet high." Emily felt caged
by those red walls: "They have covered us up in every direction,
just as if we were native women" (*UC*, p. 23), and she had already
decided, once and for all, that camp life was hateful and horrid.
She quickly named her tent "Misery Hall" and George, who shared

all her sentiments about tents, called his "Foully Palace." For Emily, it was like living inside some giant serpent, blood-red and dripping.

Leaving Benares, the long straggling march across the plains began. The bugle woke them at half-past five, and they set off exactly at six, the Governor-General and his sisters preceding the rest so as to escape the constant clouds of dust. Behind them came strings of loaded camels and elephants; as the cavalcade approached Allahabad at the end of November, there were 850 camels and 140 elephants. Next came the British members of the party, sixty in all. They travelled in carriages and buggies where the roads allowed; otherwise the men rode horses while their womenfolk were carried by native bearers in *tongas*, palanquins, *janpans* and *doolies*: all bed-like or chair-like conveyances. Next the hackeries (bamboo carts with wooden wheels) creaked by, loaded with household goods and drawn by bullocks. Then came the troops, 8,000 of them, soldiers marching, officers riding. They were followed by fakirs (religious mendicants) beating drums, and swarms of camp follow-ers, some of them dacoits (robbers) who slunk through the camp after dark stealing everything they could lay their hands on. For most of the march, there were 12,000 people.

The cavalcade was a slow-winding snake ten miles long, send-ing up puffs of dust as it inched slowly forward across the parched earth. It was on the move from six A.M. till about eight A.M. and Emily amused herself with the thought of how ridiculous they looked:

> William and I had one of our hysterical fits of laughter at the extraordinary folly of a march. We feel so certain that people who live in houses, and get up by a fire at a reasonable hour and then go quietly to breakfast, would think us raving mad, if they saw nine Europeans of steady age and respectable habits, going galloping every morning at sunrise over a sandy plain, followed by quantities of black horsemen, and then by ten miles of beasts of burden carrying things which, after all, will

not make the nine madmen even decently comfortable (*UC*, p. 248).

By eight A. M. the sun was searing and cruel and the whole cavalcade moved into camp for the rest of the day and night. An advance-guard of tent-pitchers and camel-drivers went ahead during the night – making a fearful racket in camp as they prepared to set out – to make ready the next day's campsite. It was, for Emily, a strange and dislocating life: chairs and beds snatched from under one to be loaded into the hackeries, the canvas walls of home rolled up onto the backs of elephants. One big dust-puff, *abracadabra*, and one's shaky home puffed into being; another puff and it vanished, without a trace. She preferred her world to be orderly and sane. "The worst part of a march," complained Emily, "is the necessity of everybody, sick or well, dead or dying, pushing on with the others" (*UC*, p. 37). She was to spend many a day racked with fever and headache carried forward in her palanquin. "What I hate most in a camp is the amount of human and brute suffering it induces" she would write later, after two years on the road (*UC*, p. 253).

There was, however, one comfort to camp life: she saw more of George than she had in Calcutta, but it was an unhappy George. One evening in November the two of them "went on an elephant through rather a pretty little village ... and he was less bored than usual, but I never saw him hate anything so much as he does this camp life" (*UC*, p. 37).

They reached Allahabad on November 30th and it was there, at an evening reception, that Emily and Fanny encountered one of those strong and eccentric *memsahibs* who occasionally surfaced in Early Raj days before British women arrived in force to set up tight, self-sufficient social units and corresponding pressures to conform. This extraordinary woman was Fanny Parkes, and her husband was Collector of Customs at Allahabad. Fanny Parkes was a restless romantic and adventurer who, without her husband, roamed the country on an Arab horse, wearing Turkish trousers, sleeping in

tents and ordering her servants about in fluent Hindustani. From
the day of her arrival in India in 1822, she had plunged into the
rich texture of Indian life: she celebrated Hindu festivals, learned
Persian, played the sitar and made vast collections of Indian insects,
fossils, religious icons and animal skulls. Her verandah at Allahabad
was decorated with a seven-foot stuffed alligator, and she once sailed
alone with native crew up the Jumna river to Agra, arriving fifty-
one days later to pitch her tent near the Taj Mahal.[38] Mrs Parkes
eagerly joined the Eden entourage, and from Allahabad on, tented
her way up country as far as Mussoorie, while Emily gazed in awe
at her energetic, trousered figure striding round the camp-grounds
and Fanny Eden felt envious of Mrs Parkes' gypsy freedoms and
open flouting of convention.

Christmas Day found them all at Cawnpore, and Emily, like
all *memsahibs* in India at that season, was feeling low and homesick,
with "such a horrid mixture of sights and sounds for Christmas"
that "my soul recoiled" (*UC*, p. 53). Mr Wimberley, the chaplain
travelling up-country with them, took divine service, but "still it
was in a tent, and unnatural" and "there was nobody except George
with whom I felt any real communion of heart and feelings" (*UC*,
p. 54). Still, Cawnpore had its fields of asphodel, its orange trees
and roses. The King of Oudh's palace was "the only residence I
have coveted in India," sighed Emily. "Don't you remember where
in the 'Arabian Nights' Zobeide bets her 'garden of delights' against
the Caliph's 'palace of pictures'? I am sure this was the 'garden of
delights' " (*UC*, p. 62). The Prince of Lucknow gave a breakfast
"which was quite as Arabian-Nightish as I meant it to be," with
plenty of jugglers and *nautch*-girls (dancing girls) and musicians.
The Prince was dressed in gold to match his throne, which was
canopied in gold cloth embroidered with pearls and rubies. That
was the fanciful Cawnpore.

The fearful one was the prison full of Thugs which George
and other gentlemen visited. The Thugs were members of a secret
Hindu religious society; they believed that they had been entrusted

by the goddess Kali with the duty of murdering travellers. *Thuggee* had prospered for 2,000 years before Lord William Bentinck ordered Captain William Sleeman to stamp it out, leaving only the word "thug" itself to survive in common English parlance. Thugs would join a group of travellers, joke with them round the campfire, then swiftly, silently, strangle them with a knotted cloth and dump the bodies into a shallow grave. Hundreds of travellers who set out never reached their destination, seemingly swallowed up by that parched, hungry earth. One Thug in Cawnpore prison had murdered three hundred people, so George and William reported to Emily that night at dinner.

An even more fearsome India stalked into Emily's consciousness on New Year's Day, 1838, lean and hungry, in the guise of famine: "They have had no rain for a year and a half; the cattle all died, and the people are all dying or gone away" (*UC*, p. 64), Emily wrote. The devil, says an old Muslim proverb, holds an umbrella over Delhi, and the vast plains between the Jumna and the Ganges were one brown, seared waste. As Emily travelled from Cawnpore to Agra, thousands of starving wretches lay along the roadside, or scrabbled weakly for bits of grain which had passed undigested through the bodies of the troop-horses. "You cannot conceive the horrible sights we see," shuddered Emily, "particularly children, perfect skeletons in many cases, their bones through their skin, without a rag of clothing, and utterly unlike human creatures" (*UC*, p. 65). The scales were torn from Emily's eyes at Cawnpore. She could no longer remain dreamy and detached and amused. She was wide awake now and emotionally involved, seeing clearly the pain pounded into that awesome plain and wanting somehow to alleviate it. When she found a starving baby "with glazed, stupid eyes" (*UC*, p. 66), she had it brought four times a day to the back of her tent and fed it. From the first day of 1838 until the end of her Indian stay, Emily looked head on at the suffering India exacts from its own, and from its conquerors.

If the natives were wasting physically day by day, some of the British were experiencing a different kind of attrition. Emily saw

clearly the cost of Empire for all those East India Company employees in lonely up-country stations:

> The thing that chiefly interests me is to hear the details of the
> horrible solitude in which the poor young civilians live. There
> is a Mr. G. here.... He says the horror of being three months
> without seeing a European, or hearing an English word, no-
> body can tell. Captain N. has led that sort of life in the jungles
> too, and says that, towards the end of the rainy season, when
> the health generally gives way, the lowness of spirits that comes
> on is quite dreadful; that every young man fancies he is going
> to die, and then he thinks that nobody will bury him if he
> does, as there is no other European at hand (*UC*, p. 77).

If the Arabian Nights myth was fast disappearing for Emily seeing
India at close range, so was the myth of Empire idealism. Emily
was one of the first Britons to realize that while the imaginative
ideal of empire inspires and uplifts, the actual reality enervates and
depresses.

At Delhi, Emily saw the cost of Empire in another light and
mourned the lost splendour of the Moghuls. Since 1803, the last
Emperor and King of Delhi had been a pensioner and virtual prisoner of the British, pitiful and powerless, living in Delhi's magnificent marble Palace.

> It is a melancholy sight – so magnificent originally, and so
> poverty-stricken now.... In some of the pavilions belonging
> to the princes there were such beautiful inlaid floors ... but the
> stones are constantly stolen; and in some of the finest baths
> there were dirty *charpoys* [beds] spread, with dirtier guards
> sleeping on them. In short, Delhi is a very suggestive and
> moralising place ... such stupendous remains of power and
> wealth passed and passing away – and somehow I feel that we
> horrid English have just 'gone and done it' merchandised it,
> revenued it, and spoiled it all" (*UC*, pp. 97 – 8).

This is the liberal Emily looking at India – the Emily whose political views, expressed in London drawing-rooms, were cogent enough to keep such Prime Ministers as Lord Melbourne and later, William Gladstone, hanging on her every word. Britain had exercised her commercial greed on India, had "merchandised it, revenued it, and spoiled it all." No other Lady Sahib would see more clearly than that.

Emily's serious empathy and awareness alternate with her humorous irreverence, but now the tone of her humour has changed from a means of defence to one of discovery. Emily begins to use her humour to sniff out the hypocrisy, the pretensions, the vanity of the British residents of India. The growing bitterness and disillusionment which she is feeling as the trip progresses give her humour a rasping edge. This is Jane Austen going up the country, and the various British stations along the way certainly have their quota of vain fools.

There was Mr B., an English *civilian* (Company employee) at Moradabad who was "now a bald-headed, grey, toothless man, and perfectly ignorant on all points but that of tiger-hunting" (*UC*, p. 83). There was Mrs T. who "wears long thick thread mittens, with black velvet bracelets over them. She may have great genius, and many good qualities, but, you know, it is impossible to look for them under those mittens" (*UC*, p. 87). When an English couple entertained the Edens at a "musical dinner" with flute duets, Emily was not impressed:

> The flute couple I think a failure, but they are reckoned in this country perfectly wonderful; and they whispered quite confidentially, "I suppose you are aware that before —— came out to this country, the famous Nicholson said he could teach him nothing more." I suspect when he goes back the famous Nicholson will find he may throw in a lesson or two with good effect (*UC*, p. 150).

Emily pinned English residents in India to her specimen board with her pen, and native ones with her paint brush. In addition to her letters, she left a fine legacy of portraits of native princes and soldiers and servants. Her skills are remarkable, not just in terms of technique – although one feels that Sir Joshua Reynolds himself "could teach her nothing more" – but also in terms of psychological insights. In colours still glowing, Emily has perceived and painted all the dignity and barbarity, the charm and craftiness, of her subjects.

So the march up country continued through 1838. As they climbed up into the hills en route to Simla at the end of March, Emily had to abandon "the dear open carriage, which has been the only comfort of my life in this march" (*UC*, p. 119) and climb into a *janpan*. "I get such fits of bore with being doddled about for three hours before breakfast in a sedan-chair," she complained, "I have a sort of mad wish to tell the bearers to turn back and go home, quite home, all the way to England" (*UC*, p. 121).

Simla, however, proved to be an excellent substitute. It was an entirely British creation, founded in 1819 when Lieutenant Ross built its first thatched cottage. In 1829, Lord Amherst had begun the tradition of Governors-General fleeing to Simla when the hot weather came. Lord William Bentinck gave his name to a neighbouring peak which was long known as Bentinck's Nose. Not until 1864, however, beginning with Sir John Lawrence, would the Viceroy routinely, every April to November, be resident at Simla.[39]

Simla was seven thousand feet above the sea, with its cottages perched precariously along a high ridge running round the base of Mount Jakko. One looked up at the Himalayas, snow-capped and serene against blue sky, or down through diminishing hills to brown plains veined by the Sutlej and Ganges rivers. When Emily arrived on April 3rd, scarlet rhododendrons blazed across the hills, not bushes of them, as in England, but trees, very tall trees.

At first sight, Simla, like the mythic India of bespangled elephants, appeared all very innocuous and delightful:

10 *Dost Mahomed Khan, with two sons and cousin*
(watercolour by Emily Eden)

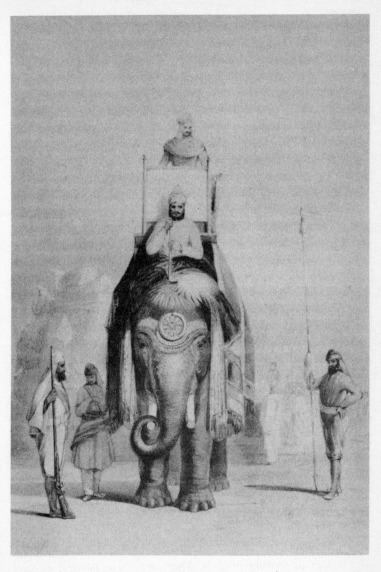

11 Rajah of Patiala on his state elephant (watercolour by Emily Eden)

12 Lord Auckland's residence at Simla
(watercolour by Captain G.F. Thomas)

It really is worth all the trouble – such a beautiful place – and our house, that everybody has been abusing, only wanting all the good furniture and carpets we have brought, to be quite perfection ... . No wonder I could not live down below! We were never allowed a scrap of air to breathe – now I come back to the air again, I remember all about it. It is a cool sort of stuff, refreshing, sweet, even apparently pleasant to the lungs. We have fires in every room and the windows open ... Good! I see this is to be the best part of India (*uc*, p. 124).

It was all terribly English. There was "a great deal of thick white fog" which "somehow has a smell of London" (*uc*, p. 144).

There was "an English cuckoo talking English – at least, he is trying, but he evidently left England as a cadet ... for he cannot get further than *cuck* – and there is a blackbird singing. We pass our lives in gardening (*UC*, p. 129). Simla appealed to Emily because, like the majority of her countrywomen in India, she never made the smallest endeavour to adapt to Indian ways.

There was another great compensation at Simla, apart from its English atmosphere. George was always close at hand. He had turned one of the rooms in their modest cottage into an office. Lately he'd been closeted there for hours with Macnaghten, discussing the sensitive issue of what to do about Afghanistan. The British needed a friendly buffer state next to their north-west provinces, but Afghanistan was being consistently wooed by Russia. It was a problem that plagued every Governor-General. On Macnaghten's urging, George decided to attempt to depose Dost Mahomed Khan from the Afghan throne and put Shah Shuja in his place. Dost Mahomed was a capable and popular ruler while Shah Shuja was a stupid weakling who, having been rejected by the Afghans three times, had slunk off to Ranjit Singh's protection in the Punjab. Dost Mahomed, however, was far too independently minded – he had dismissed from his court Sir Alexander Burnes, sent as envoy by the Governor-General in 1837, and was making friendly overtures to Russia. Shah Shuja, on the other hand, would do whatever the British told him to. Lord Auckland hated making decisions and was therefore quite content to yield to Macnaghten in the matter of ousting Dost Mahomed. It was a disastrous choice, not only for Britain and her army, but most of all for Macnaghten himself.

Lord Auckland's reluctance to become sufficiently well informed on the Afghan question to be able to make up his own mind was not his only fault as the Chief Executive of British India. It was typical of his Regency attitude to see India as a place in which to amuse and indulge himself, much as the Prince Regent had freely indulged himself by designing the extravagant orientalisms of his Pavilion at Brighton without regard to such practical matters as

13 Lord Auckland (after a painting by L. Dickinson)

finance. In India, Lord Auckland similarly kept boredom at bay by creating his own Arabian Nights atmosphere. In his case, he did it by manipulating the puppet-strings of native princes. When a jeweller showed Emily a magnificent bunch of twenty-seven emerald grapes which looked "like being the fruit in Aladdin's garden," the smallest emerald being "the size of a marble" (*UC*, pp. 177 – 78), she wanted George to present it to Ranjit Singh when they had their historic meeting. The Lord Sahib's aides wondered if perhaps the grapes should be given instead to Shah Shuja. "No," George replied, decisive for once, and enjoying the fun of it all, "we are going to give Shah Shuja a kingdom, which is quite enough without any presents" (*UC*, p. 178).

In May 1838, Lord Auckland despatched William Macnaghten, William Osborne and several others to Ranjit Singh's headquarters at Lahore, to persuade him to sign the treaty that would put Shah Shuja back on the Afghan throne. As preliminary presents – the grapes would come later – they took Ranjit Lord Auckland's portrait set in a diamond star on a string of pearls, some gold-mounted pistols, a gold-sheathed sword and two thoroughbred horses. Ranjit kept the party sweltering at Lahore in temperatures of 113° for weeks while he alternately sulked and charmed, making up his mind. Finally he signed the treaty, and the exhausted party returned to Simla in July.[40] Macnaghten went on to show the treaty to Shah Shujah, living in sad seclusion at Ludhiana, consoling himself with six hundred wives and waiting with typical Eastern fatalism for the kismet which would give him back his throne.

While these negotiations went forward in the plains, Emily was beginning to see that even Simla had its disturbing aspects. People occasionally tumbled over the precipices and were seen no more; in August the Edens' house was so overrun with fleas that Emily lost three nights' sleep; sometimes a lap-dog who strayed too far from its mistress would be mauled by a marauding leopard. And Simla's British residents, Emily was discovering, were even more snobbish and élitist than their compatriots in the plains. There was a definite line drawn between the members of the covenanted service (judges, commissioners, collectors and other top officials) and the uncovenanted ranks (clerks and assistants), and it was drawn along racist lines. The "uncovenanted service," wrote Emily with her usual asperity,

> is just one of our choicest Indianisms, accompanied with our very worst Indian feelings. We say the words just as you talk of the "poor chimney-sweepers" … the uncovenanted being, in fact, clerks in the public offices. Very well-educated, quiet men, and many of them very highly paid; but as many of them are half-castes, we, with our pure Norman or Saxon blood, cannot really think contemptuously enough of them (UC, p. 140).

In the early years of the eighteenth century, the East India Company, finding the cost of shipping out British women to India exorbitant, encouraged its employees there to take native wives and mistresses. By the end of the century, the number of "half-castes" or "Eurasians," as they were called, in Company employ outnumbered the purely British, so between 1786 and 1795 the Company took steps to bar Eurasians from the covenanted ranks of the civil service.[41] In Emily's time, at Simla, there were a great many of these cowed employees, and she deplored their social ostracism. When, in September, the British ladies of Simla were busy planning a fancy-work sale to be held among the pines of Annandale, a pretty valley reserved for fêtes and picnics, Emily offered some of her drawings, and some brisk advice. She suggested that the wives of the uncovenanted service be asked "to send contributions. This was rather a shock to the aristocracy of Simla, and they did suggest that some of the wives were very black. That I met by the argument that the black would not come off on their works" (UC, p. 159). Emily's racist views were beginning to change.

In early November, Emily and Fanny reluctantly prepared to leave Simla to make their way down to the plains for the meeting with Ranjit Singh. Emily liked the fact that they would be the only

*14 Fancy fair at Annandale, Simla, 1839
(watercolour by Captain G.F. Thomas)*

women in the large party accompanying the Lord Sahib. "We have
had seven as good months here as it is possible to pass in India,"
Emily decided, "no trouble, no heat" (*uc*, p. 180). Her longing
for England, however, never left her, not even at Simla. "We have
been here little more than half our time," she wrote to Mary the
day before leaving, "and I am sure it feels and is almost a life" (*uc*,
p. 180).

By November 27th, the Governor-General's party were en-
camped on an enormous plain near Ferozepore on one side of the
Sutlej; Ranjit's tents were pitched on the opposite bank, and near
by were the tents of the British troops, twenty thousand strong,
who would be joined by Ranjit's and a token force of Shah Shuja's
for the march on Afghanistan to depose Dost Mahomed. On November 29th, Lord Auckland, Governor-General of India, and the
powerful Lion of the Punjab, Mighty Ruler of the Sikh Kingdom,

71

met for the first time. Ranjit arrived at the Governor-General's camp on an elephant, accompanied by martial music and splendid troops. Lord Auckland went to meet him on *his* elephant, then transferred what looked like a small bundle of red cloth from Ranjit's howdah to his own, and the two men rode back to hold their Durbar, followed by a great crowd of Sikh and British officers, all of them pushing and shoving, trying to cram themselves into the inner tent where the Punjab's Lion and Britain's would stalk each other. There was a fearful crush and "the band-master, who must be a wag, played 'We met, 'twas in a crowd'."[42]

Emily peered at Ranjit as he and George talked, and decided that he looked "exactly like an old mouse, with grey whiskers and one eye" (*UC*, p. 198). He was small, wizened, plainly dressed in red silk without a single jewel. He was only fifty-five but debauchery and alcohol had aged him prematurely. He had suffered a stroke three years before, and would soon have another. His one good eye was bloodshot; his skin pock-marked and dirty-looking. He could neither read nor write, had taken eighteen wives, was routinely doctored with a medicine of powdered pearls, and got drunk on corn-brandy containing opium, musk and meat juice. (Later, Emily tried this noxious brew and declared that "one drop actually burnt the outside of my lips" (*UC*, p. 207). Ranjit was also extremely clever, courageous, remarkably astute in judging men's characters, forthright and, compared to other native rulers, positively humane. Those who crossed him were not killed, but were deprived of ears and noses.[43]

Ranjit sat in Lord Auckland's durbar tent in characteristic pose, legs curled under him, left foot held in right hand, one stocking off, one on. He seemed pleased with the portrait of Queen Victoria which Emily had painted for him before she left Simla ("it has cost me much trouble to invent a whole queen, robes and all" [*UC*, p. 175]). "I do not think he quite understood it," wrote a British officer who was present, "but seemed to think her Majesty made a very decent *Nautch* girl."[44]

On December 3rd there was a march-past of troops which

15 Maharajah Ranjit Singh (watercolour by Emily Eden)

Emily watched, a dazzling spectacle, especially "thousands of Run-jit's [sic] followers all dressed in yellow or red satin, with quantities of their lead horses *trapped* in gold and silver tissues, and all of them sparkling with jewels" (*UC*, p. 205). George and Ranjit then conversed in a *shamiana* (open-sided tent) looking out onto a compound planted not with flowers but with forty-two thousand little lamps. A beguiling land, but beyond the dazzle, Emily could still see Ranjit Singh very clearly:

> He is a very drunken old profligate, neither more nor less. Still he has made himself a great king; he has conquered a great many powerful enemies; he is remarkably just in his government; he has disciplined a large army; he hardly ever takes away life, which is wonderful in a despot; and he is excessively beloved by his people (*UC*, p. 209).

For three weeks, there were visits back and forth between the two camps, and much informal mingling. Almost too much for Emily; Sher Singh, Ranjit's second son, had an annoying habit of always dropping in on the Edens just at dinner-time. He was a handsome man, a bit of a dandy, whose tent was filled with mirrors and French scent bottles,[45] but it was his seven-year-old son, Pertab, who captivated Emily. She painted his portrait, and taught him English, the first words he learnt being "Chance, sit up." Emily's attitude had changed since her arrival in India, and was no longer the usual one of her compatriots there. The new clarity of vision and depth of feeling which she had gradually been acquiring since Cawnpore allowed her to see that natives were not clowns or clods or pieces of furniture. They were sensitive, even admirable, human beings. She saw them not only as individuals, but as friends who inspired affection, and the list kept growing: her beloved *jemadar*, Pertab and, eventually, the old Cyclops himself, Ranjit Singh.

At the end of December, the Governor-General's camp moved on for further ceremonial visits with Ranjit at Amritsar and Lahore. Five days before Christmas, Emily found herself in the Shalimar gardens, entranced to think that "it is the real Shalimar where Lalla Rookh recognised Feramorz" (*uc*, p. 223). In January 1839, the British troops marched out of camp towards Afghanistan to seize Kandahar and Ghazni and Kabul. Macnaghten went with them to act as Shah Shuja's adviser once Dost Mahomed had been routed. It was all going to be a simple matter.

Mr Wimberley, the chaplain, also left the camp; his wife, Mary, was at Simla awaiting a confinement. "He set off with some cold dinner in one hand and *Culpepper's Midwifery* in the other" reported Emily (*uc*, p. 247). She herself was very unwell; "fever in camp is about the most compendious definition of intense misery I know" she wrote on January 30th (*uc*, p. 254). "Fever," most often some form of malaria, was another of the trials which all British women in India had to endure. H.S. Cunningham describes "fever" most graphically in *Chronicles of Dustypore* as a "fiend" who "shakes his victims and racks them, and gets into their heads and beats a kettledrum there and sets a tribe of imps to dance a sort of infernal ballet all about each quivering limb; he freezes them so that the poor shivering wretches bury themselves under mountains of rugs, parches them till they feel like Dives in torture; turns their brains to mud, their high spirits to the very blackest gall."[46] India's First Ladies suffered with the rest; Emily was luckier than some; her fevers were not fatal.

By mid-March, Emily and her aching bones were back at Simla, and after four and a half months in camp "the blessing of being in a house again is not to be described," she exulted. "We had rain every week, which kept the tents constantly dripping and we were very often apparently pitched in a lake, and had to be carried through the water to dress. I was hardly a month the whole time free from ague, and how George and Fanny are so constantly well is a matter of astonishment to our doctor and every one else." (*mel*, p. 308). At the end of March, Emily reported to her English friend Elizabeth Copley that "the army is walking quietly into Kabul without opposition, the chief difficulty has been want of water in the desert ... and the officers who began by complaining that their supply of claret was cut are now in great spirits that they are on full allowance of water."[47]

On April 25th, Shah Shuja entered Kandahar in triumph, and Emily was jubilant. "A few days after my letter to you was sealed," she wrote to Mary on May 23rd, "G. [George] got the official accounts of the taking of Kandahar, or rather how Kandahar took Shah Shujah, and *would have* him for its King. There never was anything so satisfactory" (*UC*, p. 290). The officers' wives left behind at Simla were also jubilant, and saw "with their mind's eye their husbands eating apricots and drinking acid sherbet" (*UC*, p. 292). Simla was particularly gay that spring. Emily gave orders that at the celebration ball on Queen Victoria's birthday a large banner emblazoned with "Kandahar" was to be part of the decorations. She knew that would please George. But she was still able to see, underneath the Raj's burgeoning imperialistic pride, the real moral inequities of the British presence in India.

She became incensed at "a brute of a man," a British superintendent of roads, who suspected some of his native road-workers of robbery. He erected a gibbet, strung up sixteen of them with their feet off the ground, flogged them, lit straw underneath and kept them there for fourteen hours. One man died and another became insensible. The European jury brought in a "not guilty" verdict to the manslaughter charge (*LI*, II, 148 – 49). Emily deplored the insensitivity of most British towards natives now that her own empathy was in the ascendant. The indigo planters were the worst offenders. Dr Drummond told her of one who kept two dogs for "hunting the niggers." "I had a famous run this morning," the planter had reported, "after a black fellow on the course and brought him down" (*LI*, II, 252). But the natives themselves were quite as morally reprehensible as the British. The lot of Indian women made Emily furious. They were never educated in any way at all, never allowed outside their houses, never regarded as more than chattels of their menfolk. "I am quite sure I should have gone wrong," fumed Emily, "particularly wrong, if I had been one of these shut-up ladies, out of mere spite" (*MEL*, p. 336). When she overheard a male Indian remark to a male Britisher: "You are the slaves of your women, and we are the masters of ours," Emily retorted that if she "could get into their *zenana* [women's quarters] we should hear another version" (*LI*, II, 261). She also perceived the potential for violence lying dormant beneath such an innocent occasion as a Simla ball:

> Twenty years ago no European had ever been here, and there we were, with the band playing the "Puritani" ... and eating salmon from Scotland, and ... observing that St. Cloup's *potage à la Julienne* was perhaps better than his other soups ... and all this in the face of those high hills, some of which have remained untrodden since the creation, and we, 105 Europeans, being surrounded by at least 3,000 mountaineers, who, wrapped in their hill blankets, looked on at what we call our polite amusements, and bowed to the ground if a European came near them. I sometimes wonder they do not cut all our heads off, and say nothing more about it. (*UC*, pp. 293–94).

They didn't, of course, cut off heads – not that particular mountain tribe – but Emily would prove to be a prescient observer, nonetheless. Simla's spring gaiety continued, with "beautiful tableaux with music, and one or two very well acted farces" (*MEL*, p. 311). Everyone was amused, except Simla's two resident clergymen. Emily commented with her usual astringency:

> The two clergymen who are here ... have begun a course of sermons against what they call a destructive torrent of worldly gaiety. They had much better preach against the destructive torrent of rain which has now set in for the next three months, and not only washes away all gaiety, but all the paths, in the literal sense, which lead to it (*MEL*, p. 311).

On July 1st Emily was saddened to hear "of dear old Ranjit's death." He had died on June 27th, and four of his wives and five of his Kashmir slave girls had thrown themselves onto his funeral pyre. Later Emily bought back from Company stores "a little ring which Ranjit gave me, a poor diamond, but the only one within my means, for love of the old man" (*UC*, pp. 381 – 82). The genteel English spinster and the debauched Sikh despot were worlds apart in so many ways, but some silken chord – woven of mutual wit and wisdom – had bound them together.

The soldier-wives of Simla became even more jubilant on July 23rd: Ghazni had been taken. The British were proud of themselves: 500 Afghans killed, 3,500 prisoners taken, 1,800 horses captured, while they themselves had "only 180 killed and wounded, a mere nothing."[48] (The looting at Ghazni had been rather shocking. British soldiers had rushed into the inner court of the Chief's palace as soon as it was taken, smashed the beautiful carved woodwork in windows and doors, rushed out again with "cashmere shawls, ermine dresses, and ladies' inexpressibles" over "their blood-stained uniforms." "Such a scene of plunder and confusion I never saw" reported one British officer.)[49]

The triumphant British army pushed ahead to Kabul, and on August 6th routed the Afghans there as well. They placed Shah Shujah on the throne and Dost Mahomed fled north. The Shah entered Kabul in triumph, wearing a three-cornered hat with a large emerald hung from each corner. (The people of Kabul were massed on every hill and house-top to see him, but, reported the same British officer, "I neither heard nor saw any enthusiasm.")[50]

Simla celebrated with a ball on September 18th, where the decorations included, as Emily reported happily, "transparencies of the taking of Ghazni, 'Auckland' in all directions, arches and verandahs made up of flowers" (*UC*, p. 319). George beamed from his whist table, and Emily was pleased because he was. Later he would be rewarded by his Queen with an earldom for waging such a successful Afghan campaign.

At the end of October, the Governor-General's party left Simla for another dusty march which would eventually take them back, at long last, to Calcutta, stopping on the way at Delhi, Allahabad

and Benares, among other places. The whole up-country trip had
further sapped Emily's physical strength and undermined her mental health as well. She wrote to Mary of her "worn-out spirits and
battered constitution":

> G. who has always been a sort of idol to me, is, I really think,
> fonder of me than ever, and more dependent on me, as I am
> his only confidant.... Still, I have had enough of it, and as
> people say in ships, there is a difficulty in 'carrying on'.
>   "My blood creeps now only in drops through its course,
> and the heart that I had of old, stirs feebly and heavily within
> me." It is the change from youth to age, and made in unfamiliar
> scenes, so that it is the more felt (*UC*, p. 337).

Emily was only forty-two; India had aged her prematurely. In that
sere November of 1839, Emily looked at the "brown, arid plains
and browner, arider people" (*UC*, p. 338) and saw the husks of her
own life. "I feel unusually detached from the future, from having
enjoyed our young days so eagerly" she told Mary. Something had
snapped; hope and enthusiasm had drained away, leaving only a
wasteland of the spirit.

Emily had been attacked by that disease which did more harm
among British women in India than any physical debility. This
"inertia of soul" Maud Diver calls an "insidious tendency to fatalism."[51] "Anglo-Indian tissues material and spiritual," says a fic-
tional *memsahib* after twenty-two years in Calcutta, "are apt to
turn ... to a substance somewhat resembling cork."[52] "People are
born and burned and born and burned and nothing in the world
matters" sighs another *memsahib*.[53] In E.M. Forster's *A Passage to
India*, Mrs Moore falls victim to this same Indian malady in the
Marabar Caves: "Pathos, piety, courage – they exist, but are identical, and so is filth. Everything exists, nothing has value."[54]

Emily's spirits sank even further when George had to hurry
back to Calcutta at the end of January 1840 because trouble was
brewing in Afghanistan. "G's going is a great grief," she wrote to

Mary. "People who care about each other never ought to part for a day; it is all so uncertain" (*UC*, p. 385). She worried about him constantly, and wrote on February 6th: "I cannot get on at all without him. There is nobody in this country who understands me" (*UC*, p. 388). "'Oh! my coevals, remnants of yourselves' I often think of that," sighed Emily. "I am a remnant of faded yellow gingham" (*UC*, p. 389).

On March 1st, she and Fanny arrived back in Calcutta, but reunion with George lifted Emily's spirits only a little. Living in India had permanently corroded Emily's soul with bitterness. On November 17th, she dipped her pen in acid and wrote: "Karak Singh, Ranjit's successor, is dead.... I fancy Karak's wives found him rather a bore, for only one of them has thought it necessary to burn herself" (*LI*, II, 207). Rumours said that Karak, Ranjit's first-born and an idiot, had been poisoned with a potion of ground emeralds. Emily described the subsequent turmoil in Ranjit's kingdom to her brother Robert:

> His kingdom [was] a good kingdom while he was there to keep his one eye upon them, but the instant he died it all fell into confusion, and his soldiers have now murdered all their French ... and English officers, and are marauding wildly all over the country.... It might at last furnish one of those pretences for interference England delights in, and when once we begin I know (don't you?) what becomes of this country we assist – swallowed up whole (*MEL*, pp. 342 – 43).

Nine years later, Britain did indeed annex the Punjab; Emily must have felt a grim glee at her prescience. Her intelligence and her keen sense of the ridiculous are powerful probes, revealing snobbery, brutality, racism, sexist bias ... and imperial greed. She was never taken in by rhetoric or cant. For Emily there were no sacred cows.

It was a disturbing world that spring. At dinner, in February 1841, one of the sepoys on guard had gone berserk. He had come

rushing into the dining-room "to state his grievances to the Governor-General, and he had drawn his bayonet and was stabbing
away at everybody who tried to stop him.... It took ten of them
[the sentries] to hold him, and his screams were horrible" (*LI* II,
223). A month later, "poor little Chance" became so ill he had to
be put away. "I suppose it is very foolish; in short, I see it is; but
for eight years Chance has been an amusement, and he is connected
with Greenwich ... and altogether we have been through so many
vicissitudes of life together that I feel quite lonesome" (*LI,* II,
229 – 30). "Poor Jimmund has been sobbing all day," Emily continued, able to look beyond her own pain.

In April a cholera epidemic swooped down. A gentleman visiting Calcutta reported that he counted "more than 200 bearers
who had dropped down dead on the roadside," and on April 2nd,
Emily's tailor "went away from his work quite well at five
o'clock ... and was dead before morning" (*LI,* II, 232).

On May 24th there was the usual ball at Government House
to celebrate Queen Victoria's birthday; this year Dost Mahomed,
whose kingdom she had snatched away, was an honoured guest.
The British were being particularly courteous to the Dost; he was
in theory their prisoner but they were allowing him to tour about
and see British power and majesty at close range. Emily described
Dost Mahomed to an English friend as a "well-mannered man very
kingly in his ways but carrying off the present position very well.
It was the first time he had ever seen European women in society
but no native ever betrays astonishment. He and I played two games
of chess – each won one."[55]

The heat was truly unbearable that May. "Doctors who have
been in India thirty-five years say they never remember such a
season" wrote Emily.[56] She hadn't slept for three nights; it was too
hot even for a drive, or to go up river to Barrackpore. They hadn't
been for six weeks. Emily and her maid Wright fainted by turns
while dressing for breakfast.

Sir William Macnaghten, recently raised to knighthood, wrote reassuringly to George that summer from Kabul where he was acting as political agent and living in the British residency. All was well; the British garrison's commander, old General Elphinstone, was complaining rather more than usual of his gout; the 16th Lancers, who kept a small pack of fox-hounds for hunting, had had some rather good runs.[57]

Then, without warning, the blow struck. Emily reported it all on October 3rd:

> There has been a rebellion in the town of Kabul; Sir A. Burnes and his brother murdered, and a Lieut. Sturt stabbed in five places in the presence of Shah Shuja, who interfered to save him and succeeded, but seems to have little influence with his wild chiefs. All the news that comes is from a letter of Lady Sale who is in Kabul, to her husband [General Sale] who was wounded at Jellalabad. She writes very heroically, and always was an active, strong-minded woman. Many people think it impossible that any man will ever come alive from Kabul.... The women who are there are a sore subject to think of; the Afghans are such a savage set. We know most of the ladies there; one has seven small children with her, and another two (*LI*, II, 266 – 67).

Later, the heroic Lady Sale wrote that food was so scarce that they were eating the few ponies and camels left alive. Emily remembered sitting in the drawing-room at Bowood while firelight glinted on old silver and mahogany, and Alexander Burnes talked enthusiastically about Kabul. Now he'd been slashed to pieces. On November 1st, poor Burnes had called on Macnaghten whom he was to succeed as political agent, and congratulated him on keeping Afghanistan so tranquil. The next day, Burnes was hacked to death by a group of rebels headed by Dost Mahomed's son, Mahomed Akbar Khan.[58]

On Christmas day, Akbar Khan and his men seized Macnaghten and some officers while they were out riding. Macnaghten struggled vigorously with Akbar Khan, crying "For God's sake" over and over in his faultless Persian. Akbar Khan drew forth the pistol which Sir William had presented to him the day before, and shot him dead. Then the *ghazees* swarmed round and slashed at his body with their knives.[59]

"Poor Macnaghten's murder has been a great shock; we knew him so well, and it has been such an atrocious act of treachery," wrote Emily, stunned.[60] She had once described him as "our Lord Palmerston, a dry sensible man, who wears an enormous pair of blue spectacles, and speaks Persian, Arabic and Hindustani rather more fluently than English" (*MEL*, p. 300).

The terror thundered on.

At the beginning of January 1842, the beleaguered British force, starving in their Kabul cantonments, were allowed to start their return march to India. It was, as they all knew, a suicide mission; they had no food, the snow was three feet deep and there were murderous tribesmen waiting on the heights of the grim Khurd gorges. Four thousand soldiers set out, many with wives and children, to make that terrible trek. Every mile of the road was strewn with bodies, as the swords and matchlocks of hostile tribesmen slashed and thundered. Cold and hunger took their toll. Among the women were Macnaghten's widow and Lady Sale, who would later write a poignant account of the experience. Some of the women had only thin dresses; some had babies a few days old; four of them bore children on the march.[61] At the end of the third day, women and children were sent back to Kabul under the escort of Mahomed Akbar Khan. "Think of poor Lady [Macnaghten] given over to her husband's murderer," shuddered Emily (*LI*, II, 285).

There would be many more such harrowing experiences for India's *memsahibs*. If First Ladies were necessarily protected from such grisly ordeals, they also lost out on the chance to develop, and quickly, as Lady Sale had, the "masculine" virtues of quick action under stress, dauntless courage and physical stamina. Perhaps there was a hint of envy in Emily's description of Lady Sale as "an active, strong-minded woman."

In the Kabul disaster, the women were luckier than their men; they at least survived. Of the four thousand men who set out from Kabul only one survived: Dr Brydon who, wounded and weak and almost incoherent, staggered a week later into Jellalabad. His tale of horror reached Emily at Calcutta:

> Capt. —— had a letter lent to him with such horrible details of that retreat; it has made me feel quite ill. All the accounts are gathered from Dr. —— [Brydon].... He was on a pony which had had nothing to eat since they left Kabul; his sword had broken off in the last struggle, and he was very much wounded. An officer who was with him had a person mounted behind him, and they kept up nearly to the end, and were then, after being desperately wounded, carried off separately (*LI*, II, 288 – 89).

"George is looking shockingly," Emily reported. "All this worry has ... made a difference of ten years at least in his look" (*LI*, II, 292 – 93). George had good reason to look ill; he had, as one historian puts it, involved Britain in a war that "has been stamped as the most unjust, ill-advised and unnecessary that ever the British name or reputation was risked on."[62] Lord Auckland had made a terrible blunder in refusing the friendship of Dost Mahomed, a strong and able ruler. He had "plunged Afghanistan into four years of misery, saddled India with a bill for fifteen million pounds."[63] How had it happened? George poured out his feelings of disbelief and shock to his friend Charles Greville, who recorded them in his diary:

> Auckland, who writes, as is natural, in great despondency, says that the whole thing is unintelligible to him, for, as far as they know, the 5,000 British troops at Kabul were never assailed by above 10,000 or 12,000 Afghans, irregularly armed with matchlocks and spears, while our force were provided with artillery.... According to all our notions and all former

experience, a British force could always put to flight or destroy native tribes ten times more numerous.[64]

The whole thing was unintelligible, as later massacres of British by Indians would be unintelligible. How could any British person, raised on Western notions of the supremacy of reason and the sanctity of human life hope to understand? How could he or she, blinded by racist superiority, comprehend Indian minds randomly flowing, fatalistic, focused not on this life but on the one, or the hundred, still to come? "It is unintelligible," puzzled George; "inexplicable," sighed Emily, both of them craving what India would never, ever give: a rational explanation which presupposed some logical order in the world.

The Afghan disaster gave Sir Robert Peel, who had become British Prime Minister in September 1841, an excellent excuse – he had long been a sworn enemy of Lord Melbourne's – to send off letters recalling Lord Auckland as Governor-General and replacing him with Lord Ellenborough.

Emily felt little joy at the thought of being finally homeward bound. She had been too battered emotionally by her final Indian years. Fears beat at her like vulture's wings, particularly when she learned that the Hungerford would bear her home:

She has ... the particular recommendation of being the only ship that I have always declared I would never go home in, because of her age. Now, as the only other resolution I ever pronounced was declaring from the time I was seven years old that I never would go out to India, it seems that the going home from it in the "Hungerford" will be an act of great consistency (LI, II, 287).

Having felt that Indian void where courage and depravity exist side by side, both without meaning, "consistency" was something Emily craved. Her terror of "that horrid sea" wouldn't go away.

"I cannot conceal the melancholy fact," Emily wrote on March 4th, "that, whenever I think of it, I am frightened to death, and it prevents me eating anything now." "This is my birthday," she continued grimly, "and besides fright, I am nearly dead of old age" (*LI*, II, 294).

There was a six-day auction at Messrs Tallah and Company in Calcutta of gifts presented by India's rajahs to Lord Auckland. There were brilliant scarlet silks from Bhawulpore, Duknee turbans of purple and gold, embroidered scarves from Delhi, long shawls from Kashmir, swords whose hilts and scabbards were encrusted with jewels, elephant and horse trappings tinkling with emerald-drops and pearls.[65] A dazzling display of the riches of the exotic East, a dazzling river of rupees streaming into the coffers of the Company – the Company, "whose great sprawling lion is carved and stamped everywhere." (*LI*, II, 139). But Emily was no longer dazzled. Gold frogs no longer compensated for the marsh that was India. It was swallowing her whole, a fearful quagmire into which she felt herself permanently sinking.

Lord Ellenborough arrived to stay at Government House on the last day of February, 1842. The Eden party and the Ellenborough party skirted each other warily for the next twelve days. Ellenborough, who once declared that "War and Women are in reality the only fit interests for a man,"[66] had been deserted by his wife, the beautiful but wayward Jane Digby, who moved on to a long string of husbands and lovers, including the King of Bavaria, before settling down happily with a bedouin sheikh. As Governor-General, Lord Ellenborough would be autocratic and arbitrary in his power, forcing on India a measure of control he had never been able to urge on his wife. He would later incur Emily's undying hostility by publicly denouncing George's Afghan policy.

On March 12, 1842, the farewell ceremony for Lord Auckland and his sisters took place in the great marble hall of Government House. Emily and Fanny wore their travelling dresses, and all the bishops, judges and other dignitaries of Calcutta turned out to say

goodbye. " 'The snow will soon be gone,' said one bishop, referring
to the reverses suffered by the British in Afghanistan, 'we shall then
get through the passes; and *when we get at them* – ' His lordship did
not conclude the sentence, nor was it needed – every man's heart
suggested the rest."[67] The bishop was an accurate prophet: some
months later, a British force under General Pollock advanced on
Kabul, freed the prisoners, gave the Afghans a vengeful thrashing,
removed Shah Shuja from the throne and put back Dost Mahomed.

The Edens, most particularly Emily, left India feeling older,
sadder, more disillusioned than when they had come. Nor did it
lighten Emily's mood when she discovered, during the voyage
home, that the ancient, creaking *Hungerford* was deficient in everything except cockroaches, which multiplied prodigiously all the way
to England.

EMILY AND GEORGE and Fanny moved into a house in London's
Kensington Gore, opposite Hyde Park, into an elegant white villa
which they could now easily afford. They called it Eden Lodge,
and filled it with oriental carpets and furniture and other Indian
spoils. Emily found herself back in the familiar eddies of politics,
but more inclined than formerly to rock the boat. After British
honour had been restored by victory at Kabul, Lord Ellenborough
had issued, with home Government approval, a proclamation stating that in future it would be British policy not to interfere in Afghan
affairs. Lord John Russell rallied the Whig opposition at a meeting
to decide whether or not they should oppose a vote of thanks to
Ellenborough from both Houses. They decided not to oppose it.
"Auckland took no part, of course," recorded Charles Greville in
his diary, "but entirely concurred." Greville continued:

> His sister, Emily Eden, however, who has a great influence
> over him, and who is a very clever and wrong-headed woman,
> was furious, and evinced great indignation against all their

Whig friends, especially Auckland himself, for being so prudent and moderate, and for not attacking Ellenborough with all the violence which she felt and expressed.[68]

A "very clever" woman who almost always saw the world clearly – except where her brother George was concerned.

Once settled at Eden Lodge, Emily did her best to pick up her old life, but India had bruised her too deeply. She spent more and more time on her sofa, suffering a number of indeterminate ills. She was at home in the mornings to the great Whig leaders, Lord John Russell, Lord Grey and Lord Palmerston, who "came to imbibe wisdom, tolerance and common sense, for she had all these."[69]

In 1844 Emily published, to wide acclaim, a portfolio of twenty-four lithographs drawn from her Indian sketches, entitled *Portraits of the Princes and People of India*. Holding it proudly in her hands, she must have seen it as the only tangible good resulting from her Indian sojourn. There they all were, quite a rogue's gallery: Dost Mahomed, long-faced and dour, dear old Ranjit, little Pertab, solemn and round-eyed in his turban....

When Lord John Russell and the Whigs came back into power in 1846, George was again made First Lord of the Admiralty, and Emily had to be content with much less of his company. When she was well enough, she still went to Bowood, haunted for her now by Alexander Burnes's ghost.

Emily's chronic invalidism and mental depression increased after George died suddenly on January 1, 1849. He had gone down to the Grange, Lord Ashburton's seat in Hampshire, on Friday, suffered a stroke while out shooting on Saturday, and died early Monday morning. It was all so sudden, the way death had pounced in India. Emily was too ill to go to him on Saturday; Fanny went instead and was at his side when he died. "To his sisters," wrote Charles Greville, "he was a husband, a brother, and a friend combined in one, and to them it is a bereavement full of sadness almost amounting to despair."[70] George's funeral took place on January 6th, with Fanny and William Osborne, but not Emily, following his coffin to the family vault in Kent.[71] A subscription of two thousand pounds was quickly raised by his friends, and a bronze statue of the Earl of Auckland, Governor-General of India, was duly shipped off to be erected in Calcutta.[72] It was a whole year before Emily could speak of his death. Then she opened her heart to her friend Theresa:

> It was a twelvemonth yesterday since he left me to go to the Grange. I had got out of bed and was settled on the sofa, so that he might go off with a cheerful impression of me, and we had our luncheon together, and he came in again in his fine cloak to say goodbye, and I thought how well he was looking. And that was the close of a long life of intense affection. I do not know why I should feel additionally sad as these anniversaries come round, for I never think less or more on the subject on any day (MEL, p. 381).

Emily felt like a listless anachronism and lonelier than ever, for Fanny had died four months after George. Fanny had been weak and apathetic ever since her return to England and its square little cage of female conventions. She lay day after day on a sofa in Eden Lodge remembering Rajmahal's wide spaces and savage beat. Fanny seemed to have some sickness not of body – doctors examined her and could find nothing wrong – but of soul. On April 26, 1849, Frances Harriett Eden died, aged forty-eight.[73]

Emily spent the next twelve Christmas seasons in bed; various illnesses kept her there as the anniversary of George's death came round. In 1859 her first novel, *The Semi-Detached House*, a comedy of manners showing the hypocrisy and snobbery of the British, was published anonymously to much acclaim. She was pleased to report to Theresa that Sydney Herbert had called on his way to dine with that other chronic invalid, Florence Nightingale, to tell Emily that her book "had become a sort of byword in London, and that if anybody talked of having a house, the answer was, Semi-detached, of course" (MEL, p. 396). Soon everyone knew who'd written it. "They say the semi-detached," wrote Lady Stanley to her husband, "is by Emily Eden who has been so long ill, and that it is well worth reading."[74] *The Semi-Attached Couple*, a satire of high society, begun so long ago in Emily's happy Greenwich days, was published the following year.

Overall, Emily's novels are less original and sprightly than her letters, but there are some brilliant sparks. "The Baroness wore a gown of such very bright yellow that the sun was affronted and went in," Emily writes crisply in *The Semi-Detached House*, and gives this description of the hero of *The Semi-Attached Couple*, as viewed by ogling church-goers:

> Lord Teviot was exactly what they expected, so very distinguished and so good-looking. Some thought him too attentive to his prayers for a man in love, and some thought him too attentive to Lady Helen for a man in church; but eventually the two factions joined, and thought him simply very attentive.

There are flashes of the old Emily, too, in her letters; she often turned her satiric wit on her own ill health. After Lord Brougham had been to see her in 1860 she wrote to Theresa:

> But on going away he always cries so much at the prospect of our not meeting again, that he leaves me in a puzzled state of low spirits. All the more, that I have not the remotest idea whether it is his death or mine that he is crying over; but he looks so well, I think it must be mine (MEL, p. 401).

When, that same year, William Gladstone came to visit her, Emily found him "not aristocratic" and "not frivolous enough for me; if he were soaked in boiling water and rinsed till he was twisted into a rope, I do not suppose a drop of fun would ooze out."[75] Gladstone had wrapped himself in mid-Victorian High Seriousness, and Emily was never guilty of that. Her happy years at Eden Farm were now very far away; George was gone and everyone else grown far too

The Hon. Emily Eden
from a drawing by George Richmond, R.A.

solemn; it was time to depart. In 1866, Emily spent seven months in her Eden Lodge bedroom, never once going downstairs. Three years later she died, on August 5, 1869, in her 73rd year, and was buried close to George in the family vault.

Six years before her death, Emily had thoughtfully set down for the niece who would eventually edit her letters a piece of characteristic advice: "You are quite right to make your children's childhood happy, and as merry as possible, but please do not spoil them. Life does not spoil anybody, and so teach them early to take it as it comes – cheerfully." (*MEL*, p. 404). Emily had struggled always to do that, and had succeeded up until the time she went to India. Motivated only by love for her brother, she had gone there feeling, for the first time in her life, both fragile and fearful. Her fears had proved valid, for India's searing impact on her cool intelligence had precipitated an irreversible physical and psychological decline. Up-country dust had settled on her soul and stayed. Emily Eden had paid a high price for her love.

❋ II ❋

CHARLOTTE CANNING

*The peacock is regarded as the vehicle of the Hindu god of war,
variously called Kumara, Skanda or Kartikeya.*

MAJOR W.H. SLEEMAN
Rambles and Recollections of an Indian Official

S HE WAS BORN in a bed that had belonged to Pauline Borghese,
the beautiful sister of Napoleon I, Emperor of France. After the
British trounced him at Waterloo in 1815, they appropriated Pauline's palatial residence in Paris's Faubourg St Honoré for their
Embassy. Two years later, on the night of March 30, 1817, the
Ambassador, Sir Charles Stuart, was sleeping fitfully in one brocaded bedroom while his wife Elizabeth was labouring in another
to produce their first child. The Stuarts had been married for just
over a year, and wanted a son and heir for whom they had prepared
a nursery grand enough for "the King of Rome."¹ "At five this
morning," wrote Elizabeth to her mother on March 31st, "my ears
were blessed with the most welcome sound of a baby's cries. Pray
forgive her for being a girl" (Hare, I, 61). If, by being female, the
baby caused her parents pain, it was the first and last time in her
life she would do so. Her parents christened her Charlotte Elizabeth
after Queen Charlotte, George III's wife, who had graciously consented to be her godmother. Pomp strutted into Charlotte Elizabeth's life at her christening, and stayed, without lapse, till her
funeral. "Lady Mansfield stood proxy for the Queen," reported

95

Lady Granville, "and I never saw anything so ridiculous as her entry with two little pages in Highland costume holding up her train."[2] Plenty of public show and opulence: that was the first gift Charlotte's fairy godmother, as distinct from her regal one, poured over that ribboned, lace-frilled bassinet. Granddaughter of one Earl, future wife of another, named for one Queen, Lady-in-Waiting to another, the Honourable Charlotte Stuart would spend her life in palaces and mansions, her dinners served on gold plates, her letters proffered on silver salvers. Her sense of self-worth would come to her from the cool caress of her pearls, comforting and calming on her clear-skinned throat, announcing to the world by their superior size and lustre that the Hon. Charlotte deserved (but, alas, didn't always get) the very best.

When she was seven or eight years old, Charlotte drew a butterfly with red wings and a green body on a piece of paper, and carefully wrote underneath: "*Mon cher papa et ma chère maman. Je vous souhaite la bonne année et une bonne santé. Charlotte Stuart.*"[3] The adult Charlotte is already there in that little New Year's card: it is all so neat, so pretty, so proper in its sentiments, so politely and correctly phrased. "If anyone was ever born good, she was," her future sister-in-law would later claim (Hare, III, 179). Twelve years before Charlotte was born, Hannah More, that pious Evangelical spinster, had written a conduct book for another Charlotte, this one a Princess, daughter of the future George IV. In *Hints Towards Forming the Character of a Young Princess*, as she had in *Strictures on the Modern System of Female Education* (1799), Miss More set forth the sober Evangelical prescription for female conduct which would prevail through mid-Victorian times and beyond. The emphasis had shifted now from physical delicacy to mental, from propriety to piety, from deportment and embroidery to selfless duty and good works. Unfortunately, Princess Charlotte died before her character could be said to be completely "formed," but Charlotte Stuart, born that year, took up the torch with persevering zeal. She became a perfect paragon of all the virtues Hannah More prescribed and the rest of female England tried, with varying degrees of success, to practise. Plenty of pomp and parade, plenty of gracious living, great dollops of goodness: all these Charlotte Stuart would have.

She had lovely deep-blue eyes but a hurt look came into them early, and stayed. She could see with her level gaze, there amid the marble and ormulu, that her mother was unhappy. Charlotte's father, grandson of the eccentric Third Earl of Bute, who had been Prime Minister for a few months in the early reign of George III, had a roving eye and a rakish tendency to indulge himself. He was particularly partial to actresses. Charlotte's mother, who "by dint of rouge and an auburn wig looks only *not* pretty but nothing worse,"[4] tried to turn a blind eye to her husband's hectic philandering, but paid a price by talking "too much, too loud" in company.[5] Grave, sensitive and observant, Charlotte perceived her mother's chagrin and her compensating comforts: love of ceremony and love of clothes. Lady Elizabeth's father gave her an allowance of one thousand pounds a year, all of which she spent on clothes, describing them in braid-and-button detail in letters to her mother. After one long rhapsody on a red velvet ball-gown trimmed with gold embroidery and fur, Lady Elizabeth added, "Charlotte screamed with ecstasy at the brilliancy of my appearance" (Hare, I, 83). Charlotte was two at the time but already addicted to finery.

On April 14, 1818, Charlotte's only sister, Louisa Anne, had been born. "Charlotte is less of a princess than she was," her mother wrote two weeks later, "for she has had less homage of late ... and fewer opportunities of being gracious" (Hare, II, 66–67). Her grandmother predicted with some accuracy, when Charlotte was three, that she "will have her reign early" and "will chain men to her while she hangs on them for support" (Hare, I, 102).

Charlotte grew up soberly schooled in the probable disappointments of matrimony, soothed by the beautiful houses and gardens in which she found herself. There was Wimpole, the fine Cambridgeshire estate with immensely wide elm avenues leading to a huge old house where her grandparents, the Earl and Countess of Hardwicke, lived. At a children's costume party there on December 31, 1824, Charlotte was dressed as a French lady "in a court dress, with a long train, toque, and feathers, which became her extremely, and she looked like an elegant woman at a distance, and not at all like a child" (Hare, I, 141). An elegant woman: at the age of seven. There was another Hardwicke estate called Tyttenhanger, near St Albans, a noble old house with rich red-brick mouldings, splendid carved-oak staircase and ancient moat. And on the Hampshire coast was Highcliffe Castle, with its gargoyles and oriel windows carved round with saints.

Charlotte's father became madly eccentric as he aged. Once he disappeared from a crowded ballroom, jumped into a handy fishing-smack anchored in the harbour, then wrote to his frantic wife a week later from Iceland as if nothing had happened. As he grew more wildly flamboyant and romantic, Charlotte grew more con-ventional and constrained, in an effort to compensate her poor distracted mother.

By the time she made her début in London society, Charlotte was a very pretty, very poised young lady. In addition to her deep-blue eyes, she had thick eyelashes, dark, velvet-wing eyebrows and a long, slender neck. Her chestnut hair had grown so long that her maid constantly trod on it as she brushed it to shining perfection. Charlotte wore this luxuriant abundance tightly coiled and pinned around her head. According to the actress Fanny Kemble, who first saw her at a London dinner party deep in conversation with the artist Landseer, Charlotte had "modesty, grace and dignity" and "a sort of chastity that characterized her whole person and appear-ance." She had a "severely sweet expression, or sweetly stern" and "a fine-textured cheek, where the blood visibly mantles with the mere emotion of speaking and being listened to." "That she was much attached to Lord – –, whose father would not permit the marriage, I have heard repeatedly from people who knew their families," added Fanny Kemble in a gossipy aside, "and Rogers, who was very intimate with hers, told me that he considered her marrying as she did the result of mere disappointment saying: 'She could not have the man she loved, so she gave herself to the man who loved her.' "⁶

The man who loved her, and who married her in St Martin-in-the-Fields on September 5, 1835, was the Hon. Charles John Canning, son of George Canning, statesman and short-term Prime Minister. Charlotte and "Carlo," as she called him, were married on a Sunday, and having knelt and prayed and promised to "love, honour and obey" she did just that, with her usual Christian zeal, till death did them part. She was eighteen; he was twenty-two. Charles would give Charlotte a goodly measure of the riches she required to be happy – his mother Joan was co-heiress with her sister, the Duchess of Portland, of the fortune their father had made at whist-tables – and a goodly measure of homage from the *haut monde*, for in 1837 he became Viscount Canning of Kilbrahan. He would give her as well, but only in the beginning, his love. He was tall, with a marble brow, chiselled features and dignified mien. He had attended Eton and Christ Church, Oxford, where he'd obtained a first in classics, a second in mathematics. His father, George, had been on the point of accepting the Governor-Generalship of India in 1822, when Lord Londonderry's suicide had obligated George Canning to stay in England and succeed him as Foreign Secretary. George IV had offered him the post reluctantly; he disliked George Canning, suspecting he'd had – as who hadn't – adulterous relations with his consort, Queen Caroline of Brunswick.⁷ Charlotte tried to ignore that miasma of adultery that hung round the Cannings: Charles' only sister, Harriet, had married the first Marquess of Clanricarde, notorious for his love affairs. "I am very happy, and am sure I have every chance of continuing so, with such a really good and fond and kind husband," she wrote in sanguine vein to her parents on the day after her wedding (Hare, I, 191).

The young Cannings were often at sea in those early years of marriage. Their yacht, the Gondola, carried them to Spain and

18 Lord Canning (chalk drawing by George Richmond)

Greece, France and Italy. From 1841 to 1846, Charles held the post of Under-Secretary of State for Foreign Affairs in Sir Robert Peel's government and became busy and preoccupied.

Charlotte had to content herself with Perfect Wifehood. Perfect Motherhood was, alas, withheld. His Lordship longed for an heir; Charlotte doubled her goodness to compensate. In 1842, she was given an additional opportunity for abject service. Queen Victoria offered her the post of Lady of the Bedchamber, just vacated by Lady Dalhousie, and Charlotte accepted the great honour. The Queen, two years her junior, had chosen well, having perceived Lady Canning to be "a remarkably nice person, so quiet, unaffected and gentle and so ready to do anything."[8] Charlotte did her duty by her Queen for the next thirteen years, always attentive, always "ready to do anything," which included making countless wreaths of Balmoral heather for the Queenly hair, accompanying the Queenly fingers in piano duets, standing behind the Queenly chair for as much as four hours in the theatre, and walking always one step behind the Queenly train. There were exhausting Royal tours abroad: to Belgium in 1843, to France the same year, to visit King Louis Philippe and his court at Chateau d'Eu. Charlotte was engrossed that year by Eyre's book *Military Operations at Cabul, January 1842*, detailing that disastrous Afghan retreat which had so distressed Emily Eden. Charlotte found it "the most interesting thing" she had ever read.[9]

In September 1844, Charlotte accompanied the Queen to Blair Castle, Scotland, where Prince Albert shot stag, and the Queen wanted "views done for her in every direction." Charlotte painted sketch after sketch, was rewarded with "a little souvenir of himself" by Prince Albert, "the teeth of a stag set like acorns with green enamel leaves."[10]

Charlotte was troubled by Queen Victoria's bad taste in clothes. "Her bonnets would do for an old woman of seventy" and her gowns were "very decidedly badly chosen and quite unlike what she ought to have," Charlotte confided to her diary.[11] She did, however, envy Her Majesty's pearls, a gift from the East India Company, four rows of them "so very white and even, all alike, all round and very large" (Hare, 1, 316). She also envied the Queen and Prince Albert their growing family. "You never saw anything so happy as they are," Charlotte sighed, "with the five babes playing around them" (Hare, 1, 292 – 93).

In August 1845, Charlotte went with the Royals to Germany, met "no end of princes and princesses, all as civil as they can be" (Hare, 1, 289), accompanied the Queen up the Rhine to see dear Albert's birthplace, finally declared herself "almost blind and deaf with fatigue." It was excellent training in self-abnegation and service, and Charlotte performed her duties to perfection during those apprentice years, unconsciously readying herself for a far grander public role.

She was supremely good and chaste – but perhaps a little too coldly chaste within the matrimonial bed. On the surface, Charles Canning was emotionally reticent and reserved, often aloof, abstracted and silent. But underneath was a warm sensuality which stands revealed in his heavy-lidded eyes, full-lipped mouth, and in his love for the passion and panache of bull-fights.[12] He was also very fond of fishing, but "his pleasure in the latter amusement consisted exclusively in throwing the fly. His interest was gone as soon as he had hooked his fish."[13] He had wooed and won his wife ten years before; by 1845 he was ready for a fresh cast in new waters and fell obsessively in love with another woman whose identity is no longer known. He was so besotted with her that he once stood all night under her window.[14] In this one instance, Canning showed himself to be beyond reason and beyond reform. The other woman came into his life, and stayed. Charlotte bore it all, as one could have predicted, patiently, stoically, uncomplainingly. She never mentioned Charles's mistress to anyone except her sister. She smiled bravely, bowed her back to this new burden, almost enjoyed her martyr's role. When, in that same year, 1845, her philandering father died after a long illness, Charlotte wrote to Louisa: "I think Mama ... has much comfort in the memory of how very well she did her duty" (Hare, 1, 290). When Charles and Charlotte were alone, which was rarely now, her attentions grew frantic, took on an edge, sometimes, of hysteria, and succeeded only in driving him farther away.

There was one awful moment at Windsor Castle in January 1850, when Charles's mistress had unexpectedly appeared among the Royals and guests. Charlotte, at least, had kept her *sang-froid*. "Lord Canning's fainting fit whilst out shooting," reported a fellow-guest, "is attributed to the visit of a certain lady, which very considerably annoyed him, as the interview was of a stormy nature, and he had fears it might come to the knowledge of her Majesty. Lady Canning is said to be not the least disturbed about this lady."[15] The taciturn Charles often revealed his inner turmoil in fainting fits. On another occasion, while out shooting with Prince Albert, he had peppered General Grey in the face, narrowly missed shooting the infant Prince of Wales, and fainted dead away with the shock of it all.[16]

And then, miraculously, after ten years of silent suffering, came a heaven-sent reprieve and reward for Charlotte. In June of 1855, Charles was offered the post of Governor-General of India, to succeed his friend and schoolmate Lord Dalhousie. "What do you think of the news Mama told you?" Charlotte asked her sister, Louisa, breathlessly on June 9th. "I cannot tell yet what answer will be given. There are really no reasons against accepting.... But I will not take any part in the decision, only be ready to follow like a dog" (Hare, II, 2). No reasons against accepting, but a strong one in favour, from Charlotte's point of view: Charles would be separated for five whole years from his mistress, still very much in the forefront of his life. "I see *le doigt de Dieu* in it," wrote Louisa to a friend, "it will cause a want to be supplied which will be *the* right thing for her" (Hare, II, 3). *Le doigt de Dieu* was apparently aided by an earthly Lord's, for Lord Elgin, who would succeed Canning as Viceroy, claimed that "it was in order to get Lord Canning away from this [mistress'] influence that one of his most influential friends, a great statesman, old Lord Lansdowne, got the government to appoint Lord Canning to be Governor-General of India."[17]

Charlotte, with great alacrity and suppressed glee, ordered a vast number of white muslin dresses lavishly trimmed with Valenciennes lace, packed the pearls inherited from great-grandmother Baroness Mountstuart, and promised herself that she would replace them with Indian ones as large as the Queen's. In general, however, Charlotte had no thought of going to India to be entertained and have *fun*. She was prepared to do her duty as India's First Lady. In those mid-Victorian years, as George Eliot once observed, duty had almost replaced the Deity as the hub of morality. "It is a duty of paramount importance to a wife," Mrs Sarah Ellis had decreed in her immensely popular conduct book *The Wives of England* (1843), "to ascertain what is her exact position in society, and to endeavour to adapt herself to it wherever it may be."[18] The Eden sisters had taken a casual, even critical attitude to their roles as First Ladies of India, and they had never allowed that role to obscure their individuality. They were, after all, not the Governor-General's wife and helpmeet, but only his sisters; and in the 1830s, with relatively few First Ladies preceding them – many early Governors-General had left their wives in England – the role's traditions and parameters were not so firmly fixed. Even before her arrival, however, Lady Canning, personally acquainted with her predecessor, the exemplary Lady Dalhousie, was already thinking of herself primarily as the important female component of the Governor-Generalship, the consort to the throne. She went out prepared to suffer and sacrifice and serve, and to look supremely elegant while doing so, even when the temperature hit a hundred.

In addition to trunkfuls of fine clothes, Charlotte took with her to India two maids to help her get into and out of them. West and Rain were their names: hopeful reminders of what, after all the Indian sun, she would some day return to. At the end of November, the Cannings said their restrained farewells and left for India.

Twenty years earlier, it had taken the Edens five months to get there; it took the Cannings two, with plenty of sight-seeing along the way. Since the opening of the overland route through Egypt, one could sail to Alexandria, take the train via Cairo to Suez, and sail from there to India. The Cannings spent a few days in Paris for last-minute shopping, then sailed from Marseilles in early December. At Alexandria they stayed in Said Pasha's splendid palace where, as Canning noted, "the towels have gold embroidery six inches deep round them – it is like wiping one's face on a Field Marshal's uniform."[19] At Cairo, they were housed in another Pasha's palace, where one room measured 155 by 60 feet, "with all the gold papers and damask and ormulu"[20] that Paris could provide, Charlotte told her Queen. "We have revelled in the honours paid to us," she wrote to her mother (Hare, II, 6). On January 12, 1856, the Cannings sailed from Suez on board the Indian frigate ss *Feroze*; they were both journalizing frantically. Charles began his diary on January 1st, but made no mention at all of his wife until January 12th, when he noted that his sleeping cabin was on the port side, hers some distance away, with West and Rain's conveniently between.[21] There were two large cabins on the quarter deck where, during the day, Charles and Charlotte also went their separate ways. "Char and I have appropriated each one of the Poop cabins – to read, write and draw in," Charles noted in his diary. He burrowed into a pile of books on India and rarely came up for air. Charlotte tried to appear equally industrious in *her* cabin: "I have got plenty of Eastern books, and try to learn all I can about India; it is rather overwhelming to think how much there is to learn" (Hare, II, 14). So they studied and sweated as the thermometer climbed. At dinner on the night of January 17th, "four white-robed blacks" appeared with palm-leaf fans and took up their stations at the four corners of the table. "I was very grateful to the one at my corner," Charles wrote in his diary, "but Char protested violently against any such attention, and dismissed the Fan nearest to her."

Finally, on January 29th, the Cannings landed at Bombay. Charlotte felt distanced, displaced, able to see but not to feel, as one view after another slid by. There were "crowds and crowds of natives in their white dresses," she told her mother and sister, "all sorts of picturesque people" and "the native town looked most picturesque" (Hare, II, 15 – 16). She and Charles were driven to

Parell, residence of the Governor of the Presidency of Bombay, now occupied by Lord Elphinstone; Parell was five miles beyond the smells and congestion of the native quarter. They were to stay there for a week. Parell was "in a sort of park and large garden" and "I am quite charmed with it," Charlotte reported to her mother with some relief (Hare, II, 15). She hadn't known quite what to expect but Parell was very civilized indeed, positively sumptuous. The very first watercolour in her 1856 sketchbook, with "India" in large, important letters at the top of the page is, fittingly enough, of the exterior of Parell.[22] Inside were large rooms with lovely English chintzes, English-style flower arrangements and white-dimity punkahs with white-covered cords. Charlotte noted everything; she had found her pattern-book for Government House decorating.

That first night, dinner was served "in a verandah entirely draped with white muslin," while rows of "servants in scarlet and gold dresses" stood at attention. A band played while the assembled guests talked in voices "very quiet, and gentle, and low"; Charlotte decided that it must be the heat that made them all "so very piano" in tone (Hare, II, 16). Only one day into her stay, Charlotte was already aware of that bodily inertia which paralyzed so many *mem-sahibs* and which had affected Emily Eden. To that particular Indian malady, at any rate, Charlotte would prove immune.

Charlotte told her mother:

It is so amusing and curious, and I cannot tell you the strange feeling of such overpowering novelty. But it makes one feel absurdly helpless, not to know a person, or a word of the language, or manners and customs of the simplest description. Every plant being totally new to me is not at all the least strange part (Hare, II, 17).

Unlike the Eden sisters, Charlotte had no humour to use as defence against the strangeness. Instead, she made lists: of flower-names and tree-names and Hindi words and local customs. If she could order it all on clean white pages perhaps she could comprehend India. In addition to her list-making, Charlotte's other habitual defence, also unknown to the Eden sisters, would be her prudery. "Delicacy of mind" the conduct books called it, or "inner purity," by which a woman "knows herself to be clean in heart and desire, in body and soul, loving cleanness for its own sake, and not for the credit that it brings."[23] It was prudery from now until the end of the century which, far more than the Arabian Nights myth, kept British women from seeing India whole, with all its unabashed eroticism and deep unconscious urges. In the beginning of her stay, but only then, it was easy for Charlotte Canning to keep Mrs Grundy's plush curtain drawn across her mind.

While the Cannings were still at Bombay, Lord Elphinstone was a charming host and got up two expeditions to famous caves, which showed just how far Raj formality had spread since the Edens' time. On January 31st, a large party went to the caves of Keneri, where everyone had their own cave furnished with washing tubs, sofas, writing-tables "and all requisites down to pen knives and India rubber bands," as Canning noted approvingly in his diary. Lord Elphinstone's servants had laboriously carried all this paraphernalia during the night "to this desolate uninhabited, trackless spot." The Imperial Presence became even more pronounced on February 5th when the Cannings went by steamer to the caves of Elephanta. Tents and huts had been set up outside where the party all changed into evening clothes – all frightfully well organized. Dinner for fifty people was laid in the principal cave, complete with champagne coolers, finger bowls, everything. The British toasted their Queen while Hindu gods carved in the dank rock leered lasciviously.

On Sunday, the Cannings accompanied Lord Elphinstone to church, where the punkahs, as Canning noted in his diary, "drove Char nearly mad." She described their effect:

Imagine a bad dream, in which all the gallery fronts of a London church should detach and swing across to meet their opposite neighbours, all going backwards and forwards at a great pace and with no noise. At first, it was very difficult not to laugh, and then not to cry, the effect was so irritating, and one would have given anything to entreat them to stop. These odious punkahs of the church were solid, painted in stone-coloured panels, and a solid flap appended at the bottom. They pass within a few inches of one's head, and leave a sort of mesmerizing effect that one feels inside one's head (Hare, II, 26).

"Here we are really in India! It feels very like a dream" were the first words Charlotte had written on Indian soil (Hare, II, 14). But with one flick of a punkah the dream could become a nightmare, laughter could turn to tears, the solid fabric of one's life could "detach and swing." And there would be no way to make it stop.

From Bombay, the Cannings sailed in the *Feroze* to Ceylon, where Charles noted ominously in his diary for February 11th that "our European force in India is already unwisely and dangerously small." The next stop was Madras, where they stayed with its Governor, Lord Harris, who had been a class-mate of Charles at Oxford. Of course, Charlotte did a watercolour of Guindy, his large mansion, and one evening, strolling in the garden, she and Charles went to look at the two pet tigers imprisoned there, "in beautiful condition and quite ready to eat us up" (Hare, II, 40). "I thought the bars of their cages looked weak," Canning wrote in his diary, with unconscious prescience.

On February 29th the Cannings travelled up the Hooghly river and prepared to land at Calcutta. It was a very close, hot morning with a dull grey sky. Charlotte was eager to begin the duties of her regal office, and consequently was upset by the arrangements Lord Dalhousie had made for their arrival. His Lordship, whose wife had always crept into balls by a side door after his own grand entrance,[24] arranged for Charlotte to land first, with no pomp at all; it was all reserved for Charles who landed a quarter of an hour later, while she stood inconspicuously on the sidelines like any ordinary *mem-sahib*, and watched. Then an aide-de-camp bundled her into a carriage and drove her to the back entrance of Government House, where there was no one about except Lady Susan Ramsay, Lord Dalhousie's daughter, who was waiting to receive her. Lord Dalhousie's wife, as Charlotte knew, had been one of India's victims. She had died three years before, aboard the ship taking her back to England to recover her health. Lady of the Bedchamber, First Lady of India, Charlotte's life would follow Lady Dalhousie's more closely than she knew.

While Lady Susan welcomed Charlotte, Lord Dalhousie was in another part of the house, sitting at his desk writing to his Queen:

> The guns are announcing from the ramparts of Fort William that Lord Canning has arrived. In an hour's time he will have assumed the Government of India. Lord Dalhousie will transfer it to him in a state of perfect tranquillity. There is peace within and without.... Lord Dalhousie is able to declare, without reservation, that he knows of no quarter in which it is probable that trouble will arise.[25]

"Perfect tranquillity" ... but not for long. Meanwhile Lady Susan was hurrying Charlotte round to the front steps of Government House to see Lord Canning arrive with all due ceremony. Charlotte described the bustle there:

> The great flight of steps goes up to the first floor, and on it all the official people were clustered, and the hundreds of servants down the sides and at the bottom. C. drove up in Lord D's barouche, with two ADC's, and the whole body-guard as escort. Mr. Halliday, who is Lieutenant-Governor of Bengal, met him at the lowest step, and Lord Dalhousie at the top with the Council; and C. and they all went off with all the crowd to the council-room, where he was instantly sworn in. Lord

D. came to the drawing-room where I went and sat with him and – oh how sad to see the change in him, and he is but forty-three! (Hare, II, 47 – 48).

Right at the beginning of her stay, Charlotte was seeing all too clearly the terrific cost of Empire. Dalhousie couldn't walk without the aid of crutches, and his departure for England on March 6th was a moving occasion, as a later Governor-General described it:

The retiring ruler barely tottered on board with the aid of crutches, and his countenance bore traces of his physical pain and his mental emotions. There was a death-like silence and many shed tears as the doomed man waved a last adieu to the country for which he had sacrificed his health, and, as it was presently to appear, his life.[26]

Once Lord Dalhousie and Lady Susan had vacated, Charlotte took a good look round her new home, and found it not nearly luxurious enough. She was also dismayed to find that there wasn't a single toilet in the whole house, just nasty commode-affairs which the sweeper emptied out after use. She sketched the floor plan of Government House for her mother and sister, "the strangest plan of a house I ever saw, and the most uncomfortable" (Hare, II, 48). There was one recent improvement, however. Previously, the Governor-General's wife had had her bedroom in a different wing from his; now a private winding staircase had been built so that Charlotte could have her bedroom and sitting-room directly above Charles's "which is an exceeding comfort" she wrote in her diary, "and I have not to take a train of servants and pass the sentry in his hallway every time I move."

Charlotte had become accustomed to the masses of servants at Windsor Castle, so the ones trailing after her in Government House were "rather less bother than I expected." She was, however, shocked at the idea of a male sweeper in her room. "I have insisted on having

19 Tank in the Eden Gardens, Calcutta

my bed made and room swept by a woman," she told her mother, not mentioning the sweeper's less exalted duties.

The heat didn't bother Charlotte as it had Emily Eden. "Happily I have never thought ill of this climate, or hated it, as some people do," she would write later (Hare, II, 258). The worst thing for Charlotte in those early weeks was the common complaint of all *memsahibs* of having nothing to do. She wanted to show Charles how indispensable she was and to help him govern the Indian masses. "You cannot imagine the odd feeling it is to me to be so entirely and completely idle," she told her friend Viscountess Sydney (Hare, II, 76). She led, she complained to her mother, "a more idle and selfish life than I ever did before in all my days" (Hare, II, 132). In those first weeks, she didn't even go out for a drive and airing, not wanting to trouble the servants – there were so many grooms and postilions and outriders required – but later she did take a daily ride before dinner. Then she and an ADC – Charles rarely came with them – went "round the circular road" or "round and round the Eden Gardens," the public park whose shrub and tree plantings Emily had planned.

Charlotte's idleness was probably more frustrating for her, and indeed for all mid-century *memsahibs*, than it had been for the Eden sisters, due to the fact that the conduct books written in Charlotte's formative years had begun to stress the joys and rewards of diligent and bustling domesticity. "St. Paul knew what was best for woman when he advised her to be domestic. He knew that home was her safest place; home her appropriate station" writes Mrs Sandford in *Woman in Her Social and Domestic Character* (1831).[27] "The number of languid, listless and inert young ladies, who now recline upon our sofas is to me a truly melancholy spectacle," chides Mrs Ellis in *The Women of England* (1839). "The highest aim of the writer does not extend beyond the fact of warning the women of England back to their domestic duties."[28] For British women in India, all of whom had many servants at command, domestic duties consisted in arranging the flowers, filling the decanters and issuing clean dusters. Some of the servants' duties Charlotte preferred not to think about. "Cow-dung, strange to say, is used in cleaning everything," she told her mother. On her silver, her jewels – "All the last polishing touches are done by rubbing up with this strange decoction" (Hare, II, 24). For the mistress of the house, there was one more highly commendable, almost holy, domestic duty, and Charlotte eagerly embraced it. "On Monday," she told her mother self-importantly on March 3rd, "I shall begin to arrange the house" (Hare, II, 56). The house, after all, was "a sacred place, a vestal temple" for mid-century Victorians, as John Ruskin noted: "the place of Peace, the shelter, not only from all injury, but from all terror, doubt and division. In so far as it is not this, it is not home."[29]

Decorating Government House kept Charlotte busy for the next six weeks, the biggest challenge being to group the sofas and chairs in the private drawing-room in a way that was æsthetically pleasing and at the same time directly under the punkahs. "I have done arranging the drawing-room and now have it to sit in" she

*20 The drawing-room, Government House, Calcutta
(watercolour by Lady Canning)*

announced with satisfaction on April 16th. "I never had such trouble in arranging a room." The sofas and chairs were covered in chintz – blue stripes and rosebuds on a white ground; the Royal children in elaborate frames looked down from the walls, and pieces of her blue Sèvres china were put on display. "I flatter myself it is the most civilised room in India," she wrote (Hare, II, 69). Her own sitting-room was "chintzed" in a white fabric printed with lily-of-the-valley, with white punkahs like the ones at Parell. She carefully sketched both rooms in her drawing-book. She had written to Lord Elphinstone with queries about some of Parell's delightful decorating touches and on April 6th he replied:

My dear Lady Canning,

I am indeed more flattered and pleased than I can say that you should have retained so favourable an impression of the comfort of Parell, though personally I fear I have very little to pride myself upon. The chintz was chosen by Mme de Flahault, for the rest the great secret is to have an English housekeeper. Natives have no idea of *tidiness*, and even their notions of cleanliness hardly extend to dust and cobwebs. I enclose a *memo* about the table linen and another about the plants that you admired in the garden. The table cloths are very expensive ... but they make a great difference in the *look* of the dinner table and I believe they really are worth the money.[30]

Lord Dalhousie was quite right: India was in a state of "perfect tranquillity," wherein a Governor could take time to concern himself with the importance of the right table-cloths.

Once she had brought Government House up to her high standards of interior luxe, Charlotte turned her attentions to Barrackpore. The weekend trip to Barrackpore was no longer made, as in the Edens' time, by boat; the Cannings went in their carriage, properly escorted by scarlet and gold, along the new road. "The last ten or twelve miles of the road are as straight as an arrow," noted Charlotte, with approval (Hare, II, 60). "I am getting so fond of this place," she told Viscountess Sydney in October 1856, "so marvellously is it improved by 450 yards of rose-chintz" (Hare, II, 99). Charlotte had even decorated the verandahs: they now had the requisite number of small tables and potted plants and parrots in cages, all of which she reproduced carefully in a large watercolour. When the house proper was finished, she turned to the bungalows:

I am beginning to hope the day will arrive when every ADC will have his bungalow here furnished with new chintz and a Minton jug and basin, and when the whole is over, you may think I shall be happy; but no! for I cannot get the chintzes washed.... I have, however, accomplished a good deal. The dinners are improved, cotton tablecloths extinct, and there are many reforms, but we are rather barbarous still (Hare, II, 130–31).

"I have now a great deal to improve out of doors," wrote Charlotte, hardly stopping to rest, once the house and bungalows were done to her satisfaction (Hare, II, 99). She had the garden beyond her bedroom windows laid out exactly like the one at Highcliffe Castle: it was very formal with plenty of straight lines and rectangular beds and classical urns.

It was typical of newly sober Middle Raj attitudes that the menagerie, which had so occupied and amused the Eden sisters in frivolous Early Raj days, was, for Charlotte, more duty than delight. Lady Dalhousie had had a pet bear which, after it got too large to keep in her room, was moved to the menagerie. Before she left India, Lady Susan had asked Charlotte "to be kind" to her mother's bear. Charlotte took this request for charity very seriously: "I am rather at a loss how to show it [kindness]; I suppose a lump of cake now and then will do," she decided, with an earnest frown (Hare, II, 62).

The Eden sisters had wanted only to be left alone at Barrackpore, undisturbed by their guests, to pursue their own fun. Charlotte, however, turned Barrackpore into a place for good works. She invited a succession of quite humble Company officers and clergy, plus wives and children, to come to Barrackpore for rest-cures. They were lodged in the newly decorated park bungalows, but took their meals with charming Lady Canning, and, when he deigned to join them, with her slightly churlish Lord.

Charlotte still felt frustrated; interior decorating and hostessing didn't nearly fulfil her need for service. "Putting dimity in the drawing-room, or a new mat, is about the principal event I can look forward to," she complained (Hare, II, 64–65). Of course there was also "choosing thirty names out of a list for a dinner, and ditto two days later, and so on three times a week" (Hare, II, 64–65). It was terrible to feel so redundant, but it was most terrible of all to have lost Charles's company almost completely. She had hoped that once she got him away from his mistress, she could re-establish the close communion they'd had at the beginning of their marriage, but Charles had disappeared behind a wall of dispatch boxes and hardly ever came out.

"I wonder whether I shall be able to keep up journalizing at this rate, after I get into harness," he had written in his diary the day before reaching Calcutta. "I doubt it entirely," he had decided, and he was right. He made the final entry on March 2nd, two days after arriving; after that official work swallowed him up. He rose at five and hunched over his desk till dinner-time. As the pile of papers grew higher, he took to breakfasting and lunch-ing alone in his office. His Governor-Generalship was the Reign of Reason, with a vast proliferation of rules, regulations, red-tape, reams of written words, addendas to the rules, memoran-dums on the memorandums. Lord Canning was the first Gov-ernor-General, but not the last, to fall victim to the fatal power of the word. He ruled in India ink, and on paper, and the words proliferated even faster than the native population. He worked slowly and inefficiently and could not delegate or decide. "He was one of the worst men of business who ever filled the Viceroy's chair," Lord Curzon, another tireless Viceregal worker, declared. "Descriptions are extant of him," Curzon continued, "barely visible behind a vast barricade of boxes, with the accumulation of which he was powerless to cope, and on whose contents, when opened, he could not bring himself to decide."[31] Charlotte only saw Charles at dinner, where he sat mute, slumped in a perspiring heap. He even stopped accompanying her to Sunday church, hardly ever drove out with her in Calcutta, or walked with her in Barrackpore's garden. Often she stayed at Barrackpore without him, feeling intensely lonely. In her diary she always wrote a huge curving "C," for Charles, much larger than the other letters, and the entries are pathetic to read:

March 19 [1856]. The day hot and windy. C. had a sharp

21 Barrackpore park

attack of fever ... staid in his room all day. Distant thunder storms and wind.

Nov. 13 [1856]. C. had very bad nervous headache and did not dine.

Nov. 19 [1856]. C. not well. Meant to drive but he had to lie down and stay all the evening in his room.

Jan. 24 [1857]. Tried to persuade C. to walk in the Botanic Garden. At the last moment he gave it up.

In addition to her private diary, Charlotte, like the Eden sisters, beguiled the time by writing long journal-letters. Those to her mother and sister Louisa contain lists of articles to be sent out to her: lace edgings and fresh ribbons and gloves in most particular shades of white and cream, to be sent wrapped in blue paper to keep them from yellowing. Charlotte also kept up a vast correspondence with old friends in England, and with new ones in India, such as Lord Elphinstone and Lord Harris. She wrote regularly every six weeks to Queen Victoria, at the latter's request. These are her most polished pieces, but even here Charlotte's writing style is wooden and stilted, quite unlike the Eden sisters' quirky, quick-silver flow. Here is Charlotte describing the Ganges to her Queen:

> Boating is not quite a pleasure, for one's senses are cruelly offended by the numbers of floating bodies of Hindus who travel up and down with the tide till they entirely disappear. This holy river is thought the happiest of resting places but a mean propensity to economy in the wood of funerals causes many bodies to be launched into the water when hardly scorched.[32]

Charlotte had long since learned that Lord Chesterfield was quite right in realizing that "the world is taken by the appearance of things and we must take the world as it is." "People always sit in armchairs at dinner all over India," Charlotte told her mother:

I am the only person who does not, and now when I dine out I find people do me the attention of putting a small chair. The arms shut in one's crinolines and petticoats and one feels quite buried in them and one's elbows unnaturally hunched up with a general appearance of clothes out of their place in a way I greatly object to.[33]

She gave a detailed description of a splendid ball held on May 30th. Charlotte entered the ballroom on Charles's arm, thus ignoring Lady Dalhousie's precedent; she wore a newly mounted tiara and a white tulle gown. "The procession was very creditable," she wrote smugly, conscious of her regal role, and "we were quite fine enough" (Hare, II, 87 – 88). A young American, however, who attended the ball, saw her differently:

> Lady Canning did not dance while I was present, but reclining in courtly style upon the regal chair, received court from her honoured lord and the several distinguished civilians and the military officers present. The formality of her reception was freezing, for that aristocratic bow was worse than an electric shock.[34]

There was, seen in the light of Charles's previous philandering, one great comfort in Calcutta society: "It is quite a mistake to suppose that the society here is *bad*," Charlotte told her mother. "Even flirting is very rare and of the mildest description, and I really believe hardly any woman but *me* goes out riding without her husband. It is really a very proper place" (Hare, II, 132).

By April of that first year the heat was daunting, but Charlotte had vowed that she would never use a *punkah* out of pity for "the poor man who pulls it" (Hare, II, 59). It got hotter and hotter and finally she had to give the order: "We have taken to having the *punkah* pulled at night. I had slept very badly, and at last thought the world in general must have reason, and I need not deny myself what I find is a universal indulgence. The result has been that I sleep to perfection. It acted like magic" (Hare, II, 75). She wrote this on May 1st, and three weeks later was still feeling wicked: "I am shocked at being hardened now to the feeling of giving work and trouble," she agonized. "Now it never occurs to me to think of the punkah-man pulling at his rope. I believe they go to sleep, and when awake, do not mind; but it is a change for the worse in one's feelings" (Hare, II, 82).

She still felt soft-hearted, however, where insects were concerned, and since she had promised to send a collection of Indian ones to Queen Victoria's children, she had to get her maids to kill them for her. The cockroaches were "as big as mice":

> They run along the floor, and now and then spread their wings and fly upon me! I let them alone, for I could on no account kill anything so big; but Rain has no mercy, and the other night killed five as I was undressing to go to bed. Some were moving away, side by side, like pairs of coach-horses (Hare, II, 74).

Even the insects at Government House, it seems, now moved in formal mode! When the rains came "silver covers, like little pagoda roofs" were placed over all the glasses at dinner to prevent the great variety of insects thereabouts from falling in (Hare, II, 84).

Occasionally, Charlotte caught a glimpse of that violent and vulgar India which would soon threaten to engulf her. One day she saw some Hindu gods carried in procession, one of them being Kartikeya, god of war, and she shivered at the "horrid sorts of yellow dolls of all sizes ... invariably riding astride on peacocks with enormous spread-out tails.... Such dreadful creatures – I cannot imagine how any human being can respect them" (Hare, II, 129). Charlotte was quite as devout a Christian as the conduct books decreed. "There is nothing so adapted to her wants," Mrs Sandford writes "as religion. Woman has many trials ... religion is her asylum."[35] Lady Canning attended morning and evening worship every Sunday in St John's Cathedral, often went on Mondays and Wednesdays as well. St John's was just round the corner from Government

House, but at Charles's decree she always went in the carriage and four, with four bodyguards, and a runner and "a *jemadar* by way of footman" (Hare, ii, 64). The wicked segment of Calcutta society rode round the Maidan, which Charlotte likened to Hyde Park, on Sunday afternoons but "I keep to my English habits," she declared smugly, "and never ride or drive on Sunday" (Hare, ii, 126). This is a long way from Emily Eden's cavalier attitude to the gardeners at Barrackpore working on a Sunday, but the moral tone of British India was growing more sanctimonious with every passing year. Charlotte, Lady Canning, perfectly epitomized the new bias. She believed that the native population should, as quickly as possible, be converted to Christianity, not by the Government but by the missionaries. She often visited the mission schools to help them along.

This newly zealous, reforming attitude of the British in India had been given a boost by Lord Ellenborough, Lord Auckland's successor, and had been gaining ground ever since. India wasn't just a commercial matter now; India had become a Sacred Trust. The British had ceased to be merchants and turned into Empire-builders and Christian zealots. By the time the Cannings arrived, Britain's territorial conquest of India was virtually complete. During Ellenborough's reign the British had annexed Sind, and in Dalhousie's, had acquired Oudh, the Punjab and many smaller states. The British quickly, and conveniently, forgot that they had acquired all this territory by conquest. Economic greed was changed overnight into moral duty.

There were various causes for this radical change in British attitudes between the time of the Edens and the Cannings. For one thing, more and more missionaries were coming out from Britain. They mixed freely with Indians, and learned their dialects, but had nothing but horror for their religion. Their criticisms held great sway with the rest of British India, which itself was growing larger every year as transportation improved and Company services expanded. But the main reason for the change in attitude lay with the women. English women were coming out to India in ever greater numbers; the good old days of British men taking native mistresses or even wives were long gone, and the reign of the *memsahib* was now in its full despotism. The *memsahibs* lost no time in banishing the native mistresses who had brought at least some traces of Indian culture into British lives, and had instituted instead their own mid-Victorian piety and prudery. They sat behind their silver teapots, corseted, Christian and correct, dressing and behaving exactly as they would have in England, unanimously agreeing that the sooner the natives could be decently clothed and converted, the better.

Gone now was the wanton luxury and moral laxity of eighteenth-century British men in India. Gone was the motivating love of risk and adventure and the impelling image of an India where horses were living maps of emeralds and the Kohinoor diamond sparkled on Ranjit Singh's arm. "The days are gone for the gathering of pearls and peacock thrones, of rubies and pagodas" a February 4th editorial in *The Times* declared in 1847:

> The treasures of India are now to be found in the people and the soil – by improving the condition of the one and employing the resources of the other – by transporting to the climate and capabilities of the East the science and steadiness of the north – by banishing famine and introducing plenty – by substituting intelligence and comfort for ignorance and want.

The Arabian Nights had given way to the Book of Common Prayer. The new piety had even infiltrated the ranks of the British army in India. A lieutenant told Mrs Colin Mackenzie in 1849 that he regularly attended prayer meetings of the 9th Lancers where there were often forty men present, besides officers. Occasionally he visited the tent of a fellow-Lieutenant in the 5th Cavalry where eight or ten British soldiers met "every evening" to read "*Overton's Cottage Lectures on the Pilgrim's Progress*, each of which ends with a hymn and a prayer and which were very much liked by the men."[36] Mrs Mackenzie herself, whom Charlotte would invite to a Government House dinner in December 1857, and describe in her diary as "very agreeable," had prayers twice daily with her army-officer husband, and when they travelled up-country from Calcutta, they got all the way to Karnal before they found a house "in which there is no daily family worship."[37] Mrs Mackenzie voiced the typical attitude of the good *memsahib*:

> It is, I believe, almost impossible to find a native who is either truthful or pure-minded. How can they be with their impure creeds? You know the tendencies of Mohammedanism, but you are not aware of the unspeakable abominations of Hinduism.[38]

This revulsion, like the earnest Evangelical zeal, came straight from England. Hannah More's good friend, William Wilberforce, the guiding spirit behind the Evangelical movement within the Anglican church, had declared as far back as 1813 that "our religion is sublime, pure and beneficent. Theirs [the Indians'] is mean, licentious, and cruel."[39] James Mill reinforced this prejudice in 1817 by being highly critical of Indian religion and society in his *History of British India*. According to Mill, Indian religion was full of superstition, Indian history was only a collection of absurd legends, and India's only salvation lay in thorough Westernization. Thomas Macaulay, the Edens' friend, went even further, declaring that Indian literature contained

> medical doctrines which would disgrace an English farrier – Astronomy which would move laughter in girls at an English boarding school – History, abounding with kings thirty feet high, and reigns thirty thousand years long – and Geography, made up of seas of treacle and seas of butter.[40]

The British felt vastly superior to Indians culturally and politically and they were quite ready and willing, eager even, to convert the Indians to "enlightened" Western ways. The very fact that they had prospered so in India, in terms of trade and territory, indicated to them that God meant them to be there, doing His work. "Lord Gough remarked how merciful providence had been to us," noted Mrs Mackenzie, listening in 1849 to the former Commander-in-Chief's tales of how Britain won the Punjab. " 'If the victory of Chillianwala had been more complete,' " he told her, " 'the Sikhs would never have ventured down so rashly into the open plain, thus exposing themselves to the total ruin they met at Gujrat. It was all God's doing' said he devoutly."[41]

Lady Canning relished the opportunity to serve such enlightened Empire ideals; she felt purposeful and energized. "You laugh at me for saying I am better than in England," she wrote to Viscountess Sydney in September, "but nevertheless it is true. One never has a cold, hardly ever a headache, and I am never over-tired, which I used to be at least four days a week" (Hare, II, 94). She liked the fact that she had, for such a noble cause, grown thin. West and Rain had to take her gowns in "four inches in the body, if I have not worn them since I left England" (Hare, II, 100). "I am certainly getting to like India," she told the Viscountess in November, "and am now thoroughly accustomed to it" (Hare, II, 125).

The year 1857 was ushered in with champagne and due ceremony. "The dust now covers everything with a thick dark red surface," Charlotte reported on February 4th, after a daily drive (Hare, II, 141), where there had been "such bad smells intermingled with such heavy sweet ones." "A thick dark-red surface" ... an ominous note, had she but known it. A week later came another:

> The General at Barrackpore made a good little speech to the Sepoys of the regiment, who are supposed to be rather disaffected on account of the new Minie cartridges, of which they complain on the ground that the grease used in making them up is beef-suet, and that they cannot touch. There have been mysterious fires at all the places where detachments of this regiment have been quartered. (Hare, II, 141 – 42).

This regiment at Barrackpore was the Bengal Army's 2nd Native Infantry, part of the East India Company's army in India. The private soldiers, called sepoys, and the cavalry, called sowars, were both Hindu and Moslem, with a preponderance of the former. There were then 300,000 men in the whole Indian army, only 14,000 of whom were Europeans. (The sepoys were mainly officered by British men.) There were, in addition, about 23,000 men in wholly British regiments, the "Queen's regiments" as they were called, then stationed in India, most of them in the Punjab. And there was a native population of 150 million needing control.

In the early years of Company rule, the relationship of sepoy to British officer had been close and informal. But more recently the gap had widened, and from the superior and often strenuously Christian vantage point of the British officers placed over him, the sepoy came to be regarded as a lowly being, fit only to be sworn at and kicked and called "nigger" or "pig." Now the sepoys were being required to tear open with their teeth the cartridges for the newly issued Enfield rifles. The grease, so the rumours said, was either cow-fat or pig-fat, the former forbidden to Hindus and the latter to Moslems. Were the British trying to convert them to Christianity? Unrest and suspicion spread among the sepoys as fast as the flames of mysterious fires which kept breaking out in the barracks.

March ushered in the beginning of the Hindu year and marked the centenary of Clive's victory at Plassey, which had given the British control of Bengal, thus beginning their rule in India. Native pundits had long predicted that the British Raj would last only a century; now there were strange stirrings and omens, noted by Charlotte in a letter of April 8th:

There is an odd, mysterious thing going on, still unexplained. It is this. In one part of the country the native police have been making little cakes – "chupatties" – and sending them on from place to place. Each man makes twelve, keeps two, and sends away ten to ten men, who make twelve more each, and they

spread all over the country ... no one can discover any meaning
to it (Hare, II, 157).

Nor would they ever. Like so much else in India, there was no
rational explanation for the chupatties. Lotus flowers and bits of
goat flesh were also being passed from hand to hand within the
sepoy regiments; an ominous slogan *sub lal hogea hai* (everything
has become red) was being whispered everywhere; strange symbols
were being scrawled on walls; protective amulets were being sold
by the hundreds in bazaars.[42] "They are curious creatures these
Sepoys – just like children," mused Canning in a letter of April 9th.
"*Ombragen* is the word for them I think. Shadows and their own
fancies seem to frighten them much more than realities."[43]

In the midst of mysterious shadows, Charlotte re-emphasized
her rational routines. She had found a new way of recording India,
in addition to the written word and sketching, namely in photographs. She took many shots herself, commissioned others, col-
lected and categorized and labelled neatly, filling her lonely hours.
She hardly saw Charles now; he even dined alone in his room. She
went to church every day during Passion week; she began another
collection: this one of pearls. She bought them one at a time and
only the biggest and best would do. She was determined to have
"a superb necklace." "Everyone in England has diamonds but pearls
like these are rarely seen," Charlotte would later tell an aide's wife
proudly.[44] "My pearls made their first appearance," Charlotte noted
in her diary with a sense of occasion on May 7th, "and I thought
how my English friends would exclaim but here no one of course
would think an observation expected so it fell very flat. I think they
would be approved."

"An outbreak has occurred at Meerut," she noted four days
later. "The 3rd cavalry has broken into the prison, and released
eighty-five comrades imprisoned for mutiny; others have burnt
houses and killed people and were fired into and escaped" (Hare,
II, 160). That was on May 10th; the Great Mutiny had now begun
in earnest. The mutinous sepoys who had joined forces with the

cavalry had rushed into the magazine and helped themselves to the ammunition, regardless of its being the "unclean cartridges,"[45] a move as typically irrational, emotional and unpremeditated as the whole Mutiny would be. And puzzling to the logical, cool-headed British. Now they stirred uneasily in their sleep; fifty European men, women and children had been slaughtered at Meerut. Between Calcutta and Lucknow there was only one British battalion. But the British officers who commanded the sepoys felt confident that *their* men would remain loyal; others might rebel, but not the men in *their* regiment surely? The "niggers," as they called them, always lept to it when they shouted an order.

Next day, the Meerut mutineers, unpursued by British officers, pushed on to Delhi, where British blood flowed again, this time more of it. The enraged sepoys massacred every European they could find in Delhi, and persuaded the King of Delhi, Bahadar Shah II, to join their rebellion. He was then eighty-two, leading a contemplative life, writing poetry, painting miniatures, listening to the pet doves and nightingales in his delightful palace garden. His one eccentricity was "a fixed belief that he could transform himself into a fly or gnat and that he could in this guise convey himself to other countries."[46] When news of Delhi having fallen into rebel hands reached her, Charlotte's thoughts were with the women. "I hope the mother of poor Lieutenant Willoughby will be well provided for," she wrote. "I do grieve for that woman. She was so proud of her sons that she came to India to be near them.... You will remember the gallant feat of young Willoughby and the eight men with him, when they blew up the magazine at Delhi ... the other son, an engineer or artillery officer at Saugor, had both legs shot through, and died soon after" (Hare, II, 260 – 61). The mothers of British India paid a high price for Empire.

In her diary for May 11th, the day of the Delhi massacre, Charlotte's tone grew positively lyrical describing the jungle growth at Barrackpore, particularly "the brilliant emerald green of that jungly bit I admire so much.... I never saw it more dazzling in colour, like the green of May wheat and emeralds." Later, she enthused about "trees like green tinsel, or green flies or enamel" (Hare, II, 138). As everything became red with blood, and Mutiny, death and destruction spread, Charlotte had her defences ready: she stepped well back from the reports of carnage into her cool greens. Pity and fear vanished if one stared long enough at the picturesque.

She was busy buying ornaments from a merchant on May 13th when Charles burst in, sent the merchant away and showed her a terrible telegram just received, giving details of the Delhi massacre. Simon Fraser, the Commissioner, was among those murdered by the mutinous sepoys. Now the seriousness of the situation dawned on the Cannings:

> There are very few European regiments. After Barrackpore, there is only one at Dinapore, in the valley of the Ganges; none at Allahabad, Patna, Benares, Cawnpore. Meerut is the greatest strength of all, and yet that has been unable, in the suddenness of the outbreak, to prevent burning and murdering and horrors (Hare, II, 163).

There they were, caught in this paradoxical country where their army of defence, hired to keep them safe from the enemy, suddenly *was* the enemy. Who would defend them now?

On May 14th Charlotte wrote that "a package of shawls arrived from Delhi, sent to me by the poor man, Simon Fraser, of whose horrible murder we heard two days ago! We have no details of the massacre or list of names" (Hare, II, 164). "There is said not to be one European left in Delhi," she wrote on May 16th:

> I have been getting one or another [of the men visiting Government House] to come and talk to me and tell me all they can, but there is really nothing to know but our telegraphs. From morning to night they come, and require instant answers. As no papers can wait to circulate, C. acts for himself at once, but has had the Council each day to see what he has done (Hare, II, 172).

Charlotte wrote and wrote, trying to order and define, describing everything in the same flat tone, moving from murder to shawls and back to murder. At church on Sunday, May 17th, so she told her mother, they had the prayer "in time of war and tumults"; she followed this with a description of cloud-colours: ink and sepia (Hare, II, 173). She commented on "the good quiet Sepoys suddenly becoming so unmanageable" (Hare, II, 176), as if they were unruly children at a birthday party. She worried about Charles looking "worn and very tired" and fast disappearing behind a new wall of telegrams, each one bringing news of some fresh disaster. Charlotte put on a brave face, clung to her optimism, and her ordinary routines, telling her mother on May 19th:

> There is not the least cause for fear here.... Many people wish us to put off the ball for the Queen's Birthday – the 25th. I would not for an instant suggest such a thing. It may not be a cheerful ball in this time of anxiety, but we ought not to appear in a state of mourning for this temporary outbreak (Hare, II, 183).

Charles had courageously refused the offer of European soldiers to replace Government House's usual household guard, composed of sepoys. The English in Calcutta began to panic – "I never came across such a set of old women," sneered Canning.[47] But life was to proceed in an orderly fashion, he insisted on that, the same rituals and routines; nothing should change; Charlotte should continue to take her daily drive with a small escort. Lord Canning did, however, lock up the King of Oudh in Fort William because his dependents were suspected of plotting rebellion in his name. "They say he is a very horrid-looking man, bloated and of most unpleasant appearance," observed Charlotte (Hare, II, 171). Like the King of Delhi, the King of Oudh wrote verses, usually spread-eagled on floor cushions as he composed, and amused himself the rest of the time with four hundred concubines.[48]

Inside Government House, the shocking telegrams continued

to arrive. After Meerut and Delhi, in June, came the horror of Cawnpore. A month before, the Nana Sahib of Cawnpore, Dhondu Pant, had given a magnificent ball, the most splendid ball ever held in Cawnpore, and all the English had sipped his champagne and danced under his crystal chandeliers and agreed that the Nana was a fine and generous fellow. "All well at Cawnpore," General Wheeler assured Canning at the end of May. "Calm and expert policy will soon reassure the public mind."[49] Calm and expert policy: the rational Western approach. It had always worked before with the hot-blooded Indians, and the British felt confident it would work now.

Then on June 5th, led by the 2nd cavalry, Mutiny madness erupted in the native regiments stationed at Cawnpore; they murdered and burned and plundered, encouraged by Nana Sahib, now in a less genteel mood. For the next three weeks, General Wheeler and four hundred men held out against three thousand rebels. British residents who had escaped the slashing swords and whizzing bullets cowered in the garrison where the temperature often rose to 138° in the daytime, all of them dirty, starving, stinking, ragged. Horrifying stories of their sufferings reached Government House. General Wheeler's son, recently wounded, had been sitting on a sofa fanned by his two sisters one day when a round-shot came hurtling over the mud wall and decapitated him. A missionary of the Propagation Society, nursing his wounded mother, had gone mad "and used to walk about stark naked."[50]

Finally the British were forced to surrender, but Nana Sahib promised safe conduct to Allahabad for their women and children. However, on June 27th, when the ragged little band piled into boats at Satichaura Ghat and prepared to push off, sepoys fired on them at point-blank range until the river ran red with blood. Those who escaped that slaughter, about one hundred and twenty-five in number, were imprisoned by Nana Sahib in a house called Bibigarh. "Details I hear of the emaciated appearance and filth and misery of these poor women at Cawnpore have filled me with more pain and horror than anything I have heard except reports of the worst insults," agonized Charlotte.[51] "Reports of the worst insults" were

*22 Massacre of women and children in the boats off Cawnpore
(steel engraving)*

rumours (unfounded) that some of the women had been raped by
natives; for every Victorian lady, that was definitely the "worst
insult," the ultimate horror, the fate worse than death.

"By God's help, men, we shall save them," shouted General
Havelock en route with a British force to rescue the Cawnpore
women. "Think of our women and the tender infants in the power
of those devils incarnate!"[52] Then, when General Havelock was a
day's march from Cawnpore, Nana Sahib gave the order: all women
and children in the Bibigarh were to be slaughtered and their bodies
thrown down a well. When the British soldiers finally arrived, they
found the Bibigarh floor covered with clotted blood, with blood-
soaked bonnets and petticoats strewn about. "The sight of those
rooms makes strong men faint," Charlotte told the Queen.[53] There
were hanks of human hair caught on thorn-bushes between house
and well, and imbedded in the bark of one tree was a child's eyeball,

*23 A memsahib defending herself against the mutinous sepoys at
Cawnpore (steel engraving)*

marking the spot where its brains had been smashed against the
trunk.[54] Charlotte closed her mind to these grisly details; the officers
were surely exaggerating. In such days of fear and paranoia, she
told her mother, it was impossible to tell fact from rumour.

"There were fifteen young ladies in Cawnpore," wrote Charlotte, focusing on pretty details,

> and at first they wrote such happy letters, saying time had
> never been so pleasant, it was every day like a picnic, and they
> hoped they would not be sent away; they said a regiment would
> come, and they felt quite safe. Poor, poor things! not one was
> saved! I want that well where they were all thrown down to
> be consecrated, with the ground around, and a plain monument
> put over them. C. would do it – a *chapelle expiatore*. I must
> think of a design (Hare, II, 258).

Later Charlotte did, with the help of a sculptor, design an angel monument. "The thought and hope of the resurrection is the only thought can calm the sorrow or give any comfort" when it came to Cawnpore, Charlotte decided.[55]

Now British officers placed their pistols on the pews in front of them at church, and beside their plates at meals. Fear spread among the British as fast as cholera in the native quarter, a deep, instinctual, irrational fear, and it spread all the way to Government House. Charlotte tried not to look directly at the sepoy sentries standing so silently in its halls, rifles at the ready.

After Cawnpore, no more mythic East blinding British eyes with jewelled scabbards and peacocks; now naked swords ripped white flesh, and screaming peacocks carried the god of war across the Northern plains. And up until the very moment that their rifles cracked and their swords slashed, the sepoys and sowars were uncertain what line they would take – to stay loyal or rebel – then a word, a cry, an alarm, would suddenly decide them. "The fanatical mania comes on so unexpectedly and frightfully," shivered Charlotte. For the British, that was the most frightful thing of all: the fact that the Mutiny was beyond reason and beyond form. There was no agreement among leaders, no concerted plan or premeditated plotting. It was all random and chaotic, its roots hidden in superstition and shadows, in the very depths of the Indian psyche. Regiments that one would expect might mutiny stayed loyal; and vice versa. Sometimes the rebel sepoys attacked wearing *dhotis* (loincloths), sometimes wearing British uniforms and medals, with their bands playing "The British Grenadiers" and "Cheer, Boys, Cheer" and "The Girls We Left Behind Us".

A world gone mad. Charlotte had always been starved for Charles's company; now she almost dreaded to see him, standing white and shaken, in the door of her sitting-room, another telegram clutched in his hand. "The great anxiety now is for Lucknow, and the thought of it haunts one day and night," wrote Charlotte to the Queen on August 24th.[56] The carnage spread from Cawnpore to Lucknow, Oudh's capital, where in June more regiments mutineed, more swords slashed. The British residents fled to the Residency, home of Sir Henry Lawrence, Chief Commissioner of Oudh. He was a muscular, sober Christian who had once remarked after attending a dance: "What a wretched, unprofitable evening! Not a Christian to speak to. All the women decked out with flowers on their heads, and their bodies half naked."[57] Now, in the Residency, he stood firm with God on his side.

By June 30th, the rebels had effectively surrounded the Residency and its little band of soldiers, and the long siege began. "Poor little Raleigh" had been one of the Lucknow victims, "a quite young cadet" who aroused Charlotte's maternal instincts. She described how Raleigh,

> really a mere child, who dined with us lately, and whom they were laughing at because he looked tied to his sword, being so small, was killed as he rode away by himself from the cantonments.... The horrors one hears daily are worse and worse and as yet there is not a ray of sunshine in the gloom (Hare, II, 208).

When Charlotte saw a Dr Brydon's name in the Government House guest book, she enquired if it was the Dr Brydon who had been sole survivor of the 1842 Kabul massacre and retreat. No, she was told "that Dr. Brydon is in Lucknow. Only imagine any man," Charlotte wrote in her diary, "having had such scrapes and stood two such sieges!" Dr Brydon's wife and children were with him in the Lucknow Residency. When on the same day, Mrs Brydon saw the chaplain, Mr Polehampton, die and her husband wounded in the loins, she comforted herself with her mother's pet saying: "Providence is a rich provider."[58] All those inside the Residency, not just the Brydons, were feeling the horrendous cost of Empire, suffering the terrible heat, the swarms of flies, the shortages of food and water and clothing, the stench from rotting corpses and offal. And sudden death was only one round-shot away. Mrs Leguere was shot through the lungs as she drank a cup of tea; Mrs Dorin was shot dead climbing into bed.[59] And on July 4th, their gallant leader Sir Henry Lawrence was fatally wounded by a shell as he lay resting on his cot. "He is a most dreadful loss," wrote Charlotte. "He was all that could be described as most brave and chivalrous."[60]

"The reputation of England's power," wrote Canning the day of Sir Henry's death to his Queen, "has had a rude shake, and nothing but a long-continued manifestation of her might before the eyes of the whole Indian Empire ... will re-establish confidence in her strength."[61] On that same day, July 4th, Charlotte tried to sound optimistic to Viscountess Sydney:

> Things have passed their worst, we hope.... Meanwhile the details of murder and wanderings and escapes are quite dreadful, and the poor refugee civilians' wives and indigo-planters' wives and railway people are coming down in shoals by boats, and in a very deplorable state.... Certainly no history has ever surpassed this mutiny in horror (Hare, II, 227 – 28).

Next day, Charlotte wrote to her mother:

> I have been busy making a collection of clothes to send to the houses for the destitute arrivals, and at last my large trousseau has turned to good account and is nearly expended. I particularly desire that my things may go to officers' wives and others who are ladies, and not be kept merely for cases of charity. ... Rain and West and my three tailors are working hard, and have engaged four other tailors, so plenty of clothes can be made. Some of the poor ladies arrive with rags only, and others have merely a gown and *nothing* else! (Hare, II, 223)

The sepoys had murdered Major and Mrs Holmes; she was the daughter of Florentia, Lady Sale, and had watched her first husband, Lieutenant Sturt, killed before her eyes in the retreat from Kabul in 1842. Major and Mrs Holmes "were waylaid and attacked on their evening drive in a buggy.... It is indeed sad to think of all that poor woman had to go through," wrote Charlotte in her typically undramatic way. (Hare, II, 245 – 46). Why weren't the sepoys grateful, wondered Charlotte, for all the British had done for them in terms of civilizing and educating? "I really do not know what there is in which Government is not honestly and conscientiously trying to do good," she wrote in bewilderment, "and that good bores the natives very much; they certainly liked the old style of neglect far better" (Hare, II, 243). Charlotte reported on August 2nd that they now had a European guard at Government House at night, "and I think the dinner company were charmed to see it" (Hare, II, 256). There was plenty of bustle now, no more idle days with nothing to do. Charlotte felt useful and important. Telegrams still poured in day and night and she was kept busy "counting up marches and roads and distances," reading "all the Indian histories of former troubles like ours" (Hare, II, 232) and gathering clothes for the poor ladies who had suffered the penultimate horror of being reduced to one gown. It was all very terrible, thought Charlotte, trying to stay calm, as she fingered her cool pearls and smiled at the old Generals across the dinner-table, all of whom mumbled into their claret that they'd teach the sepoys a lesson they'd never forget. Through it all, terribly tired and overworked, Charles kept his cool head and his sense of justice, refusing to be rushed or to let feelings of vengeance overpower him. At the end of July he passed a resolution known as the Clemency Order, intended to ensure that captured sepoys should not be punished without regard to the gravity of their offences. "The sky is black," Canning wrote to Bishop Wilson, "and, as yet, the signs of a clearing are faint. But reason and common sense are on our side from the very beginning."[62] "Resistance over," he would later assure Lord Granville in England, "deliberate justice and calm patient reason are to resume their sway."[63] Reason would prevail. The whole Western Enlightenment tradition was behind him, and Canning would do his best to hang on to Reason's reins.

In August 1857, Sir Colin Campbell, the new Commander-in-Chief of the Indian army, arrived in India to replace General

Anson, who had died of cholera en route to the relief of Delhi. Son of a Glasgow carpenter, Sir Colin had a pink, lively face and a halo of springy grey curls. He and Charlotte hit it off at once; they became "great friends." "We find him very amiable and cheerful, an endless talker and *raconteur*," she wrote, shortly after his arrival at Government House (Hare, II, 271). "To me, he has behaved like an old courtier," she smiled, obviously enjoying the attention, and she liked the fact that "he would tell me everything, and show me every letter and telegraph," so that she felt part of the decision-making (Hare, II, 332). As the siege of Lucknow continued, Charles looked "daily more worn and bleached" and talked even less than usual to her (Hare, II, 282). "The bloodthirsty feeling of Europeans is most distressing," Charlotte noted in September (Hare, II, 292).

> It would charm the Indian-English public to hang and blow from guns any number of people, and I believe C. is terribly unpopular because he is *just* and firm too. There is a positive thirst for blood. Hardly anybody can speak about natives in a tone which does not drive me wild, so I hold my tongue (Hare, II, 296).

"Vengeance is mine saith the Lord," but now the British were more than willing to lend Him a helping hand. Up until the massacre of women and children at Cawnpore, the British had been more incredulous than angry. They were sleep-walking through impossible events, for the most part. Reason and Form had still prevailed. But to Victorian men, their women were angels, placed on pedestals and almost worshipped. The "filthy niggers" at Cawnpore had dared to defile them, to hack their rarely-seen white limbs to pieces. Now both sides had gone mad; now, for both British and Indian, the deep hidden urges had been unleashed. On July 16th, General Havelock had defeated Nana Sahib's forces at Cawnpore, and Colonel James Neill, who took command after Havelock moved on towards Lucknow, made each captured sepoy lick clean the blood from a square of Bibigarh floor before he was hanged.[64]

Now, as the tide of battle turned and the rebel forces began to

24 Blowing mutinous sepoys from the guns (steel engraving)

be routed, it was the British who slashed and murdered indiscrim-
inately and rode in triumph across the land. "I cannot consider these
sepoys as human beings," wrote Captain J.W. Wade, voicing the
general opinion, "and it is only common practice to destroy them
as reptiles."[65] Sepoys were shot on sight, without distinguishing
loyal from disloyal, without any kind of trial, however impromptu.
Even the missionaries and chaplains joined in the cry for vengeance.
The rebels had, according to the Rev. John Rotton, "imbued their
hands in the innocent blood of helpless women and children – and
that very blood was appealing to heaven for vengeance."[66] Sepoys
who weren't shot on sight were strung up on the nearest tree, or
rounded up and blown, with due ceremony, from the mouths of
cannons. Those doing the firing had to stand well back to avoid
being splattered with gouts of blood and brains and intestines.
Everything in the path of the British became red.

With their usual ability to do so, the British quickly rationalized their vengeance and violence. The rebels' blood-lust sprang from savage desires; but that of the British from the desire to preserve civilized order. "If this contest between the barbarism and fanaticism of Asiatic hordes and the civilized authority of Christian rulers must be fought," pontificated the *Edinburgh Review*, "we engage in it not only with a clear conscience and a bold heart, but with all the means which a well-disciplined and highly civilized nation can apply to the chastisement of its enemies."[67]

While this second blood-bath boiled around her, Charlotte clung to her conventional forms, as Charles did to his: the rituals of her religion, and her art. She embarked on an ambitious series of flower-paintings, later sending a hundred and thirty of them home to her mother. Lady Stuart de Rothesay showed them to Ruskin, who pronounced them "the grandest representations of flowers he had ever seen" (Hare, II, 478). "Your drawings of flowers make quite a sensation" her mother wrote to her: "I can well imagine their quieting influence on anxious days, when the hands could go on, and keep the head from working.... It is quite a wonder that the greater part should have been done in these months" (Hare, II, 250).

Charlotte never attempted portraits of people or animals, breathing and warm-blooded. She painted only static things: trees and flowers and furniture in a room. Her paintings were accomplished, beautiful enough in line and colour, but all done with a hand held rigid, a tight control. The punkah of her solid world had, with the Mutiny, tilted, swung crazily just above her head, threatening to drop. Beyond her conventions, she had glimpsed another world, all askew and absurd, where nothing mattered, nothing at all had value.

Charlotte sat on at her easel. She mustn't let herself think of Mrs Holmes, with blood on her muslin dress, or Simon Fraser, bleeding into the red dust, or little Raleigh, tumbling lifeless from his horse. Charlotte dipped her brush in vermilion, in scarlet lake,

25 *Lady Canning with her watercolours*

in burnt sienna ... one careful stroke at a time ... one flower done, another begun ... enough strokes, enough flowers, to cover up a whole Mutiny.

By the end of September 1857, the troops dispatched by ship from England were beginning to pour in. "The Fort church on Sunday morning," Charlotte noted, "was full of the tidiest men, in little brown holland short blouses, with red cuffs and collars, and white cap-covers, showing they were sent out well provided for the climate" (Hare, II, 307). There were streams of officers now to be entertained at Government House, and Charlotte was gracious and charming, and proud of her performance. "I did not at all object to leaving my monotonous London life," she told Louisa in September,

> and I took great delight in all the novelty of impressions on coming to a new country. Of late, it has been painful, and anxious, and terrible; but I do not know anything I should dislike more than to be told that C. would not have two or three or more years here, so that he might see India again prosperous, and on the way to good order, though fifty years will not put it back into the same state in which it was, so far as attempting to civilise and give liberty, and our English ideas of blessings to the country (Hare, II, 228).

The horror of the mutiny began to recede that September. Charlotte was enjoying the poignant greens of Barrackpore in company with Sir Colin Campbell when, on September 26th, a telegram arrived from Calcutta:

> I knew it must be good news and it was. "Delhi has fallen! Our troops entered by the breach on the 14th." It was a grey pleasant day, and I ventured out a little with an umbrella, under the great banyan and about some walks – a thing I had never done at that hour before. I was well repaid. The whole place was alive with the most gorgeous butterflies, of all sizes, and

colours, and shapes. The orchids on the banyans are in brilliant health.... As the elephants were at the door long before the carriage, we got upon them for a ride to the park gate. *Punch* would have made a nice vignette of Sir Colin with me in a *howdah* on the top of an elephant, talking over our great news in the greatest delight (Hare, II, 312 – 13).

There were, however, still shadows. In October, mounting discontent in Calcutta with "Clemency," Canning's cool restraint and undue leniency with the rebels reached a head, and a petition was sent to the Queen demanding his recall. "Every word of its accusations can be answered," Charlotte wrote loyally to her mother, "and it was got up by very second-rate lawyers and merchants, and was kept as secret as possible. Do not be alarmed" (Hare, II, 344). Now she had a new way of being useful to Charles. She became his staunch defender in her letters to England, where there was also plenty of opposition to what one British noble described as Canning's "kid gloves and rose-water" methods.[68] Sir Colin Campbell, too, was criticized for being too cautious in dealing with the Indian rebels, and was nicknamed Old Khabardar (Old Take Care) and Sir Crawling Camel by British soldiers.[69]

Sir Crawling had, nevertheless, on November 17th, finally routed the Lucknow rebels, re-taken the Residency, and seen to the safe conduct of the people imprisoned there for the past five months. During the final battle, a Highlander known in his regiment as "Quaker" Wallace drove his bayonet into twenty rebel bodies as he chanted verses from the 116th Psalm ("Gracious is the Lord, and righteous: yea, our God is merciful").[70]

Just before Christmas, Colonel Charles Stuart, a first cousin of Charlotte's, arrived with his wife, Minny, to take up the post of Military Secretary. "Charlotte has grown thin and aged: how could it be otherwise?" he noted (Hare, II, 375) and his wife gave a longer description of their arrival:

Bowing red men with joined hands awaited us at the door, and then we were ushered up to the drawing-room, and there in clear muslin was a *thin*, slight, pale lady Sahib, with eyes gleaming with welcome! She did indeed receive us with heartfelt cordiality and affection.... Lord Canning came upstairs to our top-of-the-house apartment to see me, and after he went down, Char. stayed and talked and talked, and kept saying, "You *must* be so tired, but *don't* send me away; I have not talked like this for ages; even letters seem nothing today" (Hare, II, 379).

There was another welcome addition to the Government House circle on January 19, 1858, when "little Johnny Stanley, the new ADC" arrived from England to take up his duties. "I sat next to Lord Canning at dinner," he wrote to his father next day, "and I hardly knew him he looks so pale and overworked.... Lady Canning I recognized directly, she looks much older but still handsome, she is very kind."[71] Johnny was the delicate, clever, high-spirited second son of Lord Stanley of Alderley. The Stanleys were an eccentric family; Johnny's brother Henry became a Mahomedan, dressing the part and wandering round the Far East for many years. A younger brother, Algernon, became a Roman Catholic priest and their sister Kate, Bertrand Russell's mother.[72] Johnny had been quite as wild and impetuous a youth as Willy Osborne, and while at Harrow was flogged for "jumping over the dinner table when Dr Vaughan [the head-master] was there." He had served in the Crimean War with his regiment, towing his bottles of champagne overboard to cool them while en route from England.[73] In India, Johnny became Lady Canning's adoring slave, her own little spaniel, soulful-eyed and eager to please. He handed her into her carriage, accompanied her on drives, printed her photographs for her, helped her with her pressed-fern collection, made her smile at dinner. "Little Johnny Stanley is like a merry page, and so civil and useful," she wrote happily, "but he requires care, for his chest is weak" (Hare, II, 416 – 17). He was the son she had never had. She needed his wild ebullience as she needed wanton jungle growth, to germinate her own barren spirit. Johnny was everything Charles was not, or at least not with her: lively, intuitive, talkative, comic, warmly loving. He was Charlotte's refuge and relief – from the frightful dark abysses of India, of her marriage, and of her own psyche.

She clung to Johnny as Charles prepared to move up-country, now that rebellion was more or less quelled, to spend most of 1858 at Allahabad. Since he had issued an edict that no women and children were to be allowed yet up-country, Charlotte, conveniently enough, could not accompany him. The day before his departure, she spent "all day packing and making preparations for C's journey," while he worked at his desk from dawn till long past midnight. Next day, January 30th, accompanied by 268 servants, his physician Dr Leckie and Colonel Stuart, Lord Canning set off. Minny Stuart stayed behind with Charlotte. "Of our sad leave-taking that morning," wrote Colonel Stuart, "the less said the better. Dr. Leckie tells me that Charlotte was in private quite upset, but she was her grand self when she came to the door of the great drawing-room" (Hare, II, 413 – 14). She wrote her first letter to Charles that very day, and went to bed feeling bereft and useless. There were still, however, ways to serve.

As the women survivors began to arrive in Calcutta from Lucknow, Charlotte visited them and heard their tales. Like the Kabul retreat of 1842, the Mutiny, for a much larger group of British women, was a terrible and traumatic testing ground. Some, like the long-suffering Mrs Holmes, perished; some went temporarily or permanently insane; some, such as Katherine Bartrum, a young woman in her twenties whose husband and child were Mutiny victims, not only survived but grew strong enough to relive their nightmare all over again on paper. Her book *A Widow's Reminiscences of the Siege of Lucknow* appeared in 1858.

As March began, Charlotte got ready for a three-month pleasure trip to Coonoor, inland from Madras in the Nilgiri hills. Minny Stuart, Johnny Stanley and another ADC were to accompany her. "I feel as if I was abandoning my post and giving in to base selfish indulgence and I see everyone else struggling to go to their husbands," she wrote to Charles on March 3rd. "Send for me back when you like and I shall be only too charmed. Pray write by land to Coonoor.... God bless you my good darling Carlo. Your own Char." She went by ship to Madras, stayed at Guindy with Lord Harris, "seeing all the Madras people in a series of grand dinners." "It seems so very strange to be here again and without you," she told Charles on March 10th. "I sometimes cannot understand how I ever came to embark on such an extraordinary and independent expedition." From Madras, Lord Harris accompanied her on the train to Vellore. ("His hair is so straggling and long and spare" wrote Johnny Stanley irreverently to his mother.[74]) Charlotte wrote almost every day to "dearest Carlo," usually eight or ten pages, fussing about his headaches, weak spells and other ills reported to her in detail, at her request, by Dr Leckie. From Vellore, she travelled by carriage, reaching Ootacamund on March 31st. "Here I am at Ootacamund very tired but I sleep here and only go on to Coonoor at six tomorrow morning," she told Charles. "I am forty-one today. Blessings on you my treasure. Your own *old* C." Charlotte's flower-flow of tenderness to her husband was, alas, not reciprocated in equal measure. "Lord C. is too overwhelmed with work to be able to write to you," Colonel Stuart apologized on April 6th, "and I will supply the blank as well as I can ... he works *fearfully*."[75]

"I have a glimpse of the burning plain," wrote Charlotte to the Queen, arriving at Coonoor, "just enough to remind me of what I have left."[76] Charlotte and the others were lodged in three charming bungalows and Johnny did his best to amuse her. But it was Charlotte's longest absence from Charles since their marriage; she fretted and pined. "I only wish she could sleep better," worried Minny. "She walks, to every one's astonishment, up and down no end of steep hills" (Hare, II, 431). Charlotte had been walking up a steep hill for most of her life; now she needed to walk off her frustrations. Lord Canning fell ill of fever at Allahabad, and although Dr Leckie tried to make light of it in his letters, she fretted even more at not being at Charles's bedside. She tried to soothe herself with Coonoor's green lushness. "I never saw more gorgeous foliage," Charlotte told her mother, "sometimes like curtains of great green leaves, looped up with coils of ropes, binding the trees together" (Hare, II, 435).

Charlotte turned, more and more, to Johnny. "He is so nice and amusing," she told his mother. "You will like to know that Mrs. Stuart and I watch over him as if we were his Grandmothers." "Johnny's spirits never flag," she wrote later, "and he enlivens our little party more than I can say.... I never saw such an affectionate creature."[77] Johnny himself told his mother on May 19th: "Lord Canning has been trying to get the only house at Allahabad for Lady C. to come to but the man, Mr. Palmer, refuses to let it. She is very angry, the poor thing will be wretched alone at Calcutta and (private) possibly he will send her home." Johnny fantasized about accompanying her to England, the two of them together on the moonlit waters: "If Lord C. stays in India *two* ADC's must be with her and even if she went home someone would have to go with her."[78] Johnny took a strong dislike to Minny, whom he thought "absurdly jealous when I show my preference for Lady Canning – Of course I like walking with her, she walks like a goat while Mrs. S. puffs and blows and requires lifting over stones one foot high."[79] A tense threesome, there in the Nilgiri hills.

At the end of June, Charlotte left Coonoor, declaring to Viscountess Sydney: "You cannot imagine the joy with which I left those charming hills, and that cool climate. Enjoyable as it all was, it became nearly unbearable, from the impossibility of knowing what C. was doing in all this complication of troubles" (Hare, II, 454). Lord Canning was now being subjected to all manner of slander and abuse in both Indian and British newspapers. *The Times* called him "a prim philanthropist from Calcutta" and spoke sneeringly of the "clemency of Canning."[80]

Back in Calcutta, Charlotte found Government House full of Mutiny echoes, and very empty without Charles. "I wish she was not so silly and obstinate about going to Allahabad," Johnny Stanley worried. "Lord C. wrote her that the country was so unsettled she *must not* come up now. I do not at all like the risk for her."[81] It was the hottest summer Calcutta had had for forty years; the sky took on a strange inky tint and the terrible furnace-winds stirred up parched clouds of brown-red dust everywhere. Finally, in August, Lord Canning consented to Charlotte's joining him in Allahabad. She set off on the four-week trip up the Ganges by barge and steamer with a light heart, accompanied by both the Stuarts, Johnny and one other ADC. "I now really feel I have seen *India*," wrote Charlotte at Benares. The domes of the great temple there "covered with sheets of gold is a curious and horrible sight with its nearly naked painted priests and Faquirs."[82]

"I must say I shall be rejoiced to be back at my post," Charlotte confided to Viscountess Sydney, a week before her arrival at Allahabad, "after having been about seven months left behind" (Hare, II, 459). "Lord Canning's greeting was most cordial," Minny Stuart reported upon arrival, "and it was very nice to see the bright look in Char's eyes, as she came in to dinner with her light step" (Hare, II, 463). "I arrived here yesterday afternoon, and find C. quite well and delighted to have me back after seven months," Charlotte exulted to her mother on August 30th. "We are in a rough sort of house here, scanty of furniture, but I shall make it better" (Hare, II, 464). She had purposely brought furniture with her from Calcutta on the barge. Johnny Stanley thought Lord Canning "not much changed but his mouth is gone in more as he never wears his false teeth now." On October 5th, Johnny wrote candidly to his mother:

(This is private.) I do not like the way the G.G. treats Lady Canning, she is so constantly thinking only of him and how to please him and he is as sulky as possible and last night at dinner he snubbed her dreadfully for nothing and her poor face looked so pained, she tried to laugh it off but it was a very agonised laugh. I would go a good way to save her such a scene as that for she is as proud as possibly can be with all her devotion to him. I never saw a man with less conversation.[83]

Lord Canning's dour mood lightened a little when, on October 17th, he learned from his Queen that henceforth he would be not just Governor-General but Viceroy of India. This was the result of all the pondering and head-scratching that had been going on in Whitehall and East India Company offices since the rebellion had died down. First the British authorities had looked for causes. Why had the sepoys mutinied? The annexation of Oudh had perhaps been rather peremptory, and no doubt had aggrieved the sepoys, so largely recruited from that province. Then too, the sepoys seemed to resent the fact that rules and red-tape and deal tables were re-placing the mythic splendour of Oriental courts, where kings could lie supine on divan cushions all day writing love-songs. The King of Oudh had, from time to time, been rather squeezed financially to pay for British campaigns. The sepoys had also feared that their British officers were going to force Christianity down their throats. The old-style officers, in the 1830s and '40s, would never have proffered a creed they hardly seemed to hold themselves. But times had changed and now, it was true, some British officers had been waving their Bibles about, and Hindus and Moslems feared for their religion, their caste, their whole way of life. If everything that had become red on India's map was to *stay* red, then some careful words of reassurance to the natives were called for. The British powers-that-be decided to draft a Royal Proclamation.

On November 1, 1858, the Queen's Proclamation, preceded by military salutes and followed by Thanksgiving services and fire-works, was read out at every civil and military station in India. Charlotte felt it a good omen that November 1st was All Saints Day. The Royal Proclamation declared that the East India Company was abolished; that the Crown and British Government now ruled India directly; that there would be no more territorial expansions, that the treaties made by the Company with Princes in the native states not under British rule would be honoured; that all rebels who had not murdered Europeans would be pardoned, and that religious toleration would be observed (the Queen felt strongly about that).

Britain now owned a large part of India, and when the bound-aries were finally fixed in 1900 with the formation of the North-Western Provinces, the British Crown would own two-thirds of

India's territory. But already, in 1858, there was plenty of red on the map vying with the yellow of the native states. In the west were the British provinces of Baluchistan and Sind; in the south, the Central Provinces and the Presidencies of Bombay and Madras; in the east, the Bengal Presidency and the province of Assam, soon to be joined by Burma. Running north-west from Bengal was a solid line of British provinces that formed the backbone of British India: Bihar, the United Provinces, the Punjab and, in due course, the North-Western Provinces. The Presidencies of Madras and Bombay were ruled by Governors; the other British provinces, by Lieutenant-Governors or Commissioners. Each province was divided into districts supervised by District Officers.

The yellow part of India's map comprised 562 native states including Rajputana, Hyderabad, Mysore, Kashmir, Baroda, Nepal and many smaller ones; some, such as Hyderabad, were as large as England and Scotland together; some were only a few dusty acres. They were nominally self-governing, ruled by a prince diversely called a Nizam, Rajah, Maharajah or Rana, each with his own army and revenues. But in actual fact, more and more as the years passed, the native states were under the thumb of the British Resident and Military Commissioner stationed in each state; they were ostensibly there to offer help and advice but they were empowered to interfere in instances of misrule or suspected treachery to the British. The British Lion was now virtually supreme throughout India.

"It is a source of great satisfaction and pride to her," Queen Victoria wrote in the conventional third person to Lord Canning, to feel herself "in direct communication with that enormous Empire which is so bright a jewel of her Crown, and which she would wish to see happy, contented, and peaceful."[84] So bright a Jewel of her Crown: the most valuable jewel, acquired by force, kept by good management, with God's approval. "With respect to the *future shawls*," wrote Queen Victoria to Charlotte shortly after the Proclamation, "I should wish *long as well as* square ones and also *sometimes one* or *two embroidered in gold*."[85]

The Kohinoor diamond, radiant symbol of the power of the

Moghul Empire, had, with the annexation of the Punjab in 1849, been quietly palmed into future Chief Commissioner John Lawrence's waistcoat pocket. From there it was sent to London to be shown at the Great Exhibition in 1851, recut by Garrard's, the fashionable London jewellers, then set in the very centre of Queen Victoria's crown. In 1656, when it had been presented to Shah Jehan, the Kohinoor had weighed 756 carats; recut by Garrards, it was reduced to 106 – fit symbol of waning Indian fortunes.[86] Emily and Fanny Eden had seen it sparkling on Ranjit Singh's arm, the final gleam of Moghul wealth; henceforth India's riches would belong more to the British Raj than to the native Rajahs. The Mutiny was the watershed. Emily Eden had played chess with Dost Mahomed and taught English to Pertab Singh, but such easy conviviality between Indian ruler and English was gone forever. Henceforth, the British in India would always walk in fear. They sensed that Indians hated them; and so they ruled with an iron hand, but one which trembled a little, which relied more and more on the impersonal and inexorable power of the written word: on regulations, rules, proliferating reams of red-tape. The Eden sisters had caught glimpses of Moghul magic and magnificence, of Peacock Thrones ablaze with light, enough to fire their imaginations, enough to see by. But the violence that lay behind the spoils had come too close, and now the British had stepped back permanently into their neat little compound, fenced and right-angled, of facts and rules. Johnny Stanley admired Lady Canning for being so "wonderfully clever in remembering names, places, etc., quite remarkable."[87] The first Viceroy's wife in this, as in all else, was the norm that all the British in Post-Mutiny India would copy. India was to be learned like a subject at school, a rather difficult and disagreeable subject; one could grasp it – as much as one needed to grasp – not through one's imagination but through memorizing facts. Lord Canning sent Indian Civil Service officers who knew how to photograph across the country, at his own expense, to record the "real" India, plainly visible to all, with its proliferating telegraph wires and railway tracks and new buildings, all of which were architecturally exactly like those going up in Victorian England. None of them bore even the tiniest resemblance to indigenous Indian architecture. No minarets on the horizon, nor in the mind. In the Mutiny clash of Eastern instinct and Western reason, the latter had won. Long live the Reign of Reason! Long live the Empire! Long live Queen Victoria and the Jewel in the Crown! "We have not been elected or placed in power by the people," admitted Sir John Lawrence, Viceroy from 1863 – 69, with modest candour, "but we are here through our moral superiority, by the force of circumstance, by the will of Providence."[88] By "the force of circumstance," and a few other kinds of force. In England, the new Gospel of Empire was a flaming torch, illuminating the virtues of duty, dedication and plain hard work. "Take up the White Man's burden/ Send forth the best ye breed," Rudyard Kipling told all England. And they did. Willingly, for the rewards, both here and in the hereafter, were great. "In their prosperity," concluded the November 1st Queen's Proclamation, referring to Indian subjects, "will be Our strength, in their contentment Our security, and in their Gratitude Our best reward."[89]

Lord Canning had espoused the new Gospel from the first day of his arrival, but he had driven himself too hard. "Tell Papa *privately* that Lord C's arrears of work are something tremendous," wrote Johnny Stanley to his mother, "his room is full of boxes not opened even, it must be known some day. The officials all over India are at a standstill, they can get no decision – his shaking mouth tells the tale."[90] One of his assistants would later speak of this as Canning's "miserable period of no-government."[91] Charlotte saw Charles failing and flagging, but couldn't, from the arm's length at which he kept her, do anything to help.

In January 1859, Lord Canning, first Viceroy of India, returned to Calcutta to shuffle through the rest of his rule. He and Charlotte did not return together; her party departed first, filling eight carriages; Lord Canning's left Allahabad later, filling eleven. Charlotte's loyal coterie, Minny Stuart, Johnny Stanley and a new admirer, Emily Bayley, wife of the new Foreign Secretary Edward Clive Bayley, worried about her. "So beautiful still but oh! so changed, sadly worn with the anxiety and distress of the Mutiny," commented Emily when she first saw Charlotte in Calcutta that January.[92] "I wish I could say she was as strong as she is kind and good," wrote Minny, "the reaction of returning here to this climate, and the utter stagnation of interest, after the intense excitement of every nerve and feeling, through which she has so bravely struggled, certainly tells upon her" (Hare, II, 487). "I do not know how Lady Canning can stand it," worried Johnny, referring to the heat. "She always says oh I can do anything, but she is not looking well at all."[93] Charlotte clung to Johnny's bright spirit as her own grew more bleached and when he stopped coming to sit alone with her, perhaps realizing that he was growing too fond, Charlotte gently requested him to "come as usual." "She is worth all the rotten people in Calcutta ten times over," he told his mother, his heart nearly bursting with love and loyalty.[94] When the terrible news came by telegram that Lord Waterford, husband of Charlotte's sister Louisa, had been killed in a hunting accident on March 29th (an end one could have predicted), it was to Johnny, not Minny, that Charlotte turned in her grief. She learned later that Louisa had painted a portrait of her dead husband lying in state, a means of distancing her emotions which her sympathetic sister could well understand. "What a thought of comfort it must be to know how very happy she made him, never ceasing to do everything for his comfort and pleasure," Charlotte wrote to her mother (Hare, III, 46), smugly aware of her own consummate devotion. "I feel she [Louisa] will be inclined," continued Charlotte, "to build a fence of little punctilios round herself" (Hare, III, 58). It was what Charlotte herself had done, beginning at Windsor Castle, driving the pickets deeper into the barren soil of her Calcutta life. But from inside her square little fence, she could still glimpse the jungle growth beyond. "I quite revel in the *luxe* of flowers and green leaves," she enthused at Barrackpore. She took to sitting out "nearly all day under the great Banyan and its creepers" that August. She stayed at Barrackpore most of the month, painting a series of tree-portraits:

26 A banyan tree (watercolour by Lady Canning, August 1859)

of the deodar, the tamarind, the Burma mahogany, the banyan. They are painted, however, not in shades of green, but in dull brown tones on buff paper. One of the few trees done in its true colours is the peepul, that sacred tree whose leaves never stopped trembling, and whose dry rustle one could so easily mistake for the sound of life-giving rain. Lady Canning's record of India: sepia drawings and piles of sepia photographs. "As for my photographs," Charlotte wrote, "they are like a nightmare, for I have now thousands of them" (Hare, III, 59). She would never catch up with the sorting and cataloguing.

In the autumn of 1859, the Cannings started a camp journey north to hold splendid durbars at Lucknow, Cawnpore, Agra and Meerut, durbars of pacification that would roll the red carpets of British Raj pomp and power over those sandy plains where so much blood had flowed. The Viceroy's retinue was as large as the Edens',

27 Lady Canning at Futtehghur, November 1859

with twenty thousand people, most of them troops. Charlotte hated
the dust and disorder of her tent life. I "can bear anything," she
sighed, "but cannot the least see the delights of camp-life."[95] Then,
between Agra and Delhi, came a worse distress. Her tent caught
fire in the middle of the night, due to an overheated stove. Charlotte
fled in her blue flannel dressing-gown, hair streaming down her
back. She lost almost everything: all her fine clothes, all her lace,

28 Lord Canning's camp at Mirzapore 1860

except for the piece of Mechlin she'd worn at her wedding, most of her jewellery, including Indian rings with "great rubies and emeralds." Worst of all, the pearls inherited from Baroness Mountstuart were badly damaged. All gone – and with them much of her identity. Her daily journals, too, were destroyed or badly scorched round the edges, including those from November 1855 to January 1859. She had taken them all up-country with her as part of her arsenal of self-assertion. Now they were brown-edged and crumbling, as sepia-sere as her Calcutta life. Sir Colin Campbell, now Lord Clyde, so dubbed for his Mutiny triumphs, wrapped her gently round with an enormous dressing-gown, and tried to comfort her. Lord Canning's reaction to his wife's safe escape from the fire is not recorded.

By April of 1860, the Cannings had finished their grand progress and reached Simla – their only visit. They stayed in a house called Barnes Court which Charlotte "chintzed" appropriately, but from the beginning she hated Simla. "The dryness makes all look

29 Lady Canning with Lady Campbell, Simla, 1860

wintry," she noted, and the mountain precipices made her nervous. Charles hated Simla too – it was too far from the centre – and returned to Calcutta after less than a month, secretly pleased that a difficulty in the new taxation scheme called him back to business. Charlotte was not allowed to return with him – too hard on her health, he told her. He sent her off instead on a wild expedition to Chini on the Tibet border. "I should have liked going with C. to Calcutta far the best of all, and would not in the least have feared the heat, but C. would not for an instant hear of it," she sighed, accepting her fate as always without a whimper (Hare, III, 100).

30 Lord Canning, 1860

So off she went into the mountains with West and two ADC's, ordered to enjoy herself. They travelled more than three hundred miles in thirty-one days, staying at *dak* bungalows (traveller's rest stops), as they climbed towards the snow. To cross and recross the Sutlej river, Charlotte had to cope with bridges made of tree-trunks, or, where there were none, with being hauled across in a swinging basket on ropes. The roads were impossibly narrow and snaking, and there were precipices that took one's breath away. The party made only four halts of a day each; the rest of the month, Charlotte was on the move, up and down, up and down, twisting, turning, carried round the sheer drops in a "sort of reclining chair" (Hare, III, 104).

She wrote daily, of course, to Charles; his replies were sporadic: "Darling Char, I know I have been very bad about writing, it is more than a week since my last letter. But I have got into the stream of business again," he apologized on June 10th.[96] She didn't like travelling without him, and she hated the mountains, so jagged and precipitous. "Certainly mountains on a moderate scale only are pleasanter," she told her mother, "these giants are detestable to live amongst." She did rather wonder at Charles recommending such a tour, "for I certainly could hardly have called the roads passable, and I should scarcely advise any of my female acquaintances to go" (Hare, III, 108). By the end of July, she was back at Government House, suffering once more through silent dinners, where Lord Canning sat mute and Charlotte's hands fluttered over the table, straightening salt-cellars and flower-stems, and Johnny Stanley, his fair skin flushing, talked nonsense, as Willy Osborne once had to fill up Lord Auckland's silences.

Charlotte's thoughts, in the spring of 1861, were turning to England. "I hope by this time next year (if we are alive)," she wrote to Viscountess Sydney on March 18th, "we shall be arriving in England" (Hare, III, 143). Johnny Stanley went back to England in April, leaving a ragged hole in Charlotte's life. He described his leave-taking to his sister:

The night before I left Calcutta I bought a little gold cross which was made to open and when I went to dear Lady Canning's room to say good-bye to her I asked her (I have often wondered since how I had the courage) if she would put a little bit of hair in it for me to keep as a remembrance of her. I did not wait for her to answer but kissed her hand and ran away. Half an hour after she sent it back with what I had so much wished for and a few very kind words at parting.[97]

"Though I have always been very *fond* I did not know what an enormous *blank* it will make in my insignificant existence not having her to speak to and look at. When you get this," Johnny told his mother just before he left Calcutta, "you might write to Lady C. and say how much I have worshipped her, for I cannot well say so to her face." Then he regained his habitual flippancy and added: "Lord C. will not break his heart, no more shall I, when we say good-bye ... I wish he had a firmer mouth, it does so spoil his face."[98]

Charlotte felt equally bereft. "I hope soon to coax C. out to Barrackpore again," she wrote. "I shall be quite low at parting with that really nice place, and have greatly enjoyed there the command of a tropical garden" (Hare, III, 148). It was all she did have command of – that and Johnny Stanley's heart. But he was far away now; she consoled herself, as she always had, with custom and ceremony. On August 26th she presided over a very grand Government House ball in honour of the new Commander-in-Chief of the army, Sir Hugh Rose, who had been invested with the Star of India, for outstanding services to India. The new order had been recently created by the Queen, at Lord Canning's suggestion. Charlotte had supplied the Order's motto: "Heaven's Light Our Guide." For the ball, she wore a white satin dress, with a spray of real ivy plucked from its luxuriance and neatly coiled in her hair. She also wore a diamond coronet befitting a Countess, for Charles had been elevated to the rank of Earl by the Queen and would soon be given the Garter. Charlotte was now Countess Canning, not just Viscountess; in peerage pecking-order, only Marchionesses and Duchesses outranked her.

A little later, the Queen graciously wrote to Canning offering him, upon his return to England, the Rangership of the Park at Blackheath, near London. This would be a fine sinecure with a house attached, a house which Charlotte was already decorating in her mind. The house, as she recalled it in the time of Lord Aberdeen's tenancy, was not a large one; she and Charles would be in close proximity there. That autumn, when Charles sent her off on another expedition, this one to Darjeeling, Charlotte took a gardener with her to help her bring back "all sorts of treasures in the way of orchids and seeds" (Hare, III, 151) to plant in the Blackheath garden. She would make Blackheath so beautiful, so snug, that Charles would never want to be anywhere else. "My grievance is still not sleeping," she wrote to him from Darjeeling. "I have often slept badly but never as badly as now and I do not know now when I shall ever sleep again." Charlotte tossed and worried through the long, sticky nights; back in England would be Charles's mistress whom he hadn't seen for five years. She felt even more anxious when Charles wrote telling her not to attempt to join him at Allahabad as planned – the roads were impossibly bad. "I feel very much ashamed," she replied on October 17th, "of being away from my post after always following like the faithful dog." Now her letters to him took on an hysterical note, stressing how cosy and contented they were going to be at Blackheath:

> All our large china and stuffed birds etc. will do so well there and the carpets. The dairy I especially like the thought of.... The very day I knew of Blackheath I had been thinking was there any use in carrying home a nice little bamboo milk can that would go charmingly in a dairy, and I was so wishing for a dairy where one could put a few rough odd things of that kind ... and we must have some Cochin fowls. Nothing was ever so convenient.

She hoped that stuffed birds and bamboo milk cans would somehow compensate for the passion she knew he craved and which she knew she couldn't give him. At Darjeeling, Charlotte grew weak from lack of sleep and finally fell ill with dysentery. The return trip to Calcutta was wearing, but she made it back on November 8th in time to welcome Charles, expected home from Allahabad on the 10th. Her route had taken her through swamp ground infested with malaria, and she had caught fever. She had to get better quickly, for she and Charles were to leave for Burma as soon as he returned. "I think I ache more than I ought and shall treat it as fever and take a calomel and opium pill and be quite well before you come. We must get bamboo milk pails in Burma for I have only one and I believe they are bigger there. Goodbye treasure, Your own Char." She wrote that to him on the day she got back to Government House. When he returned on the 10th, she struggled up to welcome him; next day she lay on the sofa; the following day she took to her bed, got steadily worse, and never rose from it again. On November 18th, Charlotte Elizabeth, Countess Canning died. She was forty-four years old. She died in her husband's arms but didn't know it as she had been unconscious for the final four days.

Lord Canning was inconsolable, wracked with guilt. He went through all her papers, her diaries, her lists, discovered the depth of her devotion and her love. He had failed her in love, ignored her in life, perhaps even caused her death by forbidding her to come to Allahabad, thus indirectly sending her through the fatal swamp. "Whether all might have gone differently if the first plan had been held to, God alone knows," he wrote to his Queen.[99] Charlotte had finally managed to do the one thing, the only thing, which would secure Charles's love and devotion forever: she had died. The faithful wife was gone, but the golden halo round her life and service began at once to take shape.

On the day of her death, Lord Canning locked himself in his room and stayed there all day. Overnight he became an old, broken man, walking with the aid of a stick. He planned her funeral carefully, saw to it that no native hands touched the body, that no non-Christians stood beside the grave. His wife was taken through bright moonlight from Calcutta to Barrackpore, where eleven English soldiers and aides stood by the grave as she was lowered into it. Lord Canning had chosen a grave-site under some casuarina trees, amid the flowers and shrubs she had loved so much. Every morning and evening, when at Barrackpore, he visited her grave; on Christmas morning he was on the spot at four A. M. He kept a light burning there always, and each morning a fresh arrangement of flowers shaped like a cross was placed on the grave. However late his work kept him in Calcutta, every Saturday evening, from the time of her death until he himself left India the following March, Lord Canning made that evening trip to Barrackpore. He had never yielded to Charlotte's pleading to join her at Barrackpore when she was alive. Now he was exemplary in his devotion, and went faithfully.

Lord Canning began the worship of his dear wife's memory, and the rest of Victorian England, and India, joined in with sanctimonious zeal. Here was one who had made the supreme sacrifice for Empire ideals of duty and devotion. Charlotte, Countess Canning had been the perfect helpmeet to a hero serving Empire: pious, brave, uncomplaining, steadfast through Mutiny troubles. The Perfect *Memsahib*, the Perfect Victorian Lady. Both in England and India, the British had found their heroine, and the myth blossomed in their hearts. Charlotte, Countess Canning, neglected during her life, had the attention, admiration and adoration of a whole nation. On the day she died, one of Calcutta's newspapers declared that her death would "cause sorrow throughout India, where no lady has ever secured a deeper respect for her high character, or a stronger personal regard than that inspired by her graceful urbanity and amiable disposition."[100] Charlotte Canning had firmly established, for all future Vicereines, the ideals of charm, dignity, self-sacrifice and charity expected of them. She who had always followed conduct-book advice to the letter had now, as it were, written her own.

The Indians themselves immortalized Charlotte by naming a sweetmeat "ledikeni" – an Indian corruption of her name. It is made of curdled milk, flour and sugar rolled tightly into a small ball and fried in hot syrup. Perhaps they knew it to be a favourite confection of Charlotte's; perhaps they thought its cloying sweetness made it an appropriate memento.

After the first shock had passed, Lord Canning wrote to his

Queen, telling her how, to the very end, her former Lady-of-the-Bedchamber had been fastidious about doing her duty:

> In the last connected conversation which he had with her, just before the illness became really threatening, she said that she must write again to The Queen, "for I don't want her to think that it was out of laziness that I was not at Allahabad."[101]

By the time she received this letter, the Queen was suffering her own immense grief; Prince Albert died a month after Lady Canning. "To lose one's partner in life is, as Lord Canning knows, like losing *half* one's *body* and *soul*, torn forcibly away – and dear Lady Canning was such a dear, worthy, devoted wife!" Her Majesty wrote to Lord Canning.[102]

A monument was designed by Charlotte's sister, Louisa, for her grave: a most elaborate white marble one with inlaid mosaics in the form of a cross. But it deteriorated so badly in the monsoon rains that it had to be moved in 1873 to the south transept of Calcutta's cathedral and was shifted in 1913 to the north portico. A simpler marble monument was made for the grave-site, where green leaves waved and whispered just out of reach above her. The grave, like Charlotte's life, was enclosed in a neat, rectangular fence, this one of cold iron, with "CC" repeated endlessly around it.

Lord Canning said his farewells to the grave on the afternoon of March 18th, the same day he boarded the *Feroze*, the frigate which had brought him out, and left India, looking "pale, wan, toil-worn and grief-stricken."[103] Back in England, he carefully cat-alogued all Charlotte's papers, making neat lists and indexes. One little blue-covered book contains an index to her letters by subject: "Cedars near Simla, May 9, '60. Descent of rocky slope, May 30, '60" ... all written in his small, precise script.[104] Such rational rem-edies, however, couldn't help the pain of his remorse. Lord Canning barely had time to visit Charlotte's mother and sister at Highcliffe Castle before he fell ill himself. Charles, Lord Canning, died on

June 17, 1862, aged forty-nine, and was buried in Westminster Abbey. He had died of abscesses of the liver – a common complaint in India, stemming from frequent bouts of amoebic dysentery. India had killed Lord Canning as it had killed his wife, as it had killed both Lord and Lady Dalhousie, as it would in less than a year and a half kill Lord Canning's successor, Lord Elgin. Three successive Governors-General of India, and two of their wives, died for Empire ideals.

After Lord Canning's death, almost everything belonging to Charlotte, who had made no will, was sold: her jewels, her blue Sèvres, her bamboo milk pails, even her pearls: all scattered.[105]

There is one final irony. A bronze equestrian statue of Lord Canning, he who had guided India through the Mutiny with a firm hand on Reason's reins and kept it British, was raised in Calcutta. In the 1960s, his bronze Lordship was moved to the burial enclosure at Barrackpore. He sits there now, stiff and silent astride his bronze horse, looking down, from his eminence, on all that remains of his devoted wife: a cold marble form inside a square iron fence. Now, finally and forever, they are together.

❋ III ❋

EDITH LYTTON

*The throne, which is still called the peacock throne, was in the
time of Akbar said to have had jewels on it to the value of 20,000
pounds ... and the peacocks which stand at each corner had each
a string of pearls in their beaks, valued at 10,000 pounds. These,
like the diamonds, are now replaced by false ones, and the jewels
on the body of the throne have descended into coloured glass.*

H. E. FANE
Five Years in India

BORN SEPTEMBER 15, 1841, Edith was the daughter of Elizabeth
Liddell, one of Lord Ravensworth's sixteen children, and Edward
Villiers, brother of Lord Clarendon, the great Foreign Secretary
who was Emily Eden's close friend. Edith's father died in Nice in
1843 of tuberculosis, leaving his wife in financial straits with four
children to raise: Theresa, Ernest, and the identical twins Edith and
Elizabeth (Lizey), then two years old. Lord Clarendon gave them
a small house, Grove Mill, on his estate near Watford, and did what
he could to help. Mrs. Villiers and her children spent frugal winters
in France or Germany or Italy, where Edith's formal education
consisted in learning foreign languages and piano-playing. Since
marriage was the career she was being groomed for, that was held
to be quite sufficient.

Edith and Lizey grew to be tall, willowy, fair-haired beauties;
they "came out" in London society in 1860, and were so alike in
looks that Mrs Villiers hung different lockets round their necks to

enable their dance partners to tell them apart. Even so, family rumour claims that Henry Loch, later Lord Loch, Governor of the
Isle of Man, meant to propose to Edith but found himself engaged
and married to Lizey.

Holidaying in Nice over Easter, 1861, Edith was courted by
a master from Harrow, who read to her under the blossoming olive
trees a long narrative poem, *Lucile,* by one Owen Meredith. Edith
rejected the young man's advances but absorbed Owen Meredith's
view of woman as "born to nurse / and to soothe and solace, to
help and to heal." In 1862, London's fashionable portrait-painter,
G.F. Watts, painted Edith as a pre-Raphaelite beauty with a wistful
expression. It was significant of Edith's nature that her hair wasn't
tightly coiled and braided as the young Charlotte Canning's was in
youthful portraits, but hung rippling and loose around her.

The summer of 1864 found Mrs Villiers and Edith alone at
Grove Mill. By then both Theresa and Lizey had married; Edith
missed her twin badly and was ready to attach herself for life to
some deserving young man. She needed emotional intimacy and
got none from her mother. At a ball Edith met Robert Lytton and
felt a strong attraction. Robert was thirty-three, Edith, twenty-
two. He was shorter than she was, but very handsome with large
dreamy blue-green eyes, dark, curly hair and beard, and the look
of a high-strung thoroughbred. If we accept Baudelaire's definition
of a dandy as a man not just concerned with fine clothes but also
with being wildly original, and with startling others, then Robert
Lytton, like his father, the novelist Bulwer-Lytton,[1] was definitely
a dandy. He strutted proudly before Edith in silk cravat, velvet
jacket and finger-rings on the weekend of June 24, 1864, invited
down to Grove Mill by Mrs Villiers. Edith sat rapt and adoring
while Robert, who amazingly turned out to be the published poet
Owen Meredith, with five books to his credit, unfurled a long,
continuous ribbon of amusing anecdotes and "the most charming
imaginative sort of Fairy tales."[2]

Five weeks later, Edith and Robert were engaged. "It was quite
the most eventful day of my life," Edith rhapsodized in her diary

32 Portrait of Lord Lytton (by G.F. Watts)

on July 30th: "The darling began and told me the feelings he had
for me and I only felt at once so ready to give him my whole heart
and was directly so happy and grateful to God for sending me such

a good husband."[3] Bulwer-Lytton, when told of the engagement, thought Robert should have found himself a *rich* wife, but as always, with Robert, romance had triumphed over prudence. "I would rather live upon black bread with her [Edith], than share with another the greatest fortune in England," he declared dramatically to his fatherly mentor, John Forster.[4] To his father, Robert wrote, with fine prescience, "I feel that my future happiness is built upon a rock,"[5] and commented to a female friend, that in Edith's hands he knew "his future was perfectly safe."[6]

The plain fact was, Robert Lytton wanted to be cosseted and mothered, and sensed that Edith, with her bountiful flow of love and tenderness, would do just that. His own mother was Rosina Wheeler, a nubile young Irish girl whom Bulwer had married in 1827 and who had proved to be a most negligent mother. Robert was born on November 8, 1831, and Rosina at once relegated him to the care of nursery maids at the top of their Mayfair house and more or less forgot him. By the time he was five, Rosina had had more than enough of domestic bliss and departed the household forever. Bulwer was much too busy producing novels and plays and illegitimate children to have time for Robert, who found a substitute father in John Forster, drama critic and later editor of the *Examiner*. Forster introduced Robert to Charles Dickens, Leigh Hunt and his other literary friends and instilled in his protégé the ambition to be a poet. In 1850, Bulwer decided on a diplomatic career for his son and dispatched him to Washington as unpaid attaché to an uncle, Sir Henry Bulwer, who was Minister there. Robert accompanied Uncle Henry on his next posting to Florence, staying from 1852 to 1854, and making friends with Robert and Elizabeth Barrett Browning. Elizabeth decided that young Mr Lytton was quite "visionary enough" to suit her, approving of his interest in spiritualism, astrology and palmistry.[7] Robert fell hopelessly in love with Harriet Wilson, who had violet eyes, tawny hair and an incensed husband. She inspired Robert's first book of poems, imitative of Browning's, improved by Mrs Browning, and published, at Bulwer-Lytton's insistence, under the pseudonym "Owen Mer-edith," in 1855. The following year, Robert moved on to the British Embassy at The Hague and another abortive love affair.

This, then, was the young man whose personal charm, little-boy-lost appeal and calculated cunning secured him a life partner who would be both mother and mistress, refuge and rock. For her part, Edith liked the idea of marrying a poet and mistakenly sup-posed she had found a good one. Robert and Edith were married on October 4, 1864, at St Paul's, Knightsbridge, in London, and went to The Grove, Lord Clarendon's estate, for a four-day hon-eymoon. "I feel more blest than any woman has ever yet been," Edith exulted to her mother, and Robert was equally ecstatic, telling his father that Edith's companionship was "like a permanent bath of sunshine which both cheers and soothes. A sweeter or more even temper, a nature more submissive in little things, more unselfish in great, more devoted, I never experienced," he wrote.[8] "I am not of a sanguine temperament, nor even naturally self-reliant," Robert wrote with modest understatement to a friend.[9] All his life he suf-fered from what he termed "almost intolerable hysterical depres-sion."[10] He needed, and appreciated, the golden balm of Edith's cheerful disposition.

After their honeymoon, Robert was posted to the British Em-bassy at Athens and from thence, after six months, to Lisbon. On June 28, 1865, Edith reluctantly left for London and her confine-ment, and letters of love flying daily back and forth replaced the real thing. Four hundred thousand words in all; he called her "pink, purring Puttens" or "Owney"; she called him "Robsy" or "Manny." Their need of each other physically and emotionally was great – his already greater than hers. On both sides the correspondence expressed with self-conscious solemnity the wonder and joy of their mutual love. It was in those mid-century years that Victorian society raised the ideal of married love beyond any other kind, and higher than it has ever been before or since. Dinah Maria Mulock (the novelist Mrs Craik) in *A Woman's Thoughts About Women* (1858) speaks glowingly of "marriage with all its sanctity, beauty and glory."[11] In "the love of married life," Mrs Ellis agrees in *The Wives of England,* "is embodied the richest treasure which this earth affords."[12] "It is so good of you to love me as you do," wrote Edith in one letter, "how I wish I were more worthy of that love, in being a *perfect* wife in every way for you."[13] It was all she wanted in the world: to shape herself exactly to Robert's needs. "I know my darling loves me almost as much as I do him and finds me very useful," she wrote. The precise nature of a wife's usefulness was spelled out in contemporary conduct books. "To make her husband happy, to raise his character, to give dignity to his house, and to train up his children in the path of wisdom – these are the objects which a true wife will not rest satisfied without endeavouring to obtain."[14] Edith was eager to carry out these duties and would prove eminently successful in all but the elevation of Robert's character – not an easy task, as she would eventually realize. For his part, he was already beginning to see, in those early days of marriage, how very dependent he had become on his wife. "Never, never again under any circumstances, dear self of myself, can I consent … to your leaving me," he told her.[15] "I need and miss her everywhere and in everything," he confided to a friend.[16]

Edith, on the other hand, far away in London, nervously await-ing the birth of a child, was slowly realizing that she had one already: she had married, it seemed, an impulsive, impractical, feckless child. There she was in England, growing more mature and independent every day, thriftily choosing carpets and curtains for their rented villa outside Lisbon, hiring maid and nurse, placating her difficult mother and Robert's even pricklier father. In Sintra, Robert was having an antique Venetian cabinet repaired at great expense, and buying silver salvers, "far preferable" to common trays, for holding cups of tea. He ordered "darling Edie" to bring back from London an ice-machine for chilling champagne. It would cost double Rob-ert's weekly salary. Edith did as she was told, then ventured a mild rebuke. "No one can feel more strongly than I do," she told him, "that we are spending too much of our income and when we are together we must think over some means of paying the debts and recovering ourselves."[17] "You are an angel of economy as well as of love," was Robert's placating caress,[18] but he did nothing, then or later, to mend his spendthrift ways. Edith wondered if she should forego the expense of a lady's maid. "Don't be anxious about me being dowdy if I do this, I will manage somehow to be well dressed for my dear Man," she assured him.[19] He liked her to be always elegantly turned out.

From Knebworth House, his ancestral home, where Edith was visiting Robert's father, she wrote: "I don't care ever to sleep in this big bed till I do so with you my darling," hinting broadly at an eroticism which all the Victorian conduct books agreed no wife ever felt, let alone expressed. A double bed was the soft, necessary foundation of Robert and Edith's marriage, where their different but equally passionate natures met. Robert's sexual desires were openly expressed – and rather too widely disseminated. Edith's were expressed more obliquely, and only to her husband. One wonders if Robert's poem entitled "Twins," unpublished in his lifetime, was written for her:

> The woman that I hate is circumspect,
> In all her intimacies pure of taint,
> In all her conduct carefully correct,
> A social saint!
>
> The woman that I love has other ways,
> Is passionate, spontaneous, quick, intense;
> No social code her wild warm will obeys,
> Nor moral sense.
>
> . . .
>
> But sometimes, when the night is lone and late,
> And done the pious days' puritanic task,
> Panting for breath, the woman that I hate
> Shakes off her mask.
>
> . . .

Then, from that hated woman's robe set free
In all her fearless fervours manifold,
The woman that I love leaps forth to me,
Naked and bold!

Up until her marriage, Edith had had no avenue of expression for her "wild warm will." Now she was two people: the world saw the social saint and Robert the sensual woman. Not until she got to India would she begin to knit her duality together into a fully integrated self.

In that second year of marriage, Edith discovered that her maternal love was quite as strong as her sexual feelings. She went into labour in mid-August, during a whist game with her mother and the Lochs. "When a sharp pain came to flush her up and make her hide her face and writhe," Edith's mother told Robert, "the moment it passed she perked up with 'Hope you have not seen my Trumps,' then we all four roared with laughter."[20] To Robert's great delight, the baby was a boy; they named him Rowland. Although it was fashionable to have a wet-nurse, Edith insisted on nursing the baby herself.

In 1866, Robert's father, now the first Lord Lytton, allowed his son to publish a book of poems, *Chronicles and Characters,* under his own name. It appeared about the same time that Edith produced a second child, Betty, but while the new baby flourished the book of poems languished unread on bookstalls, and Robert "lapsed into a lethargy of despondency."[21] The Lyttons moved on to Madrid in the spring of 1868 and to Vienna in the autumn of 1869, where Robert was made Secretary of Legation. The continual moves were very trying for Edith, who gave birth to a second daughter, Constance, shortly after their arrival in Vienna.

In the summer of 1871, while still in Vienna, Rowland "our naughty scamp," as Edith called him indulgently, a curly-haired six-year-old with "loving, clever eyes, very like those of his father,"[22] died from complications following whooping cough. Eight

months later, Edith gave birth to another son, Teddy, but he too
died, in March of 1874, before his second birthday.

These deaths left both Edith and Robert profoundly distressed
emotionally but Edith repressed her own grief in order to deal with
her husband's – he who slipped so easily into deep depression. Edith
had learned the lesson of the conduct books well: "The love of
woman," writes Mrs Ellis, "appears to have been created solely to
minister; that of man, to be ministered to."[23] This pattern of Edith
having to curb her own strong feelings out of concern for her
husband's was to be repeated many times in their marriage. Robert
let loose the flood; Edith closed the floodgate.

On January 19, 1873, Robert's father died of an ear abscess,
and Robert became second Lord Lytton. In April he was posted to
Paris as First Secretary, where he followed the example of that
earlier diplomat, Lord Stuart de Rothesay, Charlotte Canning's
father, cultivating his tastes for old wines and young women. It
was in Paris that Robert became firmly fixed in the lifelong habit
which Edith always referred to, with a rueful little smile and a
euphemism that fooled no one, least of all herself, as Robert's
"flirting."

Edith had to pack up and move again, with the new baby
Emily, at the end of 1874, for Robert had been promoted to Min-
ister of Legation at Lisbon. In November of the next year, Lord
Northbrook resigned the post of Viceroy of India, and Prime Min-
ister Disraeli cast about for a successor. Since the deaths of Lords
Dalhousie, Canning and Elgin, and of a fourth Governor-General,
Lord Mayo, who was stabbed to death by a Pathan convict in
February 1872, their British Lordships were not exactly rushing
forward to offer themselves on the sacrificial altar of Empire. Dis-
raeli tried the Earl of Powis; and Lord John Manners; both refused.
Feeling a little desperate now, he offered the Viceroy's job to Lord
Carnarvon, who declined, ever so graciously. The names of Lord
Dufferin and Lord Derby were bandied about. Then, in sudden and
sanguine inspiration, Disraeli thought of Robert, Lord Lytton.

When Disraeli's offer came, Robert had only been seven months in Lisbon and was planning to retire soon from the diplomatic service. Now that Knebworth and its rent roll were his, he could devote his life to his true vocation, namely poetry. The idea of India, however, sent his imagination soaring. He had, after all, written verses on "the black elephants of Delhi," described the East's glorious gardens in "Desire," and composed an Indian love story. Edith stood aside; Robert had to make the decision by himself, but she could think only of how devastating India's climate and fevers were for children. Robert sent off an ambiguous letter to Disraeli, stating his willingness to serve but protesting his "absolute ignorance of Indian affairs," his total want of experience in every kind of administrative business and his fears that his health might "break down at some critical moment." He confided that for years he had suffered from "a complaint" which was "extremely painful, enfeebling, and depressing."[24] The complaint was hæmorrhoids, for which nothing could be worse than a hot climate and long hours of sitting in Viceregal office-chairs or on Viceregal thrones. Robert debated long and hard with himself, but finally imagination won out over prudence. "I have not courted or willingly accepted the crushing gift of such a white elephant," he told a friend,[25] but the plain fact was: the sensuous East tempted Robert Lytton as surely as a woman, and he was not a man to hold out against seduction. He was then embarked on his *magnum opus, King Poppy,* in whose kingdom "all are dreamers, all are children," a long poem which would keep him busy for the rest of his life. Its purpose was to show "what a poor tissue of unreality human life would be if the much-despised influence of imagination were banished from it."[26] Robert laid the poem aside and went out to India to serve Queen and Empire, so he said. But in truth, he went fully intending to indulge himself. It was forty years since the Arabian Nights had propelled the Eden sisters towards India. Lord Lytton, Viceroy Elect, may well have been the last Briton to feel that strong yet silken pull.

Edith, for her part, had more to worry about than the direction Robert's fancy and "flirtations" might take in the sultry East. Her real fears centred on the children. Betty, Constance and Emily were then eight, six and one, and Edith was expecting again in August. Infant mortality was very high in India; most British children there were shipped off to England at five or six years of age to remove them from the threat of cholera, dysentery, malaria and other ills. Edith could not for a moment consider the thought of staying behind, nor of leaving the children. Her family was her life, a sacred circle that mustn't be broken. These were the years when Victorians worshipped the family – a hallowed, self-sufficient unit – with far more sincerity and fervour than they worshipped God. There were summer outings to the seaside and winter reading-aloud sessions in the evenings, where the family Bible, inscribed with the family begettings, adorned the parlour table and "God Bless our Family" worked in coloured wools hung on the wall above. Edith quickly decided that they would all go to India together, but with plenty of English servants to mitigate the strangeness and the risks. The Lyttons left their Sintra villa for Lisbon on November 4th; Edith confided to her diary that she was "feeling very sad as the bells rang the Ave Maria for the last time for me at dear Sintra."[27]

Edith hid her feelings and carried on as usual, describing in her journal how, in spite of "great anxiety and worry over packing again, and so much that was difficult to face in the future," she'd organized a "merry" Christmas dinner in 1875, with sixteen guests and Constance and Betty joining them for the first time. "Dear quiet Edie," wrote Lady Constance Stanley to her in a letter Edith copied into her journal, "your fate is not to rest, darling, for you have had very little of that since your marriage." In eleven years of wedded bliss, Edith had already moved six times and produced five children along the way. "The Telegram saying the appointment was public and well-received," she recorded in her diary, "came on January 5th [1876].... I was much upset, for as we have kept the news so quiet, I had almost forgotten about it. All now know the great change in our happy lives; certainly happiness is not allowed for long in this world, and this appointment terrifies me." "I was not at all strong," she wrote, "and I believed that probably

I should not recover a confinement in India, and might break down over the preparations before going out." Fears and forebodings filled the corners of her mind, and soon Robert would not be there to help her fend them off. He would be going to England, leaving her alone in Lisbon to sort and sell their effects, pack up all the rest, then join him with the three children. "The separation, though short, tried me very much at the time," she admitted. Being two months pregnant, she was feeling unwell, apart from all the other strains. Somehow she coped, and as with the earlier separation during her first pregnancy, grew stronger.

Robert reached London on January 19th. In the flurry of activity he didn't write to Edith until January 23rd. On the very day of his arrival, however, he sent off a warmly affectionate note to her sister Theresa Earle, suggesting a rendezvous and telling her: "I left dear Edith in good health and as brave as a lion."[28]

Edith and the children finally arrived at Southampton on February 2nd. After three frantic weeks in London, everything at last was ready. Edith and Robert and the children left for India, accompanied by Mutiny veteran Lieutenant-Colonel Owen Burne as Private Secretary, his wife, the Hon. Evelyn, sister of Lord Kilmaine, Colonel George Colley as Military Secretary and Fred Liddell, one of Edith's many first cousins, as ADC. Also in the party were an English governess, a Swiss governess, Edith's personal maid, Robert's valet, a nanny, a nursery-maid, a groom, a footman and a French chef.

They stopped off for a week in Paris so that Edith could order enough clothes from Worth, Paris's top couturier, to keep her elegantly turned out for the length of her Indian stay. After Paris, the Viceregal party stayed in Rome's British Embassy with Sir Augustus and Walburga Paget, who then accompanied them to Naples. Edith was feeling unwell; Robert and the Pagets dined without her at Lady Holland's Naples villa. Before leaving, Robert "fell on his knees for Lady Holland to bless him," a theatrical gesture which the Pagets found "intensely comical."[29] The Lyttons and their entourage sailed on a troopship from Naples to Alexandria,

arriving March 21st. Edith had been seasick the whole way, sur-
viving on brandy and mineral water. Mrs Burne was proving to
be a disappointment, being cold and reserved; this was unfortunate
for the two women would be together for the length of their Indian
stay and Edith needed close emotional bonds with all those in her
immediate vicinity. Even after many months Mrs Burne didn't
encourage intimacy.

"The 7th of April was a piping hot day for our arrival at
Bombay," Edith recorded. "It quite upset me seeing the land where
we should have to go through so much in our new life.... Betty
and Con exclaimed to each other 'We are in Asia.' " From the
moment she landed on Indian soil, Edith felt overwhelmed with
new emotions. Emily Eden and Charlotte Canning had felt distanced, displaced, able to see but not to feel. Edith, like Fanny
Eden, had more feeling than she could comfortably handle. She felt
shocked by the bombardment of colour and noise and naked, sweat-
ing bodies, yet fascinated by the blatant sensuality of everything
around her; she was confused by the foreignness of everything, yet
intensely curious; girlishly shy of her new prominence and – strange
new paradoxical emotion – proud of it as well. She felt fearful and
apprehensive and fatalistic, yet full of anticipation.

The road to Parell, where the Lyttons were to stay two nights
with Bombay's Governor, Sir Philip Wodehouse, was lined with
cheering natives "which made one feel very grand. One native,"
Edith noted with pleasure, "cried out 'God save Lord Lytton' and
I loved him for it." On April 9th, the Lyttons boarded a special
train for Allahabad; on the first day the temperature rose to 104°,
and Edith learned that the train most conveniently carried coffins
to accommodate those who died of heat prostration. "Everything
we touched was baking hot, and the bread at luncheon quite hard,
and the napkins stiff," Edith noted. At Allahabad, the Lyttons stayed
with Sir John Strachey, Lieutenant-Governor of the North-Western
Provinces; Robert charmed and cajoled him into demoting himself
to the less prestigious post of Finance Minister in the Viceroy's
Council. Robert's charm always secured him what he wanted, and

he knew that he would have great need in Calcutta of someone with a clear head for money matters. Edith and Robert were to part at Allahabad, she and the children to head straight for Simla's cool breezes while Robert went on briefly to Calcutta. "I woke at five," Edith confided to her diary on April 11th, "feeling so wretched at the thought of leaving R. He has been so dear all the journey, and is really sorry to separate from me also." As her train left the station she was "bitterly regretting my decision not to have gone to Calcutta which has haunted me ever since and will I fear all my life, but no one would allow it." Her train could only go as far as Ambala, where the railway ended. On April 14th, Good Friday, Edith and her party went by carriage to Kalka, where she was joined by Dr Oliver Barnett, the Viceregal physician who would escort her to Simla and stay on.

From Kalka, Edith was bounced forward in a tonga, a small two-wheeled covered cart drawn by ponies. Easter Sunday found her at Dhurmpore. "It does not seem like this great festival in the little white-washed bungalow," she sighed, "and the native people not keeping the day makes one realize so much that one is not in a Christian land." Edith was a devout believer and church-goer; it pained her that Robert was not. Like his father, he was an agnostic who comforted himself with a strange grab-bag of pagan super-stitions. Edith reached Simla, as the Eden sisters had, just in time to see the scarlet rhododendrons in bloom. She loved their flame-and-flash; they looked "like rosettes on quite high trees." She and the children settled into Peterhof, a five-bedroom country house rented from the Maharajah of Simur. Auckland House, where the Edens had stayed so happily, had been turned into a boarding-house and then into a fashionable girls' school.[30] Edith liked Peterhof and thought it resembled an old English rectory. "The varieties of effects of light and shade – morning, noon and night – ," she noted in her diary, "never ceased to give me intense pleasure."

Meanwhile, Robert reached Calcutta and was sworn in on April 12th. His first flouting of convention came at once, for he made a speech following his swearing-in, something no previous Governor-General had ever done. He reported in his first letter to Edith that his Members of Council looked "as if they would have eaten me without salt" and all the rest of his audience "appallingly frigid."[31] All the British tongues began at once to wag, and continued till Lord Lytton left India, for there had never been, and would never be again, a Viceroy quite like this one. "I am treading on eggs at every step," Robert told Edith, and in those first days, he broke quite a few. "I am told that I have already shocked all the social proprieties of Calcutta," he blithely told Lord Salisbury, Secretary of State for India, "by writing private notes to members of Council, calling on their wives, holding levées by night instead of by day, and other similar heresies."[32] "I am feeling very low and depressed," he sighed to his wife, "and words cannot say what a joy it will be to me to be once more with my dear comforter." When Robert wrote with his usual hyperbole that Government House was "full of cockroaches and rats as big as young elephants,"[33] Edith shivered – bugs were her *bêtes noires*. He was so nervous and insecure without Edith to bolster him that he suffered constant headaches and nausea and felt as if he were living "under the weight of an increasing nightmare."[34]

At Simla, Edith awaited Robert's arrival with impatience and in the meantime surveyed the town. Simla had grown to four hundred houses, with excellent shops selling English goods along the Mall where Christchurch Cathedral towered at one end. There were also several hotels, a library, town hall, assembly rooms for concerts, a theatre for amateur theatricals and a hall for Simla's latest craze, "rinking" (roller-skating). These fine new buildings, in Victorian Gothic style, looked strangely out of place in their Himalayan setting. "If one was told the monkeys had built all," the renowned English architect Edwin Lutyens would quip when he first saw Simla in 1912, "one could only say 'What wonderful monkeys – they must be shot in case they do it again.' "[35] In this strange, theatrical setting, Simla society was bent only on amusing itself; it

33 View of Simla from Mount Jakko

was, as another visitor noted, "like an English watering-place gone mad,"[36] a carnival scene far removed from the realities of dust and duty down below. "You will think us very larky when you hear about rinking, dancing and all our amusements," Edith told her mother.

Simla society exemplified, if in a rather pronounced form, the general change in British India's moral tone since Charlotte Canning's time; "even flirting is rare," she had written. British India still paid lip-service to those same ideals of Sacred Trust and Moral Purity which had inspired them in Middle Raj years, but the British were more hypocritical now, with a wider gap between ideals and actual conduct. Underneath the surface cant was a new note of frivolity and moral laxity. Edith heard enough of the Simla gossip and saw enough of the Simla goings-on to realize that adultery flourished there as prodigally as rhododendrons and began to fear Simla's effect on Robert.

Edith's unease in the face of British India's immorality was shared by many of India's *memsahibs*. "India's a complicated country for the man and woman relation," says a character in Maud Diver's *Ships of Youth,* which she subtitles "A Study of Marriage in Modern India."[37] "So serious are the charges made against India's morals – and the morals of her wives in particular – that it is impossible to present any adequate picture of Anglo-Indian married life without touching upon this difficult question," Maud Diver writes elsewhere.[38] "A few nice old-fashioned prejudices as to the correct line of demarcation between friendliness and flirtation are perhaps ignored," admits Mary Frances Billington in *Woman in India.*[39] The female flirt soon became a stereotype in novels of Indian life. There is, for example, the Simla siren Mrs Vereker in Cunningham's *Chronicles of Dustypore* (1875) and Mrs Muriel Smith in Steel's *Hosts of the Lord* (1900). Adultery seems to have been a fever which attacked in High Raj days and stayed around until the end of the century. In the Early Raj period, British men had attached themselves both physically and emotionally to Indian women. Since the arrival of their *memsahibs* in force, this had not been possible. So British India closed the circle, surveyed the material available within it, and cav~rted in and out of bed among themselves. Adultery offered at le₁.t a temporary antidote to official papers, if one were male, or to idle hours on a sofa if one were female. And the British were, after all, living in a hot climate where all around them were giant stone *lingams* (phalluses).

Edith turned her back on Simla's steamy atmosphere and counted off on her calendar the days till Robert's arrival on April 26th. They had a joyous reunion, but Robert was appalled by Peterhof, describing it to Lord Salisbury as "a hideous little bungalow, horribly out of repair and wretchedly uncomfortable."[40] Salisbury quickly authorized him to spend one hundred thousand pounds on improvements.

Their life at Peterhof was like the Lyttons themselves: warm and informal and impulsive. Robert treated his staff as family and invited them to Peterhof for all meals. After dinner, they would all play "Consequences" with the children, laughing uproariously, or the adults would play relaxed rounds of whist. Robert, as Edith noted approvingly, "treated it as a game to cheer him, and not too seriously, and he would tell anecdotes and amuse us between the deals."

One of the ADC's, Captain Harcourt Rose, son of Sir Philip, was a particularly good whist player. He wasn't in India long, however, before he met with a most unfortunate accident and had to be invalided, temporarily, home to England. Edith was warmly sympathetic and missed him in the evening circle. He had been bitten by a donkey – in a most sensitive area – and had been, to speak plainly, castrated. The Lyttons' best-loved ADC was Lord William Beresford, a rollicking, madcap Captain in the 9th Lancers. He was a nephew of Lord Waterford, Charlotte Canning's brother-in-law, and was quite as mad about horses as his uncle. With "Lord Bill" to smooth her path, Edith enjoyed her social duties. "At Simla I received every day for an hour," she reminisced, "which enabled me to get personally known to all the people, and sympathize in their joys and sorrows, and to appreciate all their kindness to each other under difficulties.... I got to know from the sadness in their faces those ladies whose children were parted from them, and far away in Europe."

This was Edith's first close-up view of the sacrifice the *memsahib* made for Empire. At a time when British social mores stressed the importance of the family and the joys of maternity, the poor *mem-sahibs* of India found themselves bereft not only of domestic duties but of maternal ones as well. Flora Annie Steel, whose daughter, like most British children in India, went home to England for her schooling, speaks feelingly of the "wound of having to leave a child to the care of others" – a wound which "never heals at all."[41] In her short story, "A Mother in India," in the collection entitled *The Pool in the Desert* (1903), Sara Jeannette Duncan demonstrates the unbridgeable gap which exists forever after between a mother and child separated for the latter's formative years. "So many mothers have bewailed the fact to me," writes Flora Annie Steel, "that, though their children have been good, considerate, friendly, it seemed as though something were lacking."[42] Edith was luckier than her countrywomen in India; she had her children with her. More than ever before, she appreciated the rare privileges of motherhood and suffered many a pang for the sad-eyed Simla ladies.

Simla society as a whole, Edith decided, was rather insipid and parochial. "What a contrast to the foreign societies we have been in," she complained after the first Peterhof ball, everyone "so cold, so flat, and dancing so badly, it made me feel so low after as it will be *so difficult* to congregate them often." She would do it, as she would do anything, for Robert – and with such smiles and charm and sympathy that Simla would be utterly captivated. Edith began at once to enjoy the challenge of her public role.

As for Robert, who once described the government of India as "a despotism of office-boxes tempered by the occasional loss of keys,"[43] he was relieved to find he still had plenty of leisure. "I have certainly not as yet found my daily work at all overwhelming," he noted on May 29th.[44] During his Viceroyalty, Lytton, like Lord Auckland, would often be exceedingly bored. Since the hard-working Lord Canning's time, some of the Viceroy's administrative tasks had been taken out of his hands and transferred to the government in England, facilitated by the opening of the electric telegraph between England and India in 1865, at first overland, via Teheran, then after 1870, by cable to Bombay via the Suez Canal. Now the heavy decision-making was done in Whitehall, not in Simla or Calcutta. A Viceroy, noted a contemporary satirist, "who is the axis of India, the centre round which the Empire rotates, is necessarily screened from all knowledge of India."[45] The despatches and minutes and recommendations Lord Lytton *did* write were, as one would expect, most felicitously phrased, and finely embroidered with metaphor and simile. Family legend claims that he once wrote an official despatch in verse. One official letter to Alfred

34 *Lord Lytton in Viceregal robes*

Lyall, who would later become Lytton's Foreign Secretary sand-wiched a two-page quotation from Dante's "Purgatorio" between thoughts on the latest Afghanistan crisis.[46] Queen Victoria so relished Lord Lytton's amusing and unconventional letters that she quite forgave him for writing in the first person, rather than the custom-ary third.

So the first stage of Lytton's Viceroyalty proceeded, with plenty of games and romps at Peterhof, far from the tight protocol of Calcutta's Government House. Edith's emotions, at this early stage, were lush and burgeoning; she was able, in that relaxed atmosphere, to be her warm, extroverted self. She responded to Simla's green jungle growth by putting out binding creepers of her own, giving sympathy to Simla's British residents, affection to children and staff, and erotic passion and ego-bolstering to Robert. "Dear R. was so cheered by my praise after we came to bed; he is so curiously susceptible to being appreciated even by me who always admires him so," Edith wrote in her diary, after one of Robert's banquet speeches. This relaxed Simla idyll was a good time for Edith, an easy time; the next stage of her Indian stay would be more chal-lenging, and the last one very different in tone, but that was still some years away.

There was one thorn in that broad-leaved idyll, however. Rob-ert was "flirting" far too openly in public, perhaps to compensate for the fact that private "flirting" was not possible. Viceregal se-curity and surveillance had tightened since Lord Mayo's assassi-nation; Robert complained of it bitterly in a letter to a friend:

> I cannot be for a second alone. I sit in the privatest corner of my private room and if I look through a window, there are two sentinels standing guard over me. If I go up and down stairs, an ADC and three unpronounceable beings in white and red night-gowns with dark faces run after me. If I steal out of the house by a back door, I look round and find myself steal-thily followed by a tail of fifteen persons.[47]

Philandering was definitely out of the question. It was a hard sentence on a man who'd written to his friend Wilfrid Blunt in 1869: "I think you are very wise to give yourself occasional relaxations of the nuptial knot. Variety of sensation is the sole refuge from permanent insensibility."[48] In India, Robert had to make do with innocent flirting, and no more. "I do miss the pleasant scamps and scampesses of pleasant France," he confessed to Lady Salisbury, "being of the earth, earthy, I envy you the pleasure of living amongst so many naughty people."[49] If flirting was all he was going to get, then he would perfect it to a high art. When young Mrs Birch, on being presented to him, told him that her father had been his Lordship's tutor at school, his Lordship replied: "Yes, but I never before felt inclined to kiss the rod."[50] One evening after dinner Lord Lytton made a long, flowery speech to Mrs Hatch, wife of a Calcutta lawyer, "about kissing her,"[51] while Edith talked to the nearest *memsahib* and tried not to hear. Robert singled out Simla's two prettiest women, Mrs Batten and Mrs Plowden, for prolonged attentions. Once, just as a garden party was breaking up, he waltzed Mrs Plowden around the lawn in a particularly close embrace. At a Peterhof ball on July 27th Edith reported caustically that

> Mrs Plowden's dress was very *outré* with a lovely water lily stuck just where she ought to sit ... she had great difficulty curtseying in the Lancers, and I can understand the story from England of the dress splitting and nothing being found underneath but a pair of tights.[52]

If Edith was jealous, she tried never to show it. Robert himself in his poem "The Modern Wooer" had clearly set forth the perfect wife's behaviour on that score:

> She must never coquet
> With young frivolous fellows.
> If I flirt, she may fret,
> But must never be jealous.[53]

In India, Edith did in fact have her reward for all her years of wifely tolerance. If Robert couldn't freely indulge his sensuality with other women, he still could, most freely, with her. Edith told her mother that the only times in India when she saw her husband alone were in bed, but they were memorable times.

During their stay at Simla, the Lyttons took a cottage called "The Gables" at Mashobra, five miles from Simla's eastern ridge, and went there, feeling like children out of school, for intimate weekends. In July, they were laughing together over Emily Eden's *Letters from India,* but conscious, too, of how much in India had changed. Edith was very large now with the baby due in August. Mrs Burne was expecting at the same time. "It is absurd both of us being such a size," Edith wrote, "and I'm afraid the gents among themselves must joke a great deal."[54]

On August 2nd, Robert went without Edith to Narkanda, seventy-five miles away, for a little jaunt in the hills. On August 6th, Edith received a telegram from her twin Lizey announcing she'd just given birth to a girl; the empathetic Edith went into labour herself on the 8th, and next day, at 3:15 P.M., "Victor made his appearance with a lusty shout to announce his sex," Edith wrote, worn out but jubilant. "The much-wanted son was a great joy," even if he did look "rather like an owl and a monkey, with long skinny arms." He did, however, have dark-blue eyes like Robert's "that redeem all the other features." Edith stayed in bed for the customary month after Victor's birth. The Peterhof roof leaked, and great chunks of plaster fell off the bedroom ceiling, but Edith lay there content, cuddling her new child. When typhoid fever struck nursery-maid, nanny and valet, the little girls and Robert moved into Inverarm, Colonel Colley's house, to get them away from infection. Edith only saw Robert half an hour each day; when he did come to her room he was more distracted than usual, obsessed with planning his great Imperial Assemblage to be held at Delhi at the end of December.

By October, Edith was slim and strong again, but it bothered her that, because of her busy schedule, the baby had to be breast-fed by a native wet-nurse. Edith left the children at Simla to accompany Robert on a tour round the frontier which would end at Delhi, in time for the great Assemblage. "The enjoyment," wrote Edith in her diary, of this new vagabond life, "surpassed all that I had heard of it, and riding and walking 5 or 6 miles daily with R., after all his hard work, was such a release." Robert was "like a boy let out of school," and Edith loved the spontaneity and freedom of a gypsy existence, with tents for sleeping and a constantly changing panorama. "I don't think we shall ever see anything more grand and beautiful than the scenery of these mountains," Edith noted in her diary. She craved mountainous heights and depths – they matched her temperament – just as Charlotte Canning wanted only level ground. Edith and Robert celebrated his forty-fifth birthday at Palanpur on November 8th, sleeping "in a comfortable bungalow decorated with flags, in a red-carpeted room with a double bed." At Sharpur they were entertained by the Commissioner of the District. Robert, "in good spirits would play his game, naughty boy," wrote Edith indulgently, watching his flirting with the Commissioner's wife, who was, to be sure, reassuringly plain. "I made him laugh as we said good night by telling him it was so nice his only getting ladies like 'prunes and prisms' to *look* at. He will be a worse flirt than ever when he gets home after these ladies," she decided.[55] At Jacobabad, the chief military station in Sind, Robert signed a treaty with the Khan of Khelat, a small man with "such a savage rolling eye," who sneezed into a series of yellow-green handkerchiefs handed to him in succession as he inhaled snuff, while Robert charmed him with his "graceful easy manner" and Edith watched the Khan break "into a fiendish grin now and then."[56]

At Bombay, Edith and Robert went, as the Cannings had, to see the Elephanta caves. Charlotte Canning had been shocked by the sculptured reliefs but approved of British arrogance in turning the caves into a dining-room. Edith's reaction was just the reverse. Her own sensual nature responded to the "splendid images of gods and godesses" but, since the cave had once been "a most sacred Buddhist Temple," she "was rather shocked by the festival given of a dinner, with a military band playing dance tunes."

Edith's Worth dresses had arrived in Bombay from Paris just in time for the Imperial Assemblage. Robert talked of nothing else now; he had been Viceroy for less than a month when he first conceived the fanciful idea of this pageant and wrote to Disraeli about it. The Imperial Assemblage would be, in India, rather than Robert Lytton's poetry, his supreme imaginative creation.

The purpose of the Imperial Assemblage (apart from giving Robert a greater challenge than flirting) was to declare Queen Victoria Empress of India, and to secure the continuing loyalty of the princes in the native states outside British India proper. The Mutiny had shaken the self-confidence of the British, shown them how much Indians hated them. The princes all had private armies, and if their loyalty could be counted on, the British Raj would be more secure. "Here is a great feudal aristocracy," Lytton enthused to Disraeli, "which we are avowedly anxious to conciliate, but which we have as yet done nothing to rally round the British crown as its feudal head."[57] Like Canning, Lytton felt that Britain could best maintain her position in India by conciliating and using the Indian Chiefs and nobles. Even in Canning's day, this attitude was a little out of date; now, twenty years later, the educated middle classes were fast becoming the most important element in Indian society. But Lord Lytton had only contempt for the new Indian middle-class, whom he called "baboos whom we have educated to write semi-seditious articles in the native Press and who really represent nothing but the social anomaly of their own position."[58] Lytton ignored the new middle-class as he ignored ugly women at his parties; the new middle-class couldn't spark his imagination the way the Arabian Nights princes could. "I have personally called it an 'Imperial Assemblage' instead of a Durbar," Lytton told the Prince of Wales, "because it will materially and essentially differ from all previous Durbars, besides being on a much vaster scale."[59]

And differ it did. "Lytton's proclamation schemes," Disraeli told Lord Salisbury, "read like the Thousand and One Nights."[60] Disraeli accordingly vetoed the wildest flights of fancy, such as Lytton's idea of forming an Indian Heralds' College, and of allotting to each of the great Ruling Chiefs a specific duty redolent of England's Age of Chivalry – the Maharaja of Kashmir, for instance, would be made Warden of the Marches.[61]

All during that summer and fall of 1876, Edith had listened indulgently as Robert had unrolled the colourful scrolls of his Imperial Assemblage schemes for her approval. In early December, sixty-three Ruling Chiefs (only half of those invited came) and eight hundred princes and nobles began arriving in Delhi for the fun. In addition to Chiefs and nobles, there were foreign envoys and ambassadors, English and native officials, masses of troops, European and native press correspondents, hordes of plainer folk – 100,000 when they all arrived, 68,000 of them to be entertained at government expense in the sprawling canvas cities sprouting daily in Delhi's outskirts.

Official festivities, which would last for two weeks, began on December 23rd with the Viceroy and Vicereine's arrival in Delhi. An impressive parade through city streets thronged with natives and troops would begin at the train station and end at the Viceroy's campsite. The Viceregal train stopped first at nearby Gazeeabad where Edith was re-united, after a nine-week separation, with Betty and Con. She donned a Worth dress of grey and brown silk, and the train pulled into Delhi at exactly two P.M. as planned. The procession took almost three hours to cover the six miles through Delhi to the Viceroy's camp. Edith and Robert moved slowly forward on their elephant, sitting in a magnificent *howdah* with silvergilt reliefs of Ceres and Minerva on a silver background. "R. kept in very good spirits, and we had great fun talking about all the different things we saw," Edith wrote. The native Chiefs and their troops looked splendid, their elephants gorgeously caparisoned, their gold or silver *howdahs* emblazoned with tigers or dragons. Conspicuous in the parade was the Duke of Buckingham, Governor of

Madras, in whose Presidency a terrible famine was spreading. His
two state *howdahs,* specially built for the occasion, were the most
ornate of all.

In the procession was the Khan of Khelat, he of the snuff and
yellow-green hankies. The Khan and his followers had become
much alarmed when they'd been herded into a railway train, the
first they'd ever seen. "They held on to their seats like grim death,
expecting every moment would be their end." Once lodged in their
camp, they ate up all the Pears soap which their British hosts had
supplied for their "long-neglected ablutions" and used the washing
jugs and basins for purposes of eating and drinking."[62] Since the
Mutiny, the native princes had lost power and prestige; the British
Resident in each native state kept a close eye on their activities, and
did what he could, with the help of Raj higher authority, to curtail
their privileges. The princes were conscious of their clipped wings,
of living out their days in an India no longer really Indian, and no
longer really theirs. The Rajah of Jheend, typically trying to march
to a new drummer, had a bagpipe band with "pipers as black as
soot" playing "God Bless the Prince of Wales."[63] All this was a far
cry from the proud rajahs whom Emily and Fanny Eden had seen,
still rooted in their own customs and strengths.

As the sun beat down, and Edith felt her crisp brown silk
wilting damply, the long procession wound its way along the Ridge
where the British troops had spilled their blood during the Mutiny,
passed the monument erected to those who fell, and finally, at five
o'clock, reached the Viceregal camp. It is "certainly quite perfect,
not only in size but from its excessive neatness and order," observed
Edith, "there is grass on each side of the road and then twenty-five
tents each side." She was getting her first real glimpse of impressive
Raj panoply. The camp was lit with gas manufactured by the en-
terprising Maharaja of Jaipur and the lamp standards had been designed by Rudyard Kipling's father. The Viceroy's tent was very
grand indeed, with a broad *shamiana* (canopy) in front. In the next
few days, Edith also noted the red dust which soon covered everything, and the wretched lean-tos where *mahouts* (elephant-drivers)

and servants slept, shaking and coughing all night from cold, for there was frost on the ground in the mornings.

When Emily Eden had gone up-country, she had gradually perceived India's hard truths. What Edith Lytton, sensitive and sympathetic, was seeing forty years later was not so much the real India – since the Mutiny the British had locked themselves inside their fence of protocol and rules, so that India was now very far away – but rather the real Raj: an impersonal and inflexible bureaucracy which demanded from its native and British servants an exacting toll of human suffering: painful family separations, illness and even death.

When Edith learned that a Captain Clayton had been killed by a fall from his horse during an Assemblage polo game, she lost a night's sleep, "woke with a dreadful headache," according to her diary, and cried all day in her tent. The irony was that neither the Viceregal cavalcade then passing the polo grounds nor the assembled crowd had even seen Captain Clayton fall. British officialdom was instead totally focused on the Raj's passing show and the ritual importance of it all.

On December 26th and 27th, there were state dinners with huge platters heaped high with delicious food, in honour of the Governors of Bombay and Madras. On December 30th, Robert conferred with them about the terrible famine then taking such a toll of native lives in their two Presidencies. He was especially concerned to correct the ineffectual measures being taken by the Duke of Buckingham, Governor of Madras, he of the splendid *howdahs*. Lord Lytton decided to send Sir Richard Temple off to the Madras area to see how bad things were – dispatched Sir Richard like a knight to the rescue and commemorated the occasion in verse, later to be published in *Vanity Fair:* "Wave me now thy magic wand/ Burst me now grim famine's bond,"[64] India's Viceroy ordered.

On the last day of December, Edith watched intrepid natives diving off the Delhi ramparts into a deep well, but she was not thrilled, noting only "the horror of seeing them jump down," and fearful for their lives. That night, New Year's Eve, Edith sat up in her tent hoping Robert would come to kiss her good-night and wish her a Happy New Year, but he was deep in conversation with Sir John Strachey and didn't come. In the far distance she could hear the band playing "Auld Lang Syne" and suddenly felt very low and very lonesome. She went to kiss "the dear girls in their sleep." "Thus ends the most eventful year of my life," Edith scrawled on the last page of her 1876 diary, and blew out the light.

January 1, 1877 was the Great Day upon which Robert would declare Queen Victoria Empress of India. The site for the Great Assemblage was a grassy plain about two miles north of the Viceroy's camp where two thousand coolies had been employed for weeks levelling the ground. Three structures of painted iron had been erected: a hexagonal pavilion in red and white with plenty of gold for the Viceroy, a semi-circular pavilion in blue and white with less gold for the native princes and high British officials, and a large stand with hardly any gold at all for lesser mortals. "Oh, horror! What have I to paint? A kind of thing that outdoes the Crystal Palace in hideosity," declared poor Val Prinsep when he first saw it.[65] Robert had commissioned the English artist, fat, red-haired and bearded, and who himself resembled a portrait of Henry VIII, to paint a huge picture of the Assemblage; it would be paid for by the native princes and presented to Her Majesty the Queen. All the princes who contributed would be recognizably depicted in the foreground, and would receive a lithographic copy of the painting as well. "They have been heaping ornament on ornament," wrote Prinsep, "colour on colour, on the central Viceregal dais, till the whole is like the top of a Twelfth cake. They have stuck pieces of needlework into stone panels, and tin shields and battleaxes all over the place."[66] All together, it looked, he decided, exactly like "a gigantic circus."

When Val Prinsep's controversial and candid description of the Assemblage appeared in his book *Imperial India,* Robert – and Edith, who always deferred to her husband in literary matters – refused to read it. Instead the Lyttons whole-heartedly approved of the fulsome descriptions supplied by James Talboys Wheeler whom

Robert had commissioned to write the official book on the Assemblage. The details of Wheeler's description of the viceregal pavilion are remarkable:

> The upper part was a canopy raised over the structure, supported on twelve slender clustered shafts. The Imperial Crown at the top rested upon a cushion. Beneath it depended a graceful drapery of red cloth embroidered with gold. On the upper cornice was worked a pattern of festooned laurel wreaths and Imperial Crowns. At each angle was a trophy of three satin bannerets, festooned upwards, displaying the Cross of St. George and the Union Jack. Below the cornice the canopy was continued in alternate stripes of red and white satin embroidered with golden *fleurs de lis*. There was a lower frieze with an armorial vallance hanging from it. The frieze displayed the Rose, Shamrock and Thistle, embroidered with the Lotus of India in gold, silver and colours. It was adorned at each angle by a gilded crown and silken drapery. The vallance was composed of shield-shaped forms, on which were shown alternately the Irish Harp, the Lion Rampant of Scotland and the Three Lions of England. The shafts of the canopy were hung with silver shields ... bearing the imperial monogram in gold, surmounted by bannerets of various-coloured satins.[67]

"There was nothing oriental in these structures," concluded Wheeler. "They were not borrowed from any native design."[68] No indeed – they came straight from the fertile, fanciful brain of King Poppy's creator. Lions rampant ... and Lord Lytton rampant and re-energized, on a fitting background field. He had been very busy all those months in India, bent over his Viceregal desk, but one wonders if he shouldn't have stuck to his poetry, bad though most of it was; words are cheaper than large iron structures, if one is determined to indulge oneself.

At least part of the blame for the Imperial Assemblage's excesses, its bad taste and wanton extravagance, can be laid at Edith's feet. She had far more common sense and prudence than Robert and could have looked over his shoulder and injected a quiet word of caution here and there. But Edith had always indulged her husband, as a proper Victorian wife should. In Edith's case, not only convention but the fear forever lurking at the back of her mind that her conduct might precipitate one of Robert's deep depressions combined to keep her, always, uncritically supportive.

When January 1st dawned bright and clear Edith had to keep assuring Robert that it would all go without a hitch. At exactly twelve noon, with the whole plain filled with troops and elephants and minions, and all three hideous stands filled with handsome guests, Viceroy and Vicereine drew up slowly in their carriage. Regally, solemnly, preceded by staff and trumpeters, Edith and Robert made their way towards the cast-iron dais in the Throne pavilion. Robert looked absolutely splendid, Edith thought, in spite of his short stature, in Star of India robes, his blue-velvet cape bordered in ermine, embroidered in gold stars, gold-tasselled at either shoulder, and held up by two little page-boys. Edith walked slightly behind him in her gown of purple-blue brocaded velvet and silk with purple-blue bonnet in Mary Stuart shape trimmed with pearls and soft blue feathers. Betty and Conny in blue-green velvet and "becoming hats" tripped along on either side of their mother. It was very silent as the Lyttons proceeded towards the dais, the only sounds being the rustle of silk and the clank of aide-de-camp spurs. "Having never walked except in a funeral procession and being rather shy I am afraid I felt very serious," admitted Edith, "and the whole thing was most properly solemn." When the four Lyttons and their attendants reached the dais, trumpets sounded, and massed military bands played "God Save the Queen." Then arms were presented, and all the native Chiefs and princes arose and salaamed. Lord Lytton salaamed in return, which pleased them mightily, and then everyone sat down. The Chief Herald read in English the proclamation declaring Her Majesty Empress of India. The Foreign Secretary then repeated it in Urdu, during which reading the rustling and neck-craning and whispering among the British guests increased. After that came the Royal Salute of 101 salvos from the artillery. The terrific noise of the firing caused a stampede among the elephants, who bolted in all directions, trampling and killing some of the native crowd. Edith blanched, and tried to distract the attention of Betty and Conny, while the British *mem-sahibs* on their blue-silk chairs averted their eyes from the fallen and fanned themselves rather more vigorously.

Next came the treat of the Viceroy's speech. Edith thought it superb and wrote proudly in her diary that "everyone rose spontaneously and joined the troops in giving repeated cheers. Many of the chiefs present tried to offer their congratulations, but were unable to make themselves heard." According to Val Prinsep, the Viceroy's speech "was much too long, especially as not a word could be heard by the rajahs around. He was quite half an hour praising everybody." Prinsep was finding it harder and harder not to laugh. "It was what is called a splendid sight," he decided, but "so is Myers' circus; of the really splendid and impressive there was an utter want."[69]

Like the mediæval turrets and draperies at Knebworth, the Imperial Assemblage was all fake and fustian, all arbitrary symbol without substance, mere trappings without real truths, a silly entertainment and no more. When the Edens came to India, the strings of emeralds on Ranjit Singh's horses shone forth his real wealth and power as leader of the Sikhs, as Lion of the Punjab. Now only the British lion roared. The proud peacocks on Akbar's Peacock Throne glinted with no real jewels, only coloured glass. The rajahs were displaced and disconsolate, coping with Pears soap and bagpipes, trying pathetically and ineptly to drape themselves in Union-Jack patriotism and the British way of life. The splendour of India, once genuine, now spurious, had switched camps, from Indian rajahs to British Raj, but now it sprang from no indigenous tradition, no meaningful symbol; the peacock fans and the painted elephants were borrowed and bogus, all sham and show. For Emily Eden, India's most startling contrast had been between the splendour and squalor of the real India; Edith Lytton was so focused on the tinsel splendour and artificial lighting of the High Raj stage that India pulsed unseen and unheeded in the darkness beyond. As Edith and Robert sat centre stage on their gaily bedecked dais, they looked regal and solemn enough but secretly feared that the whole iron pavilion, so carefully planned, so carefully erected, piece by piece, day by day, might, as it almost had in the course of its construction, collapse into a mere heap of twisted metal.

That night there was a state banquet and evening party. Edith wore a white ball gown whose front was all embroidered with gold and pearls. She saw the natives looking at it, thinking "the front was all real jewels" but of course they were all imitation. The native Chiefs and "swellest Europeans" mixed so well, Edith decided. Nearly all the native Chiefs asked to be presented to her, for "I have been more brought forward than any lady yet in India."[70] She had a sympathetic word for each one of them. "And so ended the greatest day in our lives," wrote Edith in her diary, "and what a position for my dear husband!"

That same night, January 1st, at Windsor Castle, Disraeli and a select party dined with Queen Victoria. The Queen was bedecked with ropes of Indian jewels, huge uncut stones and pearls which India's reigning princes had given her in the year after the Mutiny. They looked out of place on her black-clad, stout little figure. On January 1, 1877, Britain's High Raj period began in earnest, in self-conscious solemnity, and in pious hopes of future greatness.

For the next three days, January 2nd to 4th, Lord Lytton lounged on the throne in his durbar tent, under the portrait of his Queen, from ten in the morning till seven at night, receiving visits from the native princes. To each Chief he presented a silken banner, each one embroidered by the Simla ladies with a different heraldic device designed by the ingenious Viceroy himself. "To secure completely, and efficiently utilise, the Indian aristocracy is, I am convinced, the most important problem now before us," he had written to Lord Salisbury with more conviction than truth, on May 11, 1876. "Fortunately for us," he continued, "they are easily affected by sentiment and susceptible to the influence of symbols to which

35 "The Imperial Durbar at Delhi: Proclamation of the Queen as

Empress of India'' (Illustrated London News, February 10, 1877)

facts very inadequately correspond."[71] Lord Lytton could well understand that much of the Indian mind. He had, that spring of 1876, sent a man who knew about heraldry up and down the country helping to research suitable escutcheons for each rajah. "The banners' only fault, which I had not anticipated," Lord Lytton later told his Queen rather sheepishly was that "the brass poles, which are elaborately worked, make them so heavy that it requires the united efforts of two stalwart Highlanders to carry one of them; and, consequently, the native chiefs who have received them will, in future processions, be obliged, I anticipate, to hoist them on the backs of elephants."[72] The native Chiefs did no such thing. As soon as they'd returned home, they stuck the banners in dusty corners, where a later Viceroy saw them, faded and torn. When Lytton presented one Chief with his banner, saying that "he hoped the banner would never be unfurled without reminding its possessor of its weight of responsibility," the Chief desperately replied in a loud voice, " Yes, yes, Lord Sahib, quite true. But the banner is so infernally heavy that I can never unfurl it."[73]

Lord Lytton had other brilliant ideas, apart from the banners. "I believe that at the present moment an Indian Maharaja would pay anything to obtain an additional gun to his salute," he told Disraeli, "and were we not such Puritans, we might 'ere this have made all our railways with the resources thus obtained."[74] The princes were indeed pleased, at the Imperial Assemblage, to have the number of guns in their salutes increased, particularly the four who had their salute raised to twenty-one guns, equal to the Viceregal one; pleased, that is, until they learned that the Viceroy's salute was increased to thirty-one salvos and the Queen Empress's to one hundred and one. There was thus a bigger gap than ever between British Raj and native Rajah.

While the native Chiefs received their banners and their salutes, and were properly grateful, Edith received the ladies each afternoon from three to five in *her* tent. If Robert saw the Imperial Assemblage in terms of material things, painted iron and embroidered silk and other stage props, Edith saw it in terms of people, and towards its

*36 "The Viceregal Howdah" (Illustrated London News,
February 10, 1877)*

human component, both Indian and British, she was her usual warm
and caring self. The Assemblage put the Vicereine more into the
spotlight than she was used to, and Edith responded superbly. Lady
Lytton is "very popular," wrote Val Prinsep. "Some are born with
this talent to please, like our Princess of Wales. Lady Lytton has
much of this charm of manner."[75] Sketches of Edith in her Assemblage finery had already appeared in such London magazines as the
Illustrated London News. "I am not in the least afraid of you, Queenly
as you look on the Elephant with the Gold Howdah," her friend
Mary Ann Evans (the novelist George Eliot) had written to her on
New Year's Day. "I feel sure that your face is as gentle as ever,
your voice as melodiously sincere." Edith treasured this note and
later copied it into her Indian journal. The Imperial Assemblage,
and indeed all of her Viceregal life thus far, strengthened Edith's

ego. She grew not only in self-confidence and justifiable pride in her performance but also in public esteem.

On January 5th, the final Assemblage event was a march-past of native and British troops. Robert had to sit for hours on an Arab horse in the broiling sun while Edith "dreaded his falling off from sunstroke." One body of native infantry marching past were dressed in bright yellow satin from head to foot and their band played "Home Sweet Home."[76]

And so the mighty circus came to an end. The native rulers went away dragging their heavy banners after them. British India went away grumbling about the fact that the "damn niggers" had been present at every single party, and calling Lytton's Viceroyalty "the Black Raj." Val Prinsep went away shocked at the behaviour of British subalterns at those same parties, who "made loud remarks about the rajahs there present, and expressed a wish to cut their ears off to get their jewels," not caring that many understood English.[77] The native and British reporters went away to write in their newspapers that it was no time for pomp and circumstance when Southern India was starving to death. The Governor of Bombay, Sir Philip Wodehouse, had been so taken up with famine relief that he'd tried to get out of coming to the Assemblage, but Lord Lytton had written to him on his thick, monogrammed paper that "the failure of the Assemblage would be more disastrous to the permanent interests of the Empire than twenty famines."[78] The few educated middle-class Indians who'd found themselves at the Assemblage went away with some fierce thoughts of sedition, and the *Calcutta Statesman,* to its credit, ran an outspoken editorial criticizing the "tinsel pageantry," all part of the "policy of pattings and praises" which treated the natives like children and ignored the fact that many now were getting University educations and wanted only to be treated as equals.[79] James Talboys Wheeler went back to London with a sheaf of notes to write up *The History of the Imperial Assemblage at Delhi.* Lord Lytton proudly forwarded a copy to the Queen as soon as it appeared, having noted approvingly that Wheeler had reported all the Viceregal speeches word for word with "(Cheers)" or "(Loud Cheers)" inserted here and there in the text like plums in a fruitcake.

On January 6th, the great tent cities around Delhi all disappeared, and, as if to erase every trace as quickly as possible, the rains began that very day; soon the vast plain where the Assemblage had taken place with all its trumpetings and trappings was one vast sea of red mud. Edith was relieved to be leaving. "We are alive, that is all I can say," she wrote, "but we are dead tired.... The continual banging of guns, the dust, and the duties made the time very trying, still it was splendid the way everything was done, and we are most thankful." She was proud of herself, prouder still of Robert who had thought it all up, and as yet unaware of the ground swell of criticism rising against him.

O N JANUARY 13TH, nine months after her arrival in India, Edith finally reached Calcutta's Government House, and the rigidity of the Raj closed around her. This was the second and most challenging stage of her Indian sojourn. Inside the "great prison" that was Government House, with Calcutta's teeming brown millions and parched brown plains beyond, Edith sorely missed the green light-and-shade of Simla and her spontaneous emotional flowering there. She found it tiring walking about the huge palace after Peterhof's cosy rooms, but she approved of the ballroom: "a charming room for singing in; it quite gives one a voice." Edith could relax at the piano and let her constrained feelings flow out through her fingertips. She was zealous about visiting native schools, but told her mother that "the progress of Christianity in India" was very unsatisfactory for "the missionaries make but little way." Shortly after arriving in Calcutta, Edith and Robert held their first Levee (formal reception for gentlemen) and first Drawing-Room (formal reception for ladies). Robert, very conscious, since the Assemblage, of the High Raj show, decreed that ladies were to wear trains to all state occasions, regardless of the expense of all those new gowns. At subsequent Drawing-Rooms, those who had the Private Entrée,

37 Private entrance, Government House, Calcutta

the highest-ranking officials' wives, formed up like so many birds of paradise in a swishing semi-circle on either side of the Viceregal throne, their tails becomingly draped, while lesser mortals, the Public Entrée crowd, were formally presented to the Lyttons, announced by an aide-de-camp. On January 25th, Edith and Robert gave their first big dinner party with Knebworth's gold plate arranged on the sideboard. Edith had introduced a new system of receiving – "such an improvement. I am so glad I have carried it. Colonel Colley vows I have such a will."[80] She and Robert bowed and went quickly into dinner; afterwards an ADC took them round the room, having memorized the names of guests from a printed list, and introduced them to each in turn. Edith chatted conscientiously for a moment to each guest while Robert looked restlessly around to see if there were any pretty ladies. It was all very formal and very correct, befitting the High Raj style, but Edith somehow, by drawing out each guest in turn, giving them her full attention and empathy, humanized it all. It was her own unique contribution to the Lytton Vice-Reign: to warm that cold-iron Raj regimentation with her caring and her charm.

For the first time in her life, the public and private Ediths, social and sensual, meshed in a fine unity of form and feeling. But she could only go so far and no further. Edith had exactly the right temperament to respond to a country whose secret heart could only be perceived through emotion and intuition, never through reason. Her tragedy was that she had come too late. In an earlier time, she could have forged emotional ties with the Indian India, particularly its people. But Mutiny swords had sliced through all emotional bonds between Indian and British except those of fear and distrust. Edith found herself inside the locked gates of the British compound, where her compatriots had backed away from feeling and were leaning far too heavily on the supporting crutch of form. "We have got a small dinner party tonight – a gloomy prospect," wrote one Raj official. "It is not that the people are stupid; I don't think they are – but that they have the art of becoming stupid the moment they appear in 'Society'. They have a fixed notion that good manners require a series of vapid formal remarks, and that nought beyond must be risked."[81]

Edith was the exception. She tried her best, in this, the second stage of her Indian stay, to animate the forms with genuine warmth and some degree of informality. "I visited the soldiers' wives at Calcutta and Barrackpore in their barracks," she wrote. "One loves to see all one's countrywomen so far away in India. I also visited the hospitals, where there were nice English nurses, so full of courage and cheerful patience. We had a grand feast at Government House," she continued, "for 70 soldiers' wives and 150 children. It was my idea, and a great success, tea in the marble hall, then games, presents and balloons sent up in the garden."

In addition to her Calcutta social engagements, Edith was supervising the changes which Robert had concocted for Government House, now that Assemblage plans were no longer there to satisfy

38 Marble Hall, Government House, Calcutta

his artistic whims. The walls of the Throne Room were hung with blue damask imported from Paris; eleven thousand rupees were spent making an ornamental waterway and rustic bridges in the southern garden; a double iron staircase outside the house was added at Barrackpore. The Viceroy also gave orders to close down Barrackpore's menagerie which had so amused the Edens, and its final inhabitants, as dispirited and displaced as the native rajahs, were dispatched to the Calcutta zoo, where the iron bars were thicker and stronger.

In January, a few weeks after returning from Delhi, Edith was distressed, but kept it to herself, to learn that Robert had ensured the continued presence of Mrs Plowden's pretty face and figure in his vicinity by promoting her husband from Inspector General of

39 Throne Room, Government House, Calcutta

Police at Assam to Under-Secretary of Calcutta's Foreign Department. Edith turned to her children: baby Victor was plump and rosy now, and Emily, who had turned two in December, was, according to her fond mother, "at an enchanting age," being "all bows and sash."

Then, in early March, came a new worry for Edith. Two scathing articles criticizing Lytton as Viceroy appeared in *Vanity Fair*, and Edith had to face the fact that the ground swell of disapproval of Robert, both in England and in India, was growing rather alarmingly. "We forbear to write what we are told," declared *Vanity Fair*, of Viceregal "vagaries": "his strange indolence, love of personal ease, and petty egotism, his fanciful eccentricities of dress and bizarre love of finery, though all these we regard as

beneath the dignity of one who fills so high a position."[82] Edith
would have been even more upset if she had heard in detail what
the Simla and Calcutta gossips were saying about her husband.
Occasionally one of the more sibilant hisses did reach her. Lord
Lytton, so the whispers went, wore scent and outrageous clothes;
he never, ever went to church; he bedecked his conversation with
French phrases and his fingers with rings. He kissed ladies' hands
when he was introduced. If those were his *public* kisses, what did
he do in *private*? He'd sit all evening, if he could find a pretty woman,
talking to her on a sofa, sitting *very* close, never saying a word to
any of the other guests, no matter how high their rank. Lord Lytton
never showed the smallest interest in sports or shooting as a gentleman should; he put his little dogs on the table at dinner; he smoked
between courses; he even smoked at Durbars and Levees. He turned
night into day, kept his staff on duty long past midnight, lay in
bed half the morning. Lord Northbrook had been such a model of
decorum, and Lord Mayo before him. And Lord Lawrence, "honest
John," now *there* was a proper Christian gentleman.

The trouble with Lytton, British India decided, was that he
had no proper Viceregal dignity. He didn't seem to realize what
the Viceroy stood for, Queen and Empire and all that. He called
his Council members "my dearest fellow"; he'd even been seen
walking up and down in conversation with one of them, with his
arm around the other man's neck. Here was Lord Lytton, with the
Sacred Trust of governing India's millions on his ermine shoulders,
and all he could do was *laugh*. (*No* Viceroy, British India now
decided, should be seen to laugh. Since the Mutiny, governing India
was *not* a laughing matter.) And when Lytton sat on the Viceregal
throne, in front of all those black princes, he *lolled* like a sultan on
his divan. (British India didn't know about the hæmorrhoids.)

Frivolous: that was the best word for Lytton. He paid more
attention to his dinners than he did to his dispatches. He'd brought
out a French chef with him, *and* an Italian confectioner. When the
Viceroy should have been paying attention to what was brewing
in Afghanistan, he was closeted with chef Bonsard, inventing a new

40 Lord Lytton on the Viceregal Throne, Calcutta, 1877

dish called "Quenelles à la Lytton," something with a very hot sauce.

The British in India felt so truly affronted by a frivolous, flirting Viceroy because of their own guilt. They knew, deep down, that while they still paid lip-service to the old Raj ideals of solemn and Christian duty which gave them a rationale for being in India, they had become far too silly and sinful themselves. As they felt their own ideals eroding, they looked towards the man who could best shore them up and set a fine example: the Viceroy. When he failed to do so, they became slightly hysterical. There was one further reason why Lord Lytton disturbed the British so much. Since the

Mutiny, they had all become strenuously rational in attitude and action. The mutinous sepoys had clearly shown where superstition and spontaneity could lead, if they weren't repressed and hedged round with rules. Now here was a new Viceroy who embodied all those qualities which British India feared most. "The Great Ornamental" was what they called Lytton. One English satirist summed it up neatly:

> It is certainly a little intoxicating to spend a day with the Great Ornamental. You do not see much of him perhaps, but he is a Presence to be felt, something floating loosely about in wide pantaloons and flying skirts, diffusing as he passes the fragrance of smile and pleasantry and cigarette. The air around him is laden with honeyed murmurs; gracious whispers play about the twitching, bewitching corners of his delicious mouth. He calls everything by "soft names in many a mused rhyme." Deficits, Public Works, and Cotton Duties are transmuted by the alchemy of his gaiety into sunshine and songs. An office-box on his writing-table an office-box is to him, and it is something more: it holds cigarettes.[83]

All this criticism, both verbal and printed, of her husband disturbed Edith greatly. She had long since realized that she couldn't change Robert; she could instead make amends. "It was only his wife's admirable talents as a hostess that saved the situation for him. He himself had no kind of dignity," a friend observed.[84] This was Edith Lytton's generous, loving gift to Robert, to British India, to Empire. From now on, she would counter every gaffe, but to do so, she would, of necessity, have to repress her own natural warmth and rely more on convention. At this point in her Indian stay, the balance of form and feeling which Edith had managed in Calcutta began to break down. Because of Robert's behaviour, Edith had voluntarily to place herself squarely inside the iron fence of Raj repression, inside the palings of protocol and rules where the rest of British India had, since the Mutiny, crouched, alarmed at every slightest aberration from the norm. It was not an easy move for Edith – "how much more intense one's feelings become as one grows older!" – she observed to her mother in August 1877. But the free expression of them, that self-indulgent plunge into their lush tangle, was for Robert only, not for her. In Edith Lytton's final Indian phase, decorum triumphed, and she fell into step with the other regimented marchers in the High Raj parade.

When Edith came to India, she'd already been married to Robert for twelve years and had plenty of flint in her soul. She became even stronger now: the power behind the Viceregal throne, propping up the Viceroy and the Empire. Together, the Lyttons made a satisfactory and sufficient whole.

Edith gave gossiping British India everything the Viceroy wasn't and they wanted. If Robert sat talking to the same pretty woman all evening at a party, Edith went about the room speaking to every person in turn, charming them all. If he dressed outrageously, she dressed always in outfits perfectly suitable to the occasion, properly buttoned and gloved. If he lounged on the Viceregal throne, she sat on one side rigidly erect, her head held high. If Lord Lytton was superstitious and sometimes downright silly, Lady Lytton was always eminently sane and serious. British India heaved a collective sigh of relief, stopped clucking and got back on their perches. They didn't know that Lady Lytton paid the price for their composure in frequent migraine headaches. They felt only gratitude and admiration. In his memoirs, Colonel Burne spoke warmly of "Lady Lytton whose grace and charm had won all hearts in India and who, year by year, increasingly gained the affection and esteem of all who knew her."[85] "A few more gracious queens in the world to smooth things down," Colonel Colley told Edith, "would make it a much nicer place to live in."[86]

Edith cleverly performed her miracles without ever stepping out of line. British India would never have approved of that. She was, after all, only the Vicereine, and in the Raj bureaucracy, the pecking order was firmly fixed: Queen, Viceroy, Vicereine, Governors of the three Presidencies, and so on down the line … everyone had a place. A new Warrant of Precedence appeared on every Indian Civil Service official's desk in 1877, ranking everyone from Viceroy down to Inspector of Smoke Nuisances. Every hostess consulted it for such important details as who should precede whom in to dinner. So Edith very properly deferred to Robert's judgement, but a quiet word here and there often showed him what line he should take. Men, Edith later told her youngest daughter, "hate a great, strong, chaffing woman," preferring "a quiet, gentle, sentimental woman who will make a submissive wife."[87] Edith herself became quite perfect in her role, appearing to be submissive, but guiding her husband firmly.

In April 1877, when the exhausting Calcutta season was finally over, Edith and Robert had a three-week holiday at the hill station of Naini Tal, where the Viceroy was able to "give himself up to naps and novels in a delightful way in the afternoon." Then they moved on to Simla's hothouse atmosphere for the summer. Below in the hot plains, a cholera epidemic was raging, so Robert gave the order that no Rajahs were to come that summer to Simla, in case they brought germs with them.[88] Not only was there cholera down below, but famine was still spreading. Val Prinsep arrived at Simla in August to paint Lord and Lady Lytton into his grand Assemblage picture; he was worried about doing justice to his diminutive Lordship who, enveloped in his Star of India robes, looked rather "like a bundle of clothes."[89] On September 15th, Edith celebrated her thirty-sixth birthday at Simla, and Colonel Colley gave her a "beautiful carriage rug of white fox fur, lined with rose silk." Neither the Colonel nor Robert was there; they had gone off to Madras to see about the famine, the former telling Edith in a letter that "His Excellency lay awake nearly all night reading a French novel, and consequently is not quite as fresh as he might be this morning."[90] "Lord Lytton is quite depressed," Alfred Lyall, Resident in Rajputana, told his sister Barbara, "with the weight of all these famines upon him…. I wish India had never been discovered by us."[91] It was during Lytton's Viceroyalty that the more sensitive of Raj officials began to feel the first pains of disillusionment, as the White Man's Burden, more and more, bowed them down.

Famine had now spread through the Bombay and Madras Presidencies into the native states of Hyderabad and Mysore. Thousands and thousands were dying; cannibalism was common, and there were reports of men killing their own children and drinking their blood. Emily and Fanny Eden had seen famine's gaunt skeleton close at hand; but for Edith Lytton, cosseted at Simla under her white fox rug lined with rose silk, India was moving farther and farther away. And what exactly was Robert *doing* in Madras? He wrote to tell her on September 11th that he had received two anonymous letters,

> each obviously written by a woman, the one expressing a lively interest in the state of my soul, the other a tender regard for my body. The first writer informs me that she could not sleep all night for thinking whether I am prepared to meet my Maker ... the other writer declares that she couldn't sleep all night for thinking of my eyes, that the least tone of my voice, the least touch of my hand lives in her memory, and thrills her yet.... It is really a mercy you did not come.[92]

By September 28th, Robert was back at Simla; he and Edith talked "without ceasing for five hours" while he told her everything, well, almost everything, that had happened while he'd been away. He had appointed a Famine Commission under the Chairmanship of Richard Strachey to look into setting up a permanent Famine Code. Richard was an able man and would see to it all.

Leaving the children at Simla, Robert and Edith set off with their staff for their annual autumn tour, this one to Mussoorie, Agra, Lucknow and Cawnpore. At Agra they stayed with Cora and Alfred Lyall, still Resident of Rajputana, but whom Robert would persuade to become his Foreign Secretary. At Lucknow, Robert and Edith stayed with Sir George and Lady Cowper, who had been in the Residency "all the time of the siege, so they can explain everything to us. Lady C. was confined of a child in a little tiny room," wrote Edith, "and just after the baby was born a mine was sprung very near, filling the room with smoke and dust. The baby died at a month old." Edith truly sympathized with Lady Cowper, but none of it seemed quite real. At Cawnpore, Edith and Robert drove through the Memorial Gardens which had been made on the site of the bloody massacre of British women. "Such a pretty, fresh, peaceful spot, one can hardly realize the agonies experienced there," Edith wrote in her diary. It was now, two decades after the horrors of the Mutiny, a "pretty, peaceful spot," but the fear and distrust engendered there twenty years before would never really go away. Until the advent of World War II, the British saw to it that no Indians were allowed inside the gates of Cawnpore's Memorial Gardens. Since the Mutiny, strict apartheid had been the order of the day, and the British *memsahibs* of India, even more than their menfolk, remembering the terrible acts of the Bibighar and others, conceived a hatred of all Indians which came from a deep unconscious fear of the Indian's power to murder and mutilate. Now Indians were kept on separate wards in hospitals, in separate hotels, in separate compartments of trains. No more easy mingling, as in the Edens' time. Nor were natives allowed into the Indian Civil Service. The East India Company Charter Act of 1833 had anticipated the day when Indians would share in the government of their country up to the highest level, and even the diehard Company Directors had expressed therein their aversion to anything resembling a "governing caste" in India. Yet in 1870 only four Indians stood among the 916 members of the ICS. (By 1915, there were still only 63 ICS Indians, five percent of the service.[93])

Since the Mutiny, the barriers, both psychological and practical, between Indian and Briton were formidable. The Mutiny was partly responsible, but so was the Suez Canal. Since its opening in 1869, England was much more accessible to the British in India. England was home, and India was an exile reluctantly endured till time for the next furlough, or retirement, to England. "I fear that each day we are becoming more English in India," wrote a visitor in 1877:

> Each year communication becomes more easy between England and her great empire in the East. Each year greater facility is offered to the English official to visit his native land, and so that official becomes more and more a camper and sojourner in India. With his eyes constantly fixed on England, he does not identify himself with the people and the country, with which he has little sympathy.[94]

Little sympathy, or none. "You can have little idea how much India is altered" wrote a former Governor of Bombay in 1868. "The sympathy which Englishmen felt for the natives has changed to a general feeling of repugnance."[95] Indians were useful – they did, after all, through taxes, pay for the proliferating Raj bureaucracy, but they were to stay in their places. The British had levied a salt tax which brought in considerable revenue. There were, however, in some of Rajputana's native states, great salt lakes where the Indians could get salt free. To prevent them from smuggling it into British India, the British had erected a customs barrier, a thick, high hedge of prickly pear, stretching for 1,500 miles, and manned by 12,000 inspectors and tax collectors. A prickly-pear hedge: an effective barrier that kept Indians poor, subservient, and above all, at a distance, fit symbol for the Post-Mutiny India which Edith Lytton saw.

By December 1st, the Lyttons had finished their tour of Mutiny terrain and were back at Calcutta's Government House. Edith was pleased to learn that she would be given the Order of the Crown of India, recently instituted by the Queen for deserving ladies. Privately, Edith felt that she had earned it. Robert, on the other hand, had made himself unpopular with the native press, those "seditious baboos," as he called them, by passing what he himself called "a very stringent gagging Bill" for keeping Indian-language newspapers from making wild attacks on the Government.[96] From then on, native journalists fell into step behind their British counterparts in India and toed the official line so that all Viceroys were "exemplary" and all Vicereines "supremely elegant."

The Lyttons left the "seditious baboos" grumbling down below and went up to Simla on March 18th. In May, part of the Peterhof verandah was enclosed for the girls to play in. "It is a huge doll's house," wrote Edith, "and very nice for them to revel and sit in." A huge doll's house: for Lady Lytton and all future Vicereines, India was in fact becoming just that.

In November Edith and Robert visited Lahore, returning to Calcutta on December 19th. Edith was now more than seven months pregnant, and feeling unwell from a nerve pressing on her spinal cord. She was carried about Government House's cavernous rooms in a chair. In January 1879, Edith engaged a gentleman from Calcutta's School of Art to come to Government House to teach the girls drawing. They didn't, however, as Charlotte Canning had, draw flowers and trees from nature but from "plaster casts of leaves." The new baby, Neville Stephen, arrived on February 5th, between the first and second suppers of a ball taking place down below as Edith went through her labour. "I was so proud," wrote Edith, "not having had two boys alive together before."

On May 16th, Robert's friend Wilfrid Blunt and his wife Anne, grand-daughter of Lord Byron the poet, arrived at Simla for an extended visit. Blunt was handsome and "vain as a peacock,"[97] a poet and womanizer who outshone Robert in both categories, having once handed the same felicitous verse to three married women on the same day.[98] Now, at Simla, he cast a speculative eye on Edith:

> Though always a pretty woman she had not, before she went to India, made her beauty fully felt. Now *elle se faisait valoir* and with admirable effect.... Lady Lytton was splendidly attired, and the fineness of her new feathers had made of her a truly lovable and glorious bird. Not that I ventured anything of love with her – her whole heart was devoted to Robert, but she was not displeased that I should find her beautiful.[99]

41 Lady Lytton with Betty and Conny, Calcutta, 1879

Years later, when he was fifty-two, Blunt would try to seduce Edith's daughter Emily, playing that summer of '79 on Peterhof's verandah in bows and sashes, but Emily, like her mother, would keep her distance.

Over late-night cigarettes and brandy, Robert confessed to Blunt that Mrs Plowden and Mrs Batten, whose husband he had recently taken on staff as Private Secretary, were tempting morsels beyond a Viceroy's reach, but not, apparently, beyond his aide-de-camps'.[100] Blunt consoled Robert by pointing out that Mrs Batten was "gay, fond of pleasure, quite depraved" and proved his point by seducing her himself.[101] The gossiping tongues and fluttering hearts of Simla's *memsahibs* began to decelerate when the Blunts left town on July 3rd. "They have really been so nice and agreeable ... and he said he made so many friends," wrote the innocent Edith in her diary.

Blunt hadn't, however, spent his whole time at Simla flirting and telling Robert not to. He had looked closely at the Raj and made some perceptive observations, to be published in 1885 in his book *Ideas About India*. "My first visit to India was in 1879, and it was then ... living in the daily society of the highest Anglo-Indian officials, the Stracheys, the Battens, and the Lyalls, that I first conceived the thought that India was selfishly and unwisely governed" he declared in the Preface.[102] "Once under the official roof," he continued, "a veil of suspicion seemed to divide me from the people; and it was strange to meet again, almost in the position of servants, honourable native gentlemen one had met some hours perhaps before as equals and friends."[103] Then Blunt warmed to his subject:

> The "natives", as they call them, are a race of slaves, frightened, unhappy, and terribly thin.... I have been studying the mysteries of Indian finance under the "best masters", Government Secretaries, Commissioners, and the rest, and have come to the conclusion that if we go on "developing" the country at its present rate, the inhabitants will have, sooner or later, to resort to cannibalism, for there will be nothing but each other

left them to eat. I do not clearly understand why we English take their money from these starving Hindus to make railroads for them, which they don't want, and turnpike roads, and jails, and lunatic asylums, and memorial buildings to Sir Bartle Frere; or why we insist upon their feeding out of their wretched handfuls of rice, immense armies of policemen and magistrates and engineers. They want none of these things, and they want their rice very badly, as anybody can see from looking at their ribs.... I never could see the moral obligation governments acknowledge of taxing people for debts they, and not the people, have incurred.[104]

Plain speaking indeed; he felt sure the natives could govern themselves better at "a tenth part of the expense" and goes on to note "the ridiculous overhousing of the officials, and the enormous number of public buildings – churches, barracks and government offices" – built by the British for their own use and paid for by Indians. He was astonished to "note the scale of living of every Englishman employed in India:

The enormous palaces of governors and lieutenant-governors, their country houses, their residences in the hills, their banquets and entertainments, their retinue of servants, their carriages and horses, their special trains on their journeyings ... their endless dinners of imported delicacies, with libations of imported wines.

Even those at the lower levels of government service, Blunt found, lived in luxury. "No collector's wife will wear an article of Indian manufacture to save her soul from perdition, and all her furniture, even to her carpets, must be of English make."[105] Having dealt several telling blows in the direction of male officials, Blunt drew breath and turned to their wives:

The Englishwoman in India during the last thirty years has

been the cause of half the bitter feelings there between race and race. It was her presence at Cawnpore and Lucknow that pointed the sword of revenge after the Mutiny, and it is her constantly increasing influence now that widens the gulf of ill-feeling and makes amalgamation daily more impossible. I have over and over noticed this. The English collector, or the English doctor, or the English judge may have the best will in the world to meet their Indian neighbours ... on equal terms. Their wives will hear of nothing of the sort, and the result is a meaningless interchange of cold civilities.[106]

Memsahibs like Fanny Parkes, self-sufficient women of adventurous spirit and originality who had at least tried to embrace the whole India, were now a disappearing breed, and Blunt rightly assesses the sorry lot who replaced them:

The Englishwomen in India look upon the land of their exile unaffectedly as a house of bondage, on its inhabitants as outside the pale of their humanity, and on the day of their departure as the only star of hope on their horizon.[107]

Later, having spewed out this long prose criticism of the British presence in India, all of it perfectly just and pertinent, Blunt immortalized the entire British Raj in one couplet:

Their poets who write big of the "White Burden" – Trash!
The White Man's Burden, Lord, is the burden of his cash.

Blunt was only in India for a few weeks in 1879, but he had somehow managed to see, as Edith and Robert Lytton could not, that larger India beyond the British Raj compound.

Edith gave plenty of children's parties that summer of '79 after the Blunts departed, and eagerly joined in the games. Whenever possible, she escaped to Peterhof's new nurseries; there she had "an excuse to romp again and be as jolly as a big girl. It is so solemn

when there is nothing but work and serious books and papers."
Her children were, more and more, Edith's necessary relief from
the steel corset of Viceregal formality. With them she could release
her pent-up feelings in romps and squeals and general silliness. "The
servants, the police, the guards, and all the visitors make Government House at Simla so trying," she sighed. In addition to Peterhof's nursery, Edith still loved escaping to Mashobra, or Naldera:
"The change is like leaving the bustle of a beehive and resting on
a quiet flower," she wrote with a rare burst of lyric fancy. She was
at Mashobra in August when she received a charming letter from
Sir Louis Cavagnari in Kabul; he had recently gone as British Resident to Afghanistan's capital after long and delicate negotiations
with the Amir. The British were attempting, as in Lord Auckland's
time, to counter Russia's wooing of Afghanistan. "It was a great
satisfaction to me to be able to prove once more," wrote Sir Louis
to Edith that August of 1879, "that the prophets of evil were not
correct in their forecast of coming events." The prophets of evil
had forecast treachery and murder of the British mission by the
Afghans, as in 1842, but Robert felt confident of their loyalty.

Lord Lytton had come to India with firm instructions from
Disraeli to adopt a "forward policy" with regard to Afghanistan.
He had, accordingly, when his envoys were turned back at the
frontier in November 1878, begun the Second Afghan War, sending
future Field-Marshal Lord Roberts, "Bobs" as the troops called him,
as military commander. "Bobs" had thoroughly trounced the Amir,
Sher Ali, who fled north and conveniently died there in February
of 1879. Lytton then began negotiations, with Major Louis Cavagnari as mediator, with the new Amir, Sher Ali's son, Yakub
Khan. By May 1879, Cavagnari's skilled diplomacy had secured
Britain three strategically important districts on the Afghan side of
the border, and a permanent British Mission at Kabul. Disraeli was
jubilant; the Queen gave Cavagnari a knighthood, and both wrote
extravagant praises to Lord Lytton, which pleased Edith mightily.
Cavagnari was fêted by Edith and Robert at Simla, and on July 6th
left to take up his post at Kabul. "He is going to Kabul … in perfect

BELOW THE PEACOCK FAN

confidence that it will be all right," Edith wrote blithely in her journal. But Cavagnari himself had no such illusions. "When he bade farewell to his friends he told them that the chances were four to one that he would never return," wrote a contemporary.[108] On July 24th Cavagnari's mission reached Kabul; in August he wrote to Edith laughing at "the prophets of evil" and on September 3rd every member of the mission and the whole of the escort, excepting three or four men who escaped, were massacred in the Residency.

A preliminary telegram to Simla told the Lyttons of the upset in Kabul but gave no details, and arrived just as Edith and Robert were in the middle of a dinner party. "The others knew nothing of what was going on," reported Mrs Colley, "so we had to keep up appearances, even when the look that passed over H.E.'s [His Excellency's] face when he read the telegram told us pretty well that there was little hope left."[109] So, as always, form triumphed over feeling, and the dinner continued; the entrée was borne in, eaten and the bones removed; sweets and savouries succeeded. After dinner, Edith had to go on to the theatre without Robert. "What I suffered at the play I can't describe," she wrote in her journal; "it was one of the worst contrasts in life that I have ever had to go through." When she returned to Peterhof, she passed Alfred Lyall in the hall looking very glum. His head was down, and he didn't even say good-night. "I at once went to R's room," Edith continued, "and he exclaimed 'Oh, they are all lost, it is too true.' He could hardly speak for five minutes." That night Robert sat up till three A.M. and Edith "could not sleep at all." She kept seeing Cavignari's face streaming with blood, and his widow's pale one, with tears. The terrible cost of Empire ... Edith tossed through the night, trying in vain to reason with herself. Alfred Lyall's poetic soul noted the irony of it all in a letter to his sister:

The Kabul disaster ... came, as every event of the kind comes in India, like a sudden opening of the earth beneath one's feet....
I have constantly told my friends how balls and gaieties always

have to me a dangerous and weird look in India – as people dancing in ignorance of what the next hour may bring forth.[110]

Lord Lytton quickly pulled himself together, and sent the following telegram off to Cavagnari's distressed widow:

It is with inexpressible sorrow that I convey to you the intelligence of the death of your noble husband, who has perished in heroically defending the British Embassy at Kabul against an overwhelming number. Words cannot express the depth of my sympathy in your bereavement.... Every English heart in India aches with yours.[111]

The Queen, too, sent a comforting message to grieving Lady Cavagnari, who telegraphed in reply: "Husband has died the death dearest to his brave soldier's heart."[112] Edith found it harder than Robert to regain her equilibrium: "All one's spirit was knocked out of one," she told Jane Strachey, "by that dreadful blow of the Kabul massacre."[113]

Of course, Robert gave the order for General Roberts to march off to Kabul at once with a large force to avenge the deaths of Cavagnari and the other brave British. As in Mutiny reprisals, vengeance was fierce. Yakub Khan fled in exile, as Roberts's avenging army came down like a wolf on the fold, ravaging the country for supplies, burning villages and hanging the Afghans in batches. There were, in all, eighty executions, which rather dismayed Lord Lytton, who had told "Bobs" to be stern but not cruel.[114] The Kabul massacre of Macnaghten's mission in 1842, followed by the avenging British army under General Pollock ... the Kabul massacre of Cavagnari's mission in 1879, followed by the avenging British army under General Roberts. Indian history went round and round in repeating cycles, something that the Western brain, firmly implanted with the idea of history's forward progress, could never seem to learn. Only the names changed, but not the events, not the inevitable clash, over and over, of Western reason and Eastern instinct, the old, old story.

"Lord Lytton really feels he never can get over that dreadful massacre," wrote Edith to Jane Strachey from Mashobra on October 27th,[115] ignoring her own continuing pain. By November, however, resilient Robert was regaling Jane with Simla's latest jingle: "The husband is a fearful beast / He comes when you expect him least,"[116] and, when he arrived back in Calcutta, was busily getting up a production of *A School for Scandal* at Government House with Mrs Plowden as Lady Teazel and Mrs Batten as Lady Sneerwell. From November 20th to December 12th, Robert and Edith toured four of the native states in Rajputana; Robert envied the Maharaja of Jaipur, whose pink palace was "a realised dream of the Arabian Nights," and whose *zenana* quarters contained no less than four thousand women.[117]

As Robert and Edith were returning to Calcutta's Government House from the station on December 12th, a "drunken East Indian" who only wanted, according to Edith, to "salute the Viceroy" fired two pistol shots into their carriage. "I was indeed glad to have been with Robby," Edith told her mother with conscious heroism. "I always like being at his side here and if I saw anyone try to hurt him or come near him, I would go between without hesitation as his life is far more politically precious than mine."

By the beginning of March, Edith was feeling the constraints of being now so long inside the bell-jar of Raj protocol. "I don't suppose there is one in India more truly lonely than I am," she confided to her mother. "The way to be praised in a public position is to appear to all outsiders as standing quite alone.... It is all difficult to describe and a strange unnatural position...." By the end of the month, Edith's reprieve had come. On March 31, there was a General Election in England, and Disraeli and the Conservatives suffered a disastrous defeat. Gladstone had always been loud in his denunciation of Lytton's Viceroyalty, particularly his management of Afghan affairs, accusing him of financial dishonesty, trickery, treachery, tyranny and cruelty. Now that Gladstone was Prime

Minister, Lytton felt he had to resign, and he did so promptly on
April 3rd. "What a collapse it has all been!" he wrote from Calcutta
to his wife at Simla. "I feel very low and restless."[118] Edith, however, could feel only a "growing feeling of delight at going home."
The Queen, who hated Gladstone, promptly gave Robert an Earldom to show her general approval of his Vice-Reign. "It will be
but a pauper Earldom," complained Edith, now Countess of Lytton, for Robert discovered that they were in very bad financial
straits. Although Lord Lytton received twenty-five thousand pounds
salary as Viceroy, he had spent lavishly – the Calcutta theatricals
alone had cost two thousand pounds, a true School for Scandal,
and his English investments and Knebworth rent roll had shrunk
alarmingly during his absence. The Viceroy was the same careless
spendthrift who had once indulged in ice-machines he couldn't
afford. In India, the closest Lord Lytton came to putting his mind
to financial matters was to name his little dog "Budget" because
he'd arrived on the day the budget was tabled. But there was worse
financial disaster, much worse, beyond Lord Lytton's private pen-
ury. He discovered now to his horror that his Financial Department,
under Sir John Strachey, had miscalculated the cost of the Afghan
War; they had estimated it at five million pounds when it should
have been seventeen.

Edith was quite prepared to do her part by becoming very
thrifty on Knebworth's home front. "I shall live with the children
in great retirement," she told Jane Strachey,[119] and declared she
"would rather have only a tallow candle in the smallest room than
run risks" but Robert, as she knew only too well, had "extravagant
tastes, and though he may go to London as a Bachelor he may yet
spend a good deal."[120]

Gladstone ordered Lord Ripon at once to proceed to India to
succeed Lord Lytton while there were still a few rupees left in
Government coffers. Lord Lytton telegraphed huffily to Gladstone
that he couldn't possibly leave during the hot weather (it was June)
since it wouldn't be safe for his wife and children to travel to
Bombay until the rains came to cool everything down. Gladstone

ignored Lord Lytton's plea and told Lord Ripon to keep on with his packing. The Queen wrote to Lord Lytton trusting that his dear Lordship "will not move a day sooner than is safe for himself and family to do so."[121]

The innocent Lord Ripon, caught in the cross-fire, arrived promptly and rather apologetically on June 8th and took over Peterhof. The Lyttons had to move into a house General Roberts had rented from an obliging maharajah. "I would it were bed-time, and all were over," Lytton wrote. "After the fitful fever of my Indian life, my only wish is to sleep well."[122] The Lyttons left Simla on June 28th, and set sail for England from Bombay on July 3rd. Edith looked forward to a quiet life at Knebworth "with no flies, no glare, no biting things."[123] The Lyttons were met at Portsmouth on August 7th by Wilfrid and Anne Blunt, among others. "Oh, the dear drunken people in the streets!" exclaimed Edith as she came ashore, "how I love them."[124] The sight of Knebworth's "dear towers from the railroad before Stevenage," wrote Edith on the last page of her Indian journal, "was one of the happiest moments of our lives.... The next day, Sunday, the 9th of August, was Victor's fourth birthday. The fruit was all in perfection and the place seemed ideally lovely, and we rushed about quite wild with delight." The poets, Blunt and Lytton, were meanwhile looking into their crystal balls. "We are both agreed that the day of England's *empire* is fast ending – for my own part I do not care how soon. Lytton has more patriotism," Blunt wrote in his diary.[125]

With the feverish "nightmare" of India behind him, Robert returned to the ramblings of *King Poppy*, to further renovations to Knebworth and to his usual histrionic excesses. It was in that "fantastic, be-dragoned house" during an 1883 house party that "Lord Lytton and I," wrote Walburga, Lady Paget, "ended up the historical tableaux" which assembled guests were performing "as King Solomon and The Queen of Sheba. We sat together on a silver throne, which had been given him when he was Viceroy of India."[126] British India would certainly have disapproved, had they known, of such a frivolous use of a sacred High Raj prop!

To Edith's sorrow, Robert also returned whole-heartedly to his "flirting." He grew very close to Edith's sister Theresa, telling her that his "inner self " was more *"en robe de chambre"* with her than any other woman; he wrote a series of passionate letters to Alfred Lyall's sister Barbara in India. When the Rev. Whitwell Elwin became a family friend and confidante, Edith confided in his ear "her distress" over Robert's flirtations, while Robert "told him of his irritation at her somewhat nagging and disciplinary attitude."[127] Edith's migraine headaches became more frequent as bitterness and resentment grew. Gone now, forever, was the young Edith who had blossomed in feeling and spontaneity during her first nine months in India, during her Simla idyll. Like the High Raj itself, Edith, Countess of Lytton, was now totally reliant on form, on uncompromising discipline and authority, on external signs of prestige. Raj and Viceroy together had pushed her too far. Raj rigidity had stiffened her permanently and from now on there would be nothing in her environment to effect a reversal. With the children, she grew strict and domineering. She forced the boys, every morning, "much to their disgust," to read some dull, improving book. She "liked to rule those about her," her daughter Emily recalls; as the children grew into their teens, she "did not encourage intimacy, and would have had little sympathy with the problems of adolescence."[128] She enjoyed her social prominence as Countess of Lytton, former Vicereine, and chatelaine of Knebworth, and she kept those beneath her in the pecking order at a respectful distance. Edith was now far less indulgent of Robert's flirting, far more openly censorious and vocal in her displeasure. In 1883, Robert, at fifty-two, conceived a grand passion for an American actress, Mary Anderson, then acting in London in one of Bulwer-Lytton's plays. She was twenty-four, tall, beautiful, auburn-haired, Catholic – and, alas for Lord Lytton, resolutely chaste. All London loved her; fifty thousand photos of her were printed that year for her fans; Lily Langtry sent her flowers, Oscar Wilde and W.S. Gilbert wrote plays for her, the *beau monde* invited her to dine, and Lord Lytton, with Edith's grim, grudging consent, invited her to Knebworth for weekends. On one such, Mary heard someone enter her bedroom at two A.M. From the foot of the bed she heard "a deep, pathetic sigh" and felt arms grasping her shoulders. She cried out for her maid and "the ghost" fled the room.[129] When Robert went abroad in 1887, leaving Edith at Knebworth, he apologized for the brevity of one letter to Edith – a long one to Mary Anderson had consumed all his morning. In another letter to Edith, he asked her to send Mary a current magazine containing a fable he'd written, and then mentioned the ultimatum Edith had apparently given him about inviting Mary Anderson again to Knebworth. If Edith could ask guests of her choice to Knebworth, why couldn't he? "In reference to its hospitalities, Knebworth is not quite my own house," he grumbled.[130] All this was not quite like the "Robsy-dearest Puttens" letters winging from Lisbon to London twenty-two years earlier. One wonders if Robert had Edith in mind when he wrote in his poem "Madame La Marquise":

With live women and men to be found in the world –
Live with sorrow and sin, live with pain and with passion –
Who could live with a doll, tho' its locks should be curled,
And its petticoats trimmed in the fashion?

Edith felt her heart hardening and knew, remembering now with nostalgia her early halcyon days in India, how much she had lost. From 1885 on, Edith worked sporadically, whenever she felt the need, on her Indian letters, readying them for the Indian journal which would be privately printed in 1899. "My dear Children," she wrote in its Preface, "you will some day like to know something about your Father's appointment as Viceroy of India ... so in sorting my papers I have made some notes, copied parts of some letters and written out for you in the following pages what I can remember of that eventful and interesting time." Having read Emily Eden's published Indian letters, perhaps Edith felt the need to continue the tradition of First Ladies appearing in print.

*I*N 1887, EDITH and Robert moved to Paris, where he had been appointed British Ambassador, a position he held until his death. There, at last, he found a milieu where his Bohemianism and dandyism and devotion to the arts were properly appreciated. "I devoted my life to India, and everybody abused me," he mused in puzzlement. "I come here, do nothing, and am praised to the skies."[131] Edith, too, was rejuvenated in Paris: the resplendent hostess once again, charming everyone. "Edith is a great social success, and does all she has to do in perfection," Robert told Theresa.[132] He assured Edith that his flirting days were over – "I am an extinct volcano," he told her in 1889[133] – but when they went to Bayreuth in July 1891, he couldn't resist a very *small* flirtation with Wagner's widow, Cosima, and, at supper, between the last two acts of *Parsifal,* Robert's "head was already very near her shoulder."[134] In August that year, the Lyttons rented a house at Ascot, but the picture of family life which emerges is not a happy one. Edith felt "pushed into the background" by Robert's attentions to his favourite daughter, Betty. "When Betty and Father are talking," noted Emily, "they either don't listen to what she [Edith] says or else are rather inclined to laugh at it."[135]

Robert died in Paris on November 24, 1891, shortly after his sixtieth birthday, from a cerebral hæmorrhage, in the midst of writing a poem. He had been bedridden for three weeks with a bladder infection, nursed by Edith, who caught him in her arms as he fell back dead "without a word or cry."[136] He left a letter for her admitting that he had loved Mary Anderson "deeply and too much" but that his whole heart was filled with "unspeakable love" for his devoted wife.[137] Edith was brave and controlled in public, but her inner suffering was intense. "Con knocked over a chair yesterday after lunch," Emily wrote on January 7, 1892, "and poor Mother was so nervous and began to scream.... She was miserable afterwards and said it was so dreadful when nerves got beyond one's control, and she was so afraid of doing it again."[138]

Eighteen months after Robert's death, the business man to

whom he had entrusted his money went bankrupt. Edith's income was reduced to £1,900 a year; she had to let Knebworth and move to a small house near by. She hated the poverty and the loss of social prestige. Whenever the conversation allowed, "Mother brings forward her glory in India and Paris," Emily noted.[139] Now Edith felt poor and deprived, and as she aged, grew "very stingy," once scolding Con for giving a cab-driver a whole sixpence as tip. In October 1895, Edith became Lady-in-Waiting to Queen Victoria, with a salary of £300 a year. The Queen was then seventy-six, very lame, with failing sight. "My one and only wish is to please the Queen," wrote Edith.[140] She noted carefully in her diary that on October 16, 1895, "Quenelles à la Lytton" were served for dinner at Balmoral, and that on the next night there was a white frost which "reminded me of the hills in India in October." When the current Secretary of State for India, Lord George Hamilton, was at Windsor the following October, Edith recorded that he "was very nice and talked to me about India."[141]

On February 2, 1899, Neville Lytton married Wilfrid Blunt's daughter Judith. She had to be urged into the marriage by her parents, for she had given her heart to Victor Lytton, who no longer looked like an owl or monkey (as his mother had described him at birth) but rather like a film star. Victor, however, preferred to marry Mrs Plowden's daughter, Pamela, even more beautiful than her mother. They were married in 1902 and later Victor, Second Earl of Lytton, was made Governor of Bengal, residing in Calcutta's Government House where he had romped as a child. By that time, the British Raj had shifted its headquarters from Calcutta to Delhi, where the splendid new Viceregal Palace was designed in 1912 by Edwin Lutyens, the clever young architect who had married Emily Lytton, and who created in stone an expression of British Might and Majesty in India that would, most assuredly, endure far, far longer than his father-in-law's ephemeral creations of 1877.

After Queen Victoria's death, Edith served Queen Alexandra as Lady-in-Waiting with the same devotion, finally retiring from court in 1905 to a small house on the Knebworth property, designed for her by "Ned" Lutyens. There she lived until October 1936, when she died at the age of ninety-five.

She kept her exquisite manners to the end and was charming to all who came to see her even when she couldn't quite remember who they were. She hated her memory failing so quickly and so completely in those final years. Beyond all her other recollections, she tried to hang on to her Simla ones, for it had been in India that Edith, Countess of Lytton, had enjoyed the brief, high summer of her days.

IV

MARY CURZON

*Imperialism in the ordinary London man seems, and is, vanity; to
foreigners, who have never visited India and the colonies, it is
the last feather straggling on a moulting peacock. But let the satirist
come to Bombay – even for an hour – he need not go further; he
will admit freely, and no more doubt the vigour of the Anglo-Saxon
or his ability to hold a vast possession.*

JOHN OLIVER HOBBES (PEARL CRAIGIE)
Imperial India

BOMBAY'S LANDING-STAGE was covered with red carpet, crowded
with people, on that cool, clear morning of December 30, 1898.
The new Viceroy, Lord Curzon of Kedleston, had just landed from
England and was well into one of his favourite activities: making
a speech. He was a fine-looking man of thirty-nine, with a baby's
pink-and-white skin, a head so broad his hats had to be specially
made, and an "expression of enamelled assurance."[1] In repose his
mouth had a grim, almost cruel down-curve, but at that moment
he was all smiles. All eyes, however, were not fixed, as one would
have expected, on his declaiming Lordship. His audience gazed in
wonder at the woman standing quietly beside him, his wife Mary,
a woman so beautiful and ethereal that she might have floated forth
from the mists of fable and romance. "I suddenly realised why the
Greeks had besieged Troy for so many years," declared one Indian
Civil Service officer when he first beheld this "vision of loveliness."[2] Five feet, eight inches tall, with tiny waist and narrow hips,

Lady Curzon wore her hair waved into a simple love-knot at the nape of her neck. Her grey eyes were large and thickly lashed, her face a perfect oval, her head beautifully poised on her long neck. She was fully aware both of her beauty and her audience. "Her self-possession of manner," the *Advocate of India* declared,

> was as evident as her beauty, and during the half-hour that the proceedings lasted, she was pre-eminently the most self-possessed individual.... As she leaned her crossed hands on the twisted silver handle of a parasol that matched her dress one could detect no suggestion of nervousness in a single twitch of her fingers.[3]

When the Viceregal flow of long, Latinate words had finally ceased, the Viceroy and Vicereine, with becoming dignity, climbed into a shining four-horse carriage and the procession moved off, complete with military escort and Viceregal Guard of Honour. Cheering crowds and Union Jacks lined Bombay's streets as the Viceregal Pair sat beneath the Golden Umbrella, smiling to left and right. Bombay's great Clock Tower, which pealed forth hymn tunes on Sundays and "God Save the Queen" and "Home Sweet Home" on weekdays, struck eight as they passed. The Viceregal Pair had been in India exactly one hour but already they were quite perfect in their roles.

Certainly Mary Curzon was born to be a Queen, grew up, in luxury and limelight, a princess in her mind's eye, pampered heiress in the world's. Her father, Levi Z. Leiter, was an American multi-millionaire whose Midas touch turned all his real-estate and retail dry-goods ventures into gold, such mountainous piles of gold, that at the age of forty-six he retired from the capitalist mêlée. He spent the rest of his life buying up works of art, and, at his wife's urging, such famous bibelots as the Borghese rubies, for which he paid the price of £110,000 and Queen Victoria's displeasure, for Her Majesty had wanted the rubies for her own neck.[4] Levi Leiter came from Mennonite Swiss stock, grew up poor in Maryland, denied having any of the Jewish blood which the Semitic names on his family tree implied, headed for Chicago at the age of twenty, and went on to found the dry-goods empire now known as Marshall Field. "Of family, as the word is here understood," sniffed the London *Times* years later, "he had none; of position, none save that which he created himself."[5] Levi Leiter was a mythic figure: the self-made man, pursuing the American Dream in the Land of Opportunity, another Vanderbilt or Rockefeller. He could be peppery and pugnacious, but never with his eldest daughter Mary, born in Chicago on May 27, 1870. Mrs Leiter, née Mary Theresa Carver, also of no distinguished background, always stood apart from that self-sufficient twosome of loving father and daughter. Later, she would embarrass her more-polished daughter with her blatant social-climbing and her frequent malapropisms. After a stormy Atlantic crossing, Mrs Leiter declared herself pleased to be "back on terracotta" and announced on another occasion that her husband would attend a fancy-dress ball "in the garbage of a monk."[6] Mary, however, was moulded to proper gentility, attending Chicago's most select female academy where she learned how to dress becomingly and do her hair. She was a dreamy girl, given to scribbling romantic plays about handsome young knights who spent their days falling in and out of love and duels. Mary took her first trip abroad with her parents and brother Joseph in 1881. The incident which, according to her diary, impressed her most was the arrival on their Paris dinner-table one evening of "a roast pheasant complete with head, tail-feathers and wings reattached by wires."[7] Her love of theatrical show came early, and stayed. In 1883 the Leiters moved to one of the grandest houses in Washington, Blaine House, on Dupont Circle, a castle befitting a New-World princess, with its towers and pinnacles and confused pretensions to Romanesque, Gothic and Renaissance forbears. It was rather a monstrous castle, architecturally speaking, a kind of American equivalent of England's Highcliffe Castle or Knebworth House.

In her blue boudoir high up in Blaine House, Mary primped for parties, and piled up her invitation cards from the Theodore

Roosevelts, the Hays, the Whitneys, and, her most special friend, Frances, wife of President Grover Cleveland.

Having conquered Washington society, and New York's, where she became a "Gibson Girl," model for Dana Gibson's fashionable cartoons, Mary moved her headquarters to Claridges in mid-June 1890, ready for the London season and bigger game. The princess craved coronets on her invitations and ducal signatures on her dance-cards. She had come to London at the right time, for American heiresses were then immensely popular, seen to be very useful in propping up sagging ducal fortunes. If they were beautiful as well as rich, so much the better. Jennie Jerome had already snared Lord Randolph Churchill, Consuelo Vanderbilt had marched up the aisle with the Duke of Marlborough, and now here was Mary Leiter with an eighteen-inch waist and charming manners and a father worth twenty million. Mary found that London season thrilling: one long iridescent blur of powdered, liveried footmen, soaring marble staircases, azaleas in gilt baskets, white waistcoats, quail in aspic, linkmen with flaring torches, pale-blue dawns with swept pavements and smudged satin slippers. And then, on July 17th, the blur suddenly coalesced into one shining, diamond point. It happened at the Duchess of Westminster's ball, which Mary Victoria Leiter, of no distinguished family, opened by dancing the first quadrille with Prince Edward, England's future king. Then Mary Victoria was introduced to her own Prince Charming: George Nathaniel Curzon, the future Lord Scarsdale. Mary at once came under the spell of his physical attractiveness, witty talk and proud, D'Arcy-like manners. He, in turn, took note of her beauty and of her father's twenty million, for, in spite of his noble lineage, George Nathaniel had to make do with £1,500 a year. Mary had none of that aggressive self-confidence which American girls often flaunted and he deplored; she was modest, grave and, best of all, hung on his every grandiose word. She was only twenty, eleven years younger than he, young enough, he also noted, to be pliable in his autocratic hands.

*43 Portrait of Mary Leiter, afterwards Lady Curzon
(by Seraph von Lenbach)*

George Nathaniel Curzon, eldest son of Lord Scarsdale, had
been born at the Derbyshire ancestral home, Kedleston Hall, on
January 11, 1859. The family motto was: "Let Curzon holde what
Curzon helde" and they had and did, hanging on to their Derby

property for more than eight hundred years, ever since the first "Coursons" had arrived from Normandy with William the Conqueror. Kedleston Hall, one of England's most magnificent homes, had been built on the estate in the eighteenth century by the first Lord Scarsdale, who with the arrogance and ego common to male Curzons, had first moved an entire village to a more respectful distance and changed the course of the public highway. That done, he hired Robert Adam to work his classical magic in marble and stone, and Kedleston raised its impressive bulk and beauty in the damp Derbyshire dales. The present Lord Scarsdale, George Nathaniel's father, was an ordained Anglican clergyman, ascetic and eccentric. George Nathaniel's mother had died when he was sixteen, after producing eleven children in sixteen years. Showing a streak of self-pity, George Nathaniel liked to claim he had had a miserable childhood. "I suppose no children well-born and well placed," he wrote, "ever cried so much or so justly."[8] His cruel governess, he was fond of relating, used to beat him with her hairbrush, tie him to chairs and stuff him into dark closets. Kedleston Hall was luxuriously columned in alabaster, but Calvinist in tone: narrow, disciplined and cold.[9] George and his ten siblings had no toys. They learned the alphabet by laying out their scarves and mittens to form letters on the cold marble floor of Kedleston's great hall.[10] Scarves for words: a fit beginning for George Nathaniel, who would always be in love with words, particularly his own, using them to keep his ego warm and protected.

Prince Charming dazzled Eton with his public debating, then, just as he was preparing to go up to Balliol College, Oxford, George Nathaniel developed an incurable curvature of the spine. Ever after he would be forced to wear a steel corset padded with leather, to spend days in bed, to suffer constant pain because one leg was shorter than the other. The steel bit into his character, made him irritable, restless, highly critical of others. In spite of his handicap, he sailed through Balliol as he had through Eton, on pride and prizes. He was not, however, popular with class-mates. One such told George Nathaniel that he had "plenty of intellect and not enough heart," and others lampooned him in an 1881 college skit with the following verse:

> My name is George Nathaniel Curzon,
> I am a most superior person.
> My cheek is pink, my hair is sleek,
> I dine at Blenheim once a week.[11]

The epithet stuck to him for the rest of his life. "Most superior," to be sure, but never quite as superior as he held himself to be. Already, in those undergraduate years, George Nathaniel Curzon was fired with a most superior ambition: he wanted, more than anything in the world, to become Viceroy of India, to become the most superior Viceroy India had ever had. He began preparing himself for his great role by extensive Eastern travels. Between 1877 and 1895, he went four times to India, threw in Egypt, China, Japan, Turkey, Persia and Russia for good measure, kept a meticulous account of every sixpence spent, declared that "of all the necessaries of outfit" for travelling round the world "commend me ... to a suit of dress clothes."[12] When he wasn't travelling, he was quietly reading everything about India he could lay his hands on. His ambition consumed him. When a young German governess once asked him "what bounder meant as everyone called him that," the imperturbable George replied: "One who succeeds in life by leaps and bounds."[13] He had little time for women, thought of them as "inferior creatures," opposed female suffrage, calling it "the fashionable tomfoolery of the day."[14] Women were there to beguile and enhance moments of leisure. He did become engaged in 1881, but only briefly, to a daughter of the Wentworth-Vernons of Wentworth Castle, Yorkshire. He then courted Sibell Grosvenor, young widow of the Duke of Westminster's heir, Lord Grosvenor, but after three years' courtship, Sibell preferred to marry another George, George Wyndham, and did so in 1887. George Nathaniel had, the previous year, become a Conservative member of parliament, all part of his master plan, and paid a visit that year to Lord

Lytton at Knebworth. "You smoke everywhere, in all the drawing-rooms," wrote George in amazement. "I can believe that Lord Lytton smokes in bed. I am sure that he says his prayers – if he says them at all – with a cigarette in his mouth."[15] George pumped Lord Lytton for useful hints on how to be a superior Viceroy, learned instead what *not* to do. George also argued about India with his radical friend, Wilfrid Blunt. George was a member of the Crabbet Club, which met annually for a week of high-jinks at Blunt's home, Crabbet Park.

This, then, was the proud, pompous, occasionally playful young man who waltzed Mary Victoria Leiter in his strong, directing arms around the Duchess of Westminster's ballroom. Several days later, Mary went down to Ashridge, invited by Lady Brownlow to a house-party there. The princess needed a proper setting to perform well: Ashridge was a perfect backdrop. "The house is a superb palace," Mary reported, "built over a convent where Queen Elizabeth once lived," all of it "gorgeous beyond description" with Van Dycks on the walls and Italian marble in the ballroom.[16] But the best thing was right there in the foreground: George Nathaniel Curzon was among the thirty guests. He led Mary into the rose garden, filled her lap with cascading bouquets of soft words. She thought him "the most wonderful, the most charming, the most handsome, the most clever of all the men I have met. I almost died when he touched my hand."[17] She gave him her whole heart right then and there and forever. "I always think the test of affection," she later told her sister Nancy when the latter was contemplating marriage with some young man, "is if you feel that when he comes into a room the band is playing the Star Spangled Banner and that the room is glowing with pink lights and rills are running up and down your back with pure joy. Then it is all right, but don't give your heart away until you feel *all* this, which I feel when George appears."[18] Mary was ready to be wooed and won right there in Lady Brownlow's rose garden, but George Nathaniel was a cool one, and calculating. Very shortly thereafter, he wrote to a friend at Washington's British Embassy, Cecil Spring Rice, who happened

LORD CURZON OF KEDLESTON,
VICEROY . . OF INDIA.

MESS.RS BASSANO
PHOTOGRAPHERS TO THE QUEEN
COPYRIGHT

25. OLD BOND STREET. LONDON. W.

LXVI

to be in love with Mary himself, and asked "Springy" "to inform him in all possible detail of her background and family."[19] Mary only saw George once more before she had to return to America; he was either bustling about his constituency or writing his book on Persia. She gave him a pearl from her necklace "emblematic of the tear I shed at leaving London. You, I mean."[20] He gave her copies of three of his political speeches, and a photo of himself. After that, their courtship limped ahead, with ardour on her side and apathy on his, for three long years. She sent him hundreds of letters and gifts; he replied sporadically and sent her another photo, wrapped up in three more speeches.[21] In 1891, George Nathaniel became Parliamentary Under-Secretary of State for India; he had more important things on his mind than Mary Victoria, and for six months he didn't write at all. Then he wrote briefly, told her how hard he'd been working, that he was writing now, to her and to others "to work off a lot of arrears."[22] Mary Victoria was already beginning to realize that George's two main passions were for India and for words, and that she was a long way down the list. Two years into this courtship, if one could call it that, Mary wrote to a friend: "I will have him, because I believe he needs me."[23] She increased her romantic flow of letters and parcels. He sent her *Persia and the Persian Question*, his precious book, just published, all seven pounds and 1,300 pages of it; she read every word. In 1892, Curzon came to Washington – but didn't see Mary, although he inspected the outside of her house ("red brick of a peculiarly aggressive hue"). He then moved on to Virginia and flirted with Amélie Rives, whom he'd met in England. ("Oh God, the nights on the still lawn under the soft sky with my sweetheart!" he wrote of Amélie.[24])

There were two reasons for George's coolness. Mary's beauty and her father's bank account held great appeal, but George Nathaniel was immensely proud of his patrician lineage. Could he really contemplate an American called Levi Z. Leiter as father-in-law? And as mother-in-law, a woman who was more than a little vulgar and who had, at a Buckingham Palace ball, once mistaken a Guards colonel for a footman? George Nathaniel hung back. The other reason for his coolness towards Mary was that he was more actively courting another American heiress called Pearl Craigie, one with greater intellectual pretensions than Mary, if less beauty. Pearl's father, John Richards, had made *his* fortune in cigarettes, hair-restorers and patent medicines, including Carter's Little Liver Pills.[25] Pearl was then the toast of London, acclaimed author of *Some Emotions and a Moral*, a slim gold-coloured volume shaped like a cheque-book. George Nathaniel weighed Mary Victoria's bountiful letters against Pearl Theresa's bound cheque-book. Then, in 1892, Pearl did the deciding for all three of them: she became a Roman Catholic, took a vow of chastity and refused all future suitors. "I made (for me) a great sacrifice when I refused G.C. Fortunately, I had my work," wrote this Pearl beyond price some years later.[26] George Nathaniel turned back to Mary Victoria and increased his ardour.

On March 3, 1893, they met in Paris. The beautiful princess looked up at him coyly and told him how she'd waited for him for three years, faithful and adoring, how she'd rejected all other suitors, including some rich and titled ones. On a sudden impulse, swept away by her love and loyalty, George proposed, and Mary said a heartfelt "Yes!" But he swore her to secrecy concerning their engagement; she was not to tell even her parents. The princess's trials were not yet over, for the prince had one last task to perform before he could claim her: he had to make a daring journey to the wilds of Afghanistan and the Pamirs, in order to complete his first-hand knowledge of the East. Only when that was successfully accomplished could he claim the hand of his fair one. He told Mary that his trip to Afghanistan would be his "last wild cry of freedom";[27] George never did have much tact. Years before she got to be Vice-reine, Afghanistan was for Mary, as it had been for Emily Eden and Edith Lytton, a source of pain and bewilderment. During the two years of their secret engagement, the lovers saw each other for just two days and a few snatched hours, but Mary's loyalty and trust never faltered. George's letters were still infrequent; when he did write, he clearly mapped out for her the contours of their future partnership. "You are a young child, though a stately woman," he intoned, then corrected her spelling and told her to change her hairdo to a style he liked. "Give me a girl who knows a woman's place and does not yearn for trousers. Give me in fact Mary," George wrote.[28] In their marriage, he would play father; she would be his little girl. In 1889, Mary had written to her own father: "I am afraid the man will never come along whom I can look up to and love as I do you."[29] Now she had found him; after their marriage, she always called George "Pappy"; he called her "Kinkie."

She sent him a magnificent silver inkstand, perhaps hoping he would take the hint and write to her more frequently and in more romantic vein. "The fact that you have given yourself to me is a source of great pride," he told her in the autumn of 1893. "I am spared all the anxiety of what is called a great courtship, and I have merely when the hour strikes, to enter into possession of my own."[30] In the autumn of 1894, she pleaded with him: "I implore you not to go to Kabul," perhaps with the bloody ghosts of Macnaghten and Cavignari in her mind. "If the Amir dies, the danger will be terrible; it will be quite inhuman of you to go and run such a risk."[31] The Amir was Abdur Rahman Khan, eldest son of Dost Mahomed, with whom Emily Eden had played chess. George paid no attention to Mary's pleadings, and turned up at Kabul wearing a magnificent uniform emblazoned with foreign orders and gold epaulettes, all of it hired from a London theatrical costumer. Like his future bride, he understood the importance of the right props. Mary wrote to tell him that if he didn't return, she would never marry but devote her life to good works, beginning with paying off all Kedleston's debts. "I am serious, George, *very* serious and my mind has an inherent faculty of not changing – save for you! I have no will which would not yield to you," she told him.[32] No letters came from George between his arrival in India in mid-August and his return to Chitral on October 12th; he was much too busy sending back articles to *The Times*. Mary worried and waited and read Max Muller's *India and What It Can Teach Us* and Sir Alfred Lyall's *India*, and a life of Lord Lawrence by Sir Richard Temple. "My feminine philosophy," the princess told her knight bravely, "believes in tests and patience greatly improving and developing a woman. I believe we shall be eternally happy."[33] George returned safely from Afghanistan, but rather the worse for wear. "I am rather a crock, and have led a hard-working exhausting life which has taken it out of me," he wrote from his bed in February 1895. "I want to be looked after, and to have a little comfort and some repose. It will be so sweet if you will help me to this. I think you will."[34] The map of their marital set-up was now complete and Mary agreed to its outlines. She would be docile and dependent at all times, would serve and comfort and cosset her dearest "Pappy."

In the 1890s such willing self-abnegation was no longer the norm for females. Mary had grown up in America at a time when many of her contemporaries were getting on the feminist bandwagon and demanding new rights for women. In March 1886, just down the street from Mary's house, Susan B. Anthony had rallied the forces at a huge Female Suffrage Convention. In England too, from the 1870s through to the end of the '80s, there were growing demands of a legal nature, including property rights for women, voting privileges and fair wages. In the 1890s, on both sides of the Atlantic, the main focus of the feminist movement shifted from legal rights to a whole new structuring of the female personality. The new streamlined model was called the New Woman, and she was to be neither angel nor child but fully autonomous human being, asserting her independence by going to college, choosing a career, riding a bicycle, playing tennis, shortening her dragging skirts and smoking in public.

On this feminist ground swell, Mary Leiter turned her back, and found some social sanction for her reactionary stance. In 1883, Mrs Lynn Linton had published *The Girl of the Period and Other Social Essays*, dedicated to "all Good Girls and True Women." The essays had first appeared in the *Saturday Review* and fought a brave rearguard action in defence of the good old mid-Victorian female virtues of service and submission to men espoused by Mrs Sandford, Miss Mulock and others. The first lesson to be learned by all good girls and true women was dependence. "A really sensible woman,"

Mrs Sandford had written "feels her dependence. She does what she can; but she is conscious of inferiority, and therefore, grateful for support."[35] "To resign one's very self totally and contentedly into the hands of another; to have no longer any need of asserting one's rights or one's personality," Miss Mulock had exclaimed, "how delicious is all this!"[36] The True Woman, Mrs Lynn Linton reaffirms, "loves her husband too well to wish to be his rival or to desire an individualized existence outside his. She is his wife, she says; and that seems more satisfactory to her than to be herself a Somebody."[37] We don't know whether or not Mary Leiter read Mrs Lynn Linton or her like-minded predecessors, but Mary certainly, either directly or through George, absorbed their message, and decided to opt for the True Woman rather than the New one. If George wanted an old-fashioned girl who never "yearned for trousers," that was what he would get.

Finally, five years after their first meeting, the great day on which Mary would promise to obey arrived, and on April 22, 1895, she and George were married in Washington. She wore white satin, old lace and a coronet of Kedleston diamonds, receiving the guests after the ceremony at Blaine House, under her portrait, its frame wreathed in forget-me-nots.[38] George had spent two whole days with Levi Leiter's lawyers, drawing up the marriage settlement. Levi gave his favourite daughter seven hundred thousand dollars and his new son-in-law a guaranteed income of six thousand pounds a year. George was now one step nearer his goal: Viceroys needed a large private income, since expenses, in luxurious Late Raj times, could exceed the Viceregal salary. The Amir of Afghanistan, to whom George had sent Mary's photo, sent the happy bridegroom a telegram of congratulations: "Though you have only married one wife she is competent. From my knowledge of Phrenology she is very wise and a well-wisher of yours and better than 1,000 men."[39] Among the two thousand wedding presents, Mary received one which would influence her profoundly: George's friend Augustus Hare had sent his book *The Story of Two Noble Lives*, detailing the life and sad demise of Charlotte Canning.[40]

George and Mary sailed for England on April 27th; she would never see the United States again, but her feelings for her homeland never changed. "One's country is always one's country. Laws may change one's nationality, but they cannot change the heart, and mine is *and ever will be* American," she later told her mother.[41] From now on, Mary would be acting a new role, no longer that of fairy-tale princess but of English aristocrat. She did it supremely well. "I thought that she had shed her American characteristics more completely than I was to find myself able to do," wrote Consuelo, Duchess of Marlborough, who saw Mary at various weekend house parties.[42]

As soon as they reached England, George and Mary went to Kedleston Hall, which impressed Mary with its palatial proportions. Lord Scarsdale was less impressive; he had a disconcerting habit of sticking out his tongue in every mirror, and examining it closely, and was such a stickler for detail that at dinner he kept the silver gravy spoon warm in a bowl of hot water at his elbow. Above them, as they dined, was a ceiling painted by Angelica Kauffman to show Love embracing Fortune. (Lord Scarsdale had once raised his glass of port to Fortune, with the invocation "Come down, old girl, come down!"[43]

After their visit to the ancestral seat, the newlyweds moved into one of London's most splendid town houses, 5 Carlton House Terrace, overlooking St James Park. Mary was shocked to find that George had already seen to every detail of the interior decor and engaged all the servants, two tasks reserved for wives. She felt it unfair that she couldn't even choose carpets and curtains for their town house, nor for their country house at Reigate, Surrey, since her father was paying for it all.

It was at this point that the first significant erosion of Mary Curzon's self-esteem occurred. Even the most hidebound of conduct books endorsing the ideal of the submissive wife agreed that there was one area where she was to have complete autonomy. "A man has no business to meddle in the management of the house," decrees Miss Mulock.[44] Mrs Ellis supports "the principle, which allows to every wife a little sphere of domestic arrangements, with which the husband shall not feel that he has any business to interfere. Unless a husband can feel sufficient confidence in his wife, to allow her to rule with undisputed authority in this little sphere," Mrs Ellis continues, "her case must be a pitiable one indeed."[45] For the duration of their marriage, George would continue to rule on the domestic front as he did beyond it and Mary's inner sense of self-worth and identity would continue to crumble. More and more she would come to rely on the comforting knowledge of her external beauty to offset the dwindling ego within.

For the first three years of her marriage, Mary was banished to the wings, while George did nothing but work. He had become Under Secretary of State at the Foreign Office in June of 1895. "He sits and sits at those Foreign Office boxes until I could scream!" Mary told her family.[46] Apart from the birth of her daughter Irene on January 20, 1896, these were dismal years for Mary. She was neglected, homesick, bored. "Wholly absorbed in her husband's career," wrote Consuelo of her friends, the Curzons, "she had subordinated her personality to his to a degree I would have considered beyond an American woman's powers of self-abnegation."[47] Mary was already paying the price for her choice of old-fashioned girl rather than New Woman; she was frequently unwell and began to get the severe migraine headaches which would plague her for the rest of her life. One day at Reigate, she saw two ducks trapped by ice in the middle of the lake, unable to move in any direction. Next morning the ducks were frozen solid; Mary knew exactly how they felt.[48] George worked so hard that the Curzons had little social life, and Mary missed the adulation and affluent settings. George made sure, however, that Pearl Craigie often came to dinner, and in the fall of 1897 she stayed with the Curzons for two rather tense weeks at Beldorney Castle.

George had written to the Prime Minister, Lord Salisbury, that spring to tell him that when Lord Elgin finished his term as Viceroy, George was ready and willing to succeed him. Lord Salisbury replied in a non-committal vein. In April 1898, George wrote to him again: "For twelve years I have worked and studied and thought – with a view should the chance ever arise – to fitting myself for the position," he told the PM.[49] "Would Mrs Curzon who is an American do to represent a Vice Queen?" Queen Victoria asked Salisbury when the appointment was pending.[50] He assured her that Mrs Curzon would be perfect in the role. Her Majesty then obligingly knighted George Nathaniel: henceforth he would be Baron Curzon of Kedleston. Levi Leiter provided three thousand pounds and a tiara for Mary. "It takes my breath away," Mary gasped to him, announcing George's appointment,

> for it is the greatest position in the English world next to the Queen and the Prime Minister, and it will be a satisfaction, I know, to you and Mamma that your daughter Maria [sic] will fill the greatest place ever held by an American abroad. Heaven knows how I shall do it, but I shall do my best to be a help to George and an honour to you and Mamma, and I shall put my trust in Providence and hope to learn how to be a ready-made Queen.[51]

After a short run as English Aristocrat, Mary was now to play the role of the second most prominent Englishwoman in the entire British Empire. It would be her greatest challenge.

On August 11th, George's appointment was made public; Mary went to Worth in Paris to buy a magnificent trousseau even though she was too advanced in second pregnancy to try things on. Cynthia was born on August 28th, a slight disappointment for George who longed for a son. "We begin to be treated like grandees," wrote Mary, before they left England, loving every minute of it. "Station masters always meet us, carriages are reserved, and low bows and crowds staring" were the order of the day.[52] At last, after three languishing years, Mary was on stage again! The Crabbet Club, dedicated to discouraging a serious view of life, had a rule that any member who became Viceroy of India had to resign forthwith. "I trust that you may prove the best, the most frivolous (even remembering Lytton) and the *last* of our Viceroys," Wilfrid Blunt told George.[53] In November, the Curzons paid an overnight visit to Windsor Castle. Shortly after their arrival, Edith, Lady Lytton, then serving as Queen Victoria's Lady-in-Waiting, came to their rooms and told them something of what to expect in India. Next day, the new Lady Curzon met a real Queen:

> Nothing could exceed the Queen's wonderful kindness to me, and I was quite overcome ... she produced a large pair of glasses and said I must put on my glasses to have a good look at you. I felt shy. When George came in for his audience she said I must congratulate you for your wife is both beautiful and wise! Wasn't that nice.[54]

George, of course, not Mary, interviewed and hired the nurse-maids and other servants who would accompany them to India. Then came the three-week voyage on the SS *Arabia* and the very formal, and gratifying, landing at Bombay when Mary Leiter from Chicago, whose father was in trade, stepped onto the red carpet and into an engrossing new role which she eagerly embraced on that 30th day of December 1898. For the next seven years she would know exactly who she was: Vicereine of India.

That evening, Mary shone her radiance on 112 dignitaries whom the Governor of Bombay had invited to meet the Curzons at dinner. Later that night, 1,400 more filed respectfully past with their bows and curtsies at a reception where Mary and George stood on a magnificent gold carpet "with immense gold chairs behind us."[55] Mary loved the Viceroy's special train which took them on to Calcutta next day. It was white and gold, "as long as the New York Limited" and she and George each had a splendid carriage "just like an American private car." Mary's was divided into saloon, bedroom, bathroom, maid's room and box-room. Viceregal magnificence had been increasing steadily since the Lyttons' day. At every important station along the route there were guards of honour, and cheering crowds.[56] When they arrived at Calcutta, the royal pair were escorted to Government House by a squadron of cavalry, a company of infantry, and the 120-strong Viceroy's Bodyguard, splendid tall Sikhs in white breeches, scarlet coats and blue-and-gold turbans, each man carrying a pennanted lance. There were a hundred thousand cheering natives along the route. Mary waved and smiled happily, then floated, swan-like, over the red carpet and up the broad steps of Government House, to be received at the top by Lord and Lady Elgin, three Maharajahs and their suites, and top British officials. In the distance the cannons of Fort William sounded the Viceroy's salute.

Mary found Government House itself quite grand enough. "My bedroom is so big you can just see from one end to the other!" she told her parents.[57] It seemed fitting, too, that Government House was copied from Kedleston Hall, but surpassed it in grandeur, having four wings instead of only two, and corridors an extra storey high. Mary was ready to overlook the fact that Government House was painted brick, not stone like its original, that its Great Hall pillars were plaster, not alabaster. And she heartily approved when George gave the order to paint its exterior wedding-cake white – far more appropriate for a fairy-tale palace than "dirty yellow."[58] There *were* disadvantages, of course. Her bedroom was so dark that it was difficult to dress for her public; she had to do her hair in the morning "with a hand mirror on a little upper balcony" and in the evening with smoky candles.[59] It was not long, however, before George gave the order for electric lights to be installed throughout Government House, and in the following year for electric fans, keeping the punkahs, for tradition's sake, only in the state rooms. Things had improved noticeably since Edith Lytton's day, for Government House also had proper plumbing, electric bells and elevators. The squalid India beyond could never be banished completely, however. Bats, fever-laden mosquitoes and even wild civet cats occasionally still appeared among the brocade and ormulu.

As those first weeks passed, Mary found her new role exciting, demanding and utterly absorbing. "I am getting used to the new life," she told her father, sailing through her queenly paces, "and it is all very wonderful."⁶⁰ Protocol was difficult to remember, but she was determined never to slip up. She knew that "all English women are ready to pounce" if she made a mistake "as my being here excites such jealousy in many hearts."⁶¹ Seen from her republican point of view, the whole Raj pageant was, after all, just a show, all a bit silly and contrived. "The lot of a Viceroy is one of absolute aloofness and everyone is in mortal funk of the august being," declared Mary. "Being a Yankee I can't understand it but I manage to assume the necessary amount of awful respect for his Excellency when we appear in public."⁶² She had to remember to let George go through every door first, and to let him climb first into the Viceregal carriage whenever they drove out, with eighteen postilions, guards and outriders accompanying them. Every night at dinner, all the ladies present had to curtsey to the Viceroy as they entered the dining-room, curtseying being a new formality introduced after Lord Lytton's time.

As she gradually mastered the protocol, Mary increasingly relied on it. Like many professional actresses, she liked to hide behind an assumed role and felt most comfortable with a script in her hand. To be sure, the Vicereine's script in this Late Raj period had plenty of stage directions. In Early Raj days, there had been far fewer rules to follow; the Eden sisters had merely laughed at them and more or less ignored them. But Viceregal conventions had been proliferating ever since. Mary knew that Charlotte Canning had given a very correct performance, one long remembered and loudly applauded. Lady Dufferin, in the 1880s, had given another. Mary knew that she had been raised in a real castle in Ireland inhabited by her family since 1610. No wonder she was "so regal and so essentially the *grande dame*."⁶³ After Lady Dufferin had come the equally haughty Marchioness of Lansdowne "one of the very few able to do ... as well as her predecessor."⁶⁴

All those British blue-bloods were a hard act for Mary Leiter from Chicago to follow, but she was determined, with her beauty to help her, not to feel intimidated. She was, after all, not quite centre stage, being only George's consort; he was the central figure in the golden pageant. With George taking it all so seriously, the Raj regalia began to seem less ridiculous to Mary. She was particularly impressed when she watched his first Durbar, with the red-and-gold-garbed attendants behind his throne, holding peacock fans, *chowries* and maces, "quite twenty of them."[65] Mary began to look at the Viceroy from a Raj perspective, rather than a republican one: "George is treated *exactly* like a reigning sovereign," she told her father. "Everyone bows and curtseys – ADC's precede him – the only difference is that he has a great deal more power than most kings, and ruling India is no sinecure – and a Viceroy has it in his power to be a *very* great force."[66] Mary soon realized that while she had to play Queen in public, all gracious dignity, she had to play concubine in private, all kittenish wiles, allowing her king to step down from his dais and relax, and she had to perform both roles so well that his basilisk-glance would never fall on *her*. Like all Vicereines, Mary found herself caught in the double bind of adapting not only to a new country and role but also to a husband in process of adapting.

Initially, Mary felt buoyed up by her success, *their* success, in their regal roles. "We look so young and happy and bow and smile unceasingly when we are out," she told her father, "and this pleases everybody."[67] In this same letter to her father of January 17, 1899, Mary unknowingly sounded the first ominous note in her Indian drama. She told him that on a visit to Barrackpore she "saw Lady Canning's tomb, which is beautifully placed by the river."[68] Every time thereafter, arriving at Barrackpore by steam launch, preferring always to travel by river rather than road, Mary walked past Charlotte's tomb.

That initial year, Mary threw herself whole-heartedly into her social role as India's foremost Hostess. "From the first," the *Daily Telegraph* would later declare, "she seconded in every way her husband's ambition to revive all the glories of the Viceroyalty, and she entertained lavishly."[69] By February 17, 1899, G. W. Steevens was writing in the *Daily Mail* that the new reign "socially and person-ally" was "already an assured triumph." Mary deserved these ac-colades. She was only in Calcutta for January and February 1899 before going up to Simla for the summer, but during that time she presided at a Drawing Room, a State Ball for 1,600, a State Evening Party for 1,500, a Garden Party, several lesser balls for 600, many official dinners for 100 or more, smaller dinners and informal eve-ning dances.

The etiquette for large dinner parties was now very formal indeed. "As we come to the door," Mary told her mother and sisters, "an ADC says 'Their Excellencies' and all the guests bow."[70] Then, following the procedure begun by Edith Lytton, their Excellencies went slowly round the room while an ADC introduced each guest by name. Sometimes the ADC had not studied his list of names quite long enough. One such presented four ladies in a row under the same unpronounceable name. When he came to the fifth lady, she, anticipating a similar unjust fate, cried out "I am not Mrs. Petrocochino!"[71] Edith Lytton would have been shocked to see how completely form had triumphed. "After dinner," Mary explained,

> I have to walk out of the room alone, preceded by an ADC, the ladies coming behind. The men smoke, and when George comes into the drawing-room we all get up and stand till he sits down, and have to jump up every time he does. We each sit and talk to guests, ADC's bringing up relays.[72]

For each social event, Mary had the perfect costume. At her first Drawing Room, attended by over five hundred ladies, she wore white satin embroidered with lotus leaves, the lotus being a central motif in Indian art. It was the only part of the Indian India that Mary chose to embrace. That India, in any case, was farther away from the Vi-ceregal court than ever before. Lady Curzon had no wish to bridge the gap and link herself with native customs and people; dress designs were as far as her Ladyship was prepared to go.

Like Edith Lytton, Mary was proving to be the more popular half of the Viceregal team, and George, like Lord Lytton, was the butt of most of the criticism. "Mary is adored by everyone here, and I am regarded with mingled bewilderment and pain," George told Pearl Craigie.[73] "His guests never saw George Nathaniel Curzon," declared Sir Walter Lawrence, his Private Secretary, "but always the Viceroy."[74] The carping gossip began to circulate, and one wag dashed off a clever verse:

> On a throne of Alabaster our Re-Incarnated Master
> Daily exercises his Vice-regal craft:
> Supervising now the Amir or apportioning a Pamir
> Or composing some quite devastating draft.
> From a cup of gold (not brass) he discovered in Kumassi
> See him quaffing some exhilarating thing,
> And amorously glancing at the houris that are dancing
> For the pleasure of the Peacock King.[75]

Lord Curzon was far too pompous, too proud, British India decided. He couldn't unbend. Whereas Lord Lytton had sprawled on the Viceregal throne, Lord Curzon was the stiffest, straightest Viceroy British India had ever seen. (They didn't know about the steel corset.) He was too short-tempered with his staff, too overbearing, too preoccupied with work. Once, at a large dinner party, Lord Curzon had sat at table oblivious to his guests, correcting a set of proofs.[76] Mary heard these critical mutterings and, like Edith Lytton, soon realized that part of her social role was to counter the Viceroy's faults and ommissions. But whereas Edith had had to be very formal and dignified to counter Lytton's Bohemian frivolity, Mary's role was just the opposite: George was the straight man, so Mary had to be the clown, with just the right amount of laughter and teasing and plenty of radiant smiles.

Mary soon realized that George was totally engrossed in his desk-work, that she had the entire weight of social obligations on *her* slim shoulders; he was the work-horse and she was the party-girl. He routinely returned to his desk after dinner, stayed there till two or three in the morning, worked all day Sunday, worked and worked, had a Napoleon complex which made him feel that he had to run an Empire, govern three hundred million people, three-fifths of the human race, all by himself, that no one under him could be trusted to get anything right. As in England, George usurped Mary's domestic duties and even wrote out the place-cards for dinner-parties. He painstakingly wrote all his dispatches and minutes by hand, just as Lord Canning had, he who was also married to the Word. Mary often thought of poor Charlotte, feeling neglected, longing for her beloved's company, sitting in the gloaming all alone where Mary sat now. Mary's identification with Charlotte grew.

Like Charlotte, Mary had no choice but to accept her fate where George's work was concerned. When he did turn to her for distraction and approval and solace she was always there for him, ready to calm him down after he had demolished a few egos. After one of his "angry days," as he called them, Lord Curzon would ask his Private Secretary what had gone wrong. "Too much *hubris*," wise Walter would candidly reply.[77] But Mary never, ever criticized George with his aching leg and ego. She gave him, always, total approval. He couldn't concede and she couldn't criticize.

Mary watched George growing every more despotic on the public front, and feared, rightly, a corresponding tightening and rigidity on the home front. The Raj had always been a benevolent despotism, but with Lord Curzon cracking the whip, the benevolence had all but disappeared. He ruled India as he ruled its Vicereine: with the expectation of perfect obedience, and no questions asked. He was Supreme Ruler, as Akbar and Aurungzeb had been. "From his [the Viceroy's] lips the Indian people look to learn how and wherefore they are governed," decreed Lord Curzon from the heights,[78] and the Indian people were a long way below. When his Lordship was asked to appoint an Indian, any Indian, to his Council, he replied shortly that none was qualified, nor did he make any protest against the social ostracism of even the most highly educated natives. "We cannot take the Natives up into the administration," he wrote to a friend. "They are crooked-minded and corrupt. We have got therefore to go on ruling them.... I daresay I am talking rather like a schoolmaster, but after all, the millions I have to manage are less than school children.[79] To Mary Indians were *most* inferior persons, there to be laughed at. Lady Curzon, as the *Standard* would note in her obituary, "made a point of collecting any amusing attempts made by Hindus to write English that came under her notice, and had many ludicrous specimens in her scrap-book." Lord Curzon opposed suggestions that Indians be allowed into the higher ranks of the Civil Service as he opposed their growing demands to play an active role in governing. His Excellency refused to heed Sir Walter Lawrence's warning that British rule "rests on an illusion of infallibility and invulnerability."[80] To Lord Curzon it was no illusion. "To me the message is carved in granite, it is hewn out of the rock of doom," his Lordship thundered, "that our work is righteous and that it shall endure."[81]

Nor was the Viceroy alone in his hauteur. Other top Raj officials shared in it. What had begun in Early Raj days as crass commercialism, then changed in Middle Raj to sanctimonious ideals of moral and sacred duty was now, in the Late Raj period, bloated into overweening pride and arrogance – but only in those at the top. Lord Curzon crushed the initiative of those below, the members of the Indian Civil Service, and they responded with growing disillusionment and detachment. Despotism worked better on wives than on bureaucracies and nations. Wives had their love to keep them docile, and to spur them on. The ICS had only their loyalty to keep them plodding ahead, and the native Indians, under Imperious George's rule, had neither. In native hearts, the seeds of resentment and rebellion began to sprout. The Indian National Congress had first met in 1885, and the voices demanding some measure of self-government were growing stronger all during Curzon's reign. The bomb-throwing and shooting incidents which would plague the Raj from now until its end in 1947 had already begun. Four

45 Lord Curzon with his staff and the Rajah of Nabha

years after the end of Curzon's reign, in 1909, would come the first concession to Congress's escalating demands for self-government: the Indian Councils Act, usually known as the Morley-Minto reforms. But as long as Lord Curzon reigned, there would be no concessions. There was no room in India for any will but his; the rest of the Raj, and the natives, would have to learn the lesson Mary had been taught: the binding steel was always there.

Mary would have need of her love and her desire to serve, for the first snaking crack in the Perfect Vicereine's mask had already appeared little more than a month after her arrival. In February, Mary caught a severe fever, had a temperature of 106° and was very ill. Winston Churchill came to stay at Government House that month, and wrote home to his mother: "You would be shocked to see how Lady C. is changed. She has had a sharp attack of fever and will not, I think, stand the climate."[82] Mary was still feeling unwell in March and complained: "I can never have ten days in which to rest and recover from my fever in February but I go working on."[83] It was shortly after this that Mary perversely began, as Charlotte Canning had, to clutch her martyr's mantle of suffering around her, and to enjoy it. "Yesterday I had one of my head-aches," Mary told her parents, but she was duty-bound to attend a formal dinner to which she and George were invited:

> I nearly fainted twice dressing, and nothing but my will carried me through. I was carried to the carriage and had to drive 3 1/2 miles to the house. I thought at times that I should die, as when I arrived I had to shake hands with 70 people and talk all through dinner, and afterwards I had to talk to each lady. The only thing I ate was a water-biscuit and a teaspoonful of brandy. I collapsed in a heap in the carriage on our way home. Our doctor met me at the door and I was carried up to bed.[84]

On March 6th, pale and thin, Mary left for Simla with the children, George to follow later. It was a Simla more splendid than any earlier Vicereine had seen, where civilization had finally con-quered nature. The golden eagles had retreated to more remote areas; little dogs weren't carried off by leopards any more; there were fewer wild flowers on the hill-slopes, for too many *memsahibs* had dug them up for their herbaceous borders. But Simla, now known as "The Abode of the Little Tin Gods," had acquired its Great House. Viceregal Lodge – more palace than lodge – had been built in 1888 by the ruling Viceroy, Lord Dufferin, on Simla's highest hill, so that its lofty inhabitants could look down on the lesser mortals clustered in small bungalows below. The headquar-ters of the Late Raj's Supreme Ruler had expanded to match Late Raj arrogance. Viceregal Lodge had its banqueting hall and ball-room, its towers and cupolas, its gun firing salutes from a shed near the entrance-gates, its acres of garden employing forty gar-deners, with ten more to keep the monkeys from damaging the

46 Viceregal Lodge, Simla

plants, its out-buildings on the grounds for Chief Electrician, the Household Band, the Personal Bodyguard. The Raj had come a long way since Emily Eden had decorated the walls of their modest Simla cottage with paper designs, and the Lyttons had crammed themselves into Peterhof's five bedrooms. Mary set about changing her new castle to suit her own luxurious tastes. She approved of the fact that the Viceroy's work-room upstairs was next to her own sitting-room. "For this thank God and the architect," she wrote happily to George, still in Calcutta.[85]

Mary felt lonely at Simla without George, and too far from the centre spotlight. "My heart has stayed behind so completely that the void in my breast never stops aching," she told him. "Oh! I miss you, and miss you, and have to keep on the jump not to cry."[86] "You made me so happy by telling me you thought I had made a good start the first two months in India," wrote Mary. "Anything I do seems so minute besides all I *want* to do to help."

George reached Simla in mid-April and began at once to raise Simla's pomp to a level only a little less intimidating than Calcutta's. There were now as many servants at Viceregal Lodge as at Government House: four hundred being the necessary complement. The Viceroy saw to it that even the guests at a garden party were properly deferential. Lady Curzon appeared first, receiving guests one at a time as they were announced by an ADC; meanwhile the band played, and people sipped their cold drinks and chatted on the lawn. Then, suddenly a hush came over the crowd and all eyes turned in one direction. The band struck up the National Anthem, and the Viceroy made his dramatic entrance:

> Up walked Lord Curzon in a frock-coat and top-hat, preceded by a single *aide-de-camp* in uniform. The men bared their heads in the sun and made an avenue, through which the Viceroy ... walked to a large *shamiana* and sat down.... Then the band returned to its ordinary promenade music, the people resumed their walking and talking, the refreshment tents regained their crowds, cheerful conversation resumed its buzz, and presently Lady Curzon moved out to converse pleasantly with friends.[87]

The Viceroy permitted no relaxation of formality at Simla, nor of work-load. And as Late Raj social rigidity grew, so grew the bureaucratic forms. For even a simple proposal, there would be twenty pounds of accompanying papers giving comments and addendums. Mary soon came to resent the orderlies who, right after dinner, in long scarlet gowns trimmed with gold lace, marched in single file into the Viceroy's study carrying huge piles of paper for His Excellency's long night's work. "I have perused these papers," wrote Lord Curzon of one particularly high mound, "for two hours and twenty minutes. On the whole, I agree with the gentleman whose signature resembles a trombone."[88] Retreat to formalism:

both socially and politically, the Raj was now, in its final phase, all form and no feeling. The official Word, and the official Rule had triumphed. And Universal Decorum buries All.

But not quite all. Mary's sisters, Daisy and Nancy Leiter, arrived at Simla in April for a visit. "I told them," Mary noted sternly, fearing the worst from their free American ways and high spirits, that "we were the first Americans they had ever seen out here and we could just show them how nice and quiet Americans could be."[89] But the girls didn't listen. They thought the forms hilarious, there to be parodied. At one public ceremony, Nancy and Daisy prostrated themselves in exaggerated homage before their brother-in-law, the august Viceroy. Simla tongues clucked their disapproval: How *dare* these colonial rebels ridicule the Raj! Like naughty schoolchildren, Nancy and Daisy were sent by the Viceroy to their rooms in disgrace. But they were irrepressible. When a Rajah invited them to visit his palace in a remote part of the country, they started off in secret, pursued by a telegram from the Viceroy explaining that this particular Rajah was not *persona grata* with the Government and ordering them to return at once. Sir Walter Lawrence noted sadly in his diary: "Socially the advent of the Leiters has done great harm."[90] Western newspapers got wind of the scandal, and *Vanity Fair* tut-tutted. Mary was very distressed. She herself had managed so magnificently, and now her sisters were negating her fine performance. Even their appearance was at fault: "I am very sorry," Mary disapprovingly told her mother on April 12th, "they have not brought their strings of pearls – they would be as safe as mine and I do not like them to wear those huge sham rows as they are very vulgar and they need their own nice ones. I shall lend them mine whenever I can spare them."[91] Nancy and Daisy departed after seven nervous weeks; Mary heaved a sigh of relief and carried on her Simla social season. She was looking forward to her first Viceregal autumn tour. George, for his part, as October came, was dashing off a note to Pearl Craigie: "My dearest," he began. "One of the few things that have pained us at all – indeed the only thing that has pained us much – since we came to this country, has been your silence. If there was any human being in England ... upon the outward expression of whose affection we relied, it was yourself."[92] That done, he got down to meticulous hour-by-hour planning of the autumn tour. The same inability to relax which kept George chained to his desk for twelve hours a day, kept him, every autumn, criss-crossing India. All Viceroys, after winters in Calcutta and summers in Simla, were expected to go on tour, but no previous one covered as much ground as Lord Curzon. He and Mary visited forty native states, went to remote places no Viceregal pair had visited, chalked up ten thousand miles a year, rarely slept two consecutive nights in the same place. Most of the travelling was done on the Viceregal train, with its twelve massive coaches hauled by two steam engines. The Private and Military Secretaries, two doctors, various servants and some eighty other staff were accommodated on board. Fresh food and hot water for baths boiled up in large vats were taken on at prearranged points. Mary enjoyed these tours more than any other part of her Indian existence, and hardly ever got ill while travelling. She kept a detailed journal of each tour, to be typed up and sent off to her parents. Her diaries reveal her relish of the ever-changing panorama, of the cheering crowds, of her own high energy and excitement. To her the Raj was surely the greatest show on earth. And George was always there at her side, sharing it all.

That fall of 1899 took Mary and George on an eight-week royal progress through Rajputana, ending up at Agra, Cawnpore and Lucknow. On every page of Mary's journal, she mentions the awesome preparations and panoply that attended them. Coolies were set to work weeks ahead building and landscaping so as to please Viceregal eyes; herds of elephants were rounded up, painted in bright colours, given new coverings. An ADC went on ahead to make sure Viceregal protocol was perfect. Books were printed setting out the detailed program for Viceregal happenings. Stationmasters were instructed to hold up traffic while the Viceregal train chugged by. And everywhere there were admiring crowds and splendid retinues. Mary and George laughed together over some

47 Interior of a tent for the Viceregal staff

of the welcoming banners. "God Bless our Horrable Lout" read one, and "A Gal a Day" proclaimed another. They laughed even harder at the native attempts at pomp, so vastly inferior now to Viceregal ones. "It was impossible not to laugh at the grotesque show" was Mary's habitual reaction; "I laughed till I cried" was her school-girlish habitual refrain.[93] Mary's sense of humour, unlike the sophisticated wit of the Eden sisters, relished slapstick more than irony. At a Gwalior military review on November 30th, the native nobles sat on silk-cushioned saddles, and "by the side of everyone who was a sufficiently great swell stood a man holding a giant umbrella of red or yellow satin on the end of a long stick. The effect was *killing*, and I never saw anything so amusing," observed Mary.[94] On every possible occasion, of course, George made one of his inimitable speeches. "George Curzon," declared one friend, "is the only man I know who could make a speech in his

pyjamas without looking ridiculous,"[95] and another friend pronounced George's words "a size too big for his thoughts."[96] Mary,
however, listened attentively to George's every word and gave him
unqualified approval.

So the triumphal autumn tour of 1899 rolled on to its final
frame, and the Calcutta social season clicked into place. "My life
is real hard work I can tell you," Mary remarked at the end of
February 1900. "I get wearied by this incessant entertaining six
months in Simla, three in Calcutta and three on tour," she added,
with a martyr's sigh. She wanted some reward and told her parents
"how awfully I need a brooch or some stomach adornment ... my
'busam' is yearning for 'jools.' "[97] The 1900 autumn tour took
George and Mary along the western coastal regions from Karachi
to Bangalore, a tour of just under six thousand miles by rail, river,
road and sea – six thousand miles and forty more of George's speeches.
The heat that autumn was terrible. "Dressing in it is simply awful,"
complained Mary, "and with broad, swift rivers running down all
over you, it is hard to appear dry and smiling at a daily dinner
party."[98] There were still, however, great compensations. "This
afternoon," she boasted on November 8th, "we drove through the
native town with the Governor's bodyguard and an escort of Bombay cavalry. Millions turned out and cheered us for six miles, and
I believe the enthusiasm has never been equalled in Bombay."[99] She
felt that Viceroy and Vicereine were still riding the crest of their
popularity in spite of the slight undertow of gossip. As they drove
through Calcutta's streets on their return in December, the arches
erected to welcome them "opened just at the right moment and
dropped rose petals on our heads, while on every side cheering
crowds waved signs saying: 'Hail to the Indefatigable Viceroy.' "[100]

It was fortunate for them that the Viceregal Pair couldn't see
what Sir Walter Lawrence, one of a growing body of disenchanted
Raj officials, was writing in his diary on January 7, 1901. "Travelling in the pomp and ceremony of the Viceroy's train," he commented on the tour just ended, "one sees India garnished and white-
washed and men are not real but are playing a game of pageants.

... It is all show and play-acting and I get sick of it." "Our Government," he continued, "is out of touch with the country.... Office work and frequent transfers are making our officials real aliens and we have lost influence and power ever since I left India in 1895." "There is a general consensus abroad," he added, "that the Viceroy is of an imperious temperament and he has often admitted to the possession of a large amount of *hubris*. They call him Imperial George but they fear and respect him. Everywhere, I feel that my Chief is unpopular."[101]

While Sir Walter penned his morose sentiments, his Chief slept soundly and smugly in his bed. Two weeks later, however, on January 23, he was awakened abruptly at four A. M. to be told of Queen Victoria's death. Sixty-four years had passed since Emily and Fanny Eden had eagerly read their English letters at Rajmahal giving news of the young Queen's accession. Now, in the days following Her Majesty's death, the Viceroy received eight hundred telegrams of condolence from his loyal subjects. It was a relief, "like the clowning in one of Shakespeare's tragedies," according to Sir Walter, to come across one telegram which read: "In the words of the poet we shall never look like her again."[102] Within a week of the Queen's death, George was circulating a letter to heads of local governments outlining his Grand Scheme: to build the Victoria Memorial Hall in Calcutta, a huge museum to commemorate the Raj and its long-lived Empress. It was to be, according to Lord Curzon's decree, "the finest structure that has been reared in India since the days of the Moghuls, and the most splendid and concrete monument of British rule."[103] A large statue of Lord Curzon, Viceroy Extraordinary, who had thought it all up, would stand at the entrance. Mary, for her part, started a memorial to Queen Victoria of a more humble, self-effacing nature than George's, a fund for providing Indian women with midwives. Later Mary expanded her scheme to include nursing care for Europeans in up-country stations. She convened a committee at Simla, attended all their meetings, raised a great deal of money; Lady Minto, her successor, who brought the scheme to fruition, received most of the credit.[104]

48 Lord Curzon in Star of India robes.

In March of that year, 1901, Mary was feeling the debilitating effects of such strenuous socializing in such a difficult climate. She was also pregnant again. She knew how desperately George wanted a son and heir for Kedleston. So, as a precaution, Mary and her two little daughters sailed for a six-month stay in England.

It was a terrible wrench for Mary to leave George. She was now experiencing, whether or not she realized it, one of the worst trials for the *memsahibs* of British India. "Separation is the dark cloud which hangs over an Indian existence," writes H.S. Cunningham in *Chronicles of Dustypore*, "husbands and wives, mothers and children, forced asunder, perhaps at the very time when union is most delightful."[105] Mary had already experienced the milder form of separation common to most *memsahibs* who routinely repaired to hill stations while their husbands stayed working in the hot plains. Now Mary was feeling that more painful parting: taking the children to England while the husband stayed in India. Maud Diver sees this "tragic shadow of separation" hanging over husband and wife as the "keynote" of life in British India, and "always a tragedy."[106] For the woman "whose heart is balanced equally between the two great loves of her life," namely husband and child, it is a terrible choice, for no matter which way she chooses, the *memsahib* cannot "escape the poisoned arrows of regret."[107] In this respect, Mary was perhaps luckier than most; George had probably made the decision for her.

Her mental suffering, nevertheless, was intense and affected her health. En route to England, Mary was suddenly taken so ill that she felt sure she was dying, and dictated her will. She had a miscarriage, and her spirits floundered in that desert familiar to Charlotte Canning, also unable to give her husband the son he wanted. "Never mind, my husband, next time, next time," Mary wrote to George, when she could bear to write at all,[108] but her tears still flowed. She had never felt so desolate.

"This is your great Budget speech day," she wrote to George on March 27th, trying to rekindle her interest. "I shall tingle with impatience until I can read the great speech." George obliged by sending her newspaper reports of his sixty-five minute oration.[109] "Darling, before you think of coming back in August do regard your health," he wrote from Simla in mid-May. "You must recover it, build it up, lay the scaffolding for itty boy – sacrifice everything to that."[110] Mary had her orders; she spent a miserable time that July at Ems, a spa guaranteed to induce fertility. "I have never known so foul a place – and I never leave this little brown coloured room save for a bath or a gargle of vile water," Mary complained to George. "I hope the patron saint of Ems will not retaliate and give me no twin sons because I hate the place so."[111] George sent her additional orders: "There is no limit to the influence which you can exercise at home, as you have done in India," he told Mary, "smoothing down those whom I ignore or offend."[112] She did as she was bid: she took on a new role, became George's conciliator and mediator with the London powers-that-be, doing what she could to plump up his sagging popularity and explain his motives, echoing all his judgments like a parrot. She heard "the silly tales" circulating in London "about our foolish formality and stiffness."[113] King Edward himself was circulating a story that "old Sandbags" (Colonel Sandbach) had left India because Lord Curzon made him stand behind his chair at lunch and dinner, "Sandbags" being his Military Secretary. "I really would almost prefer it were said that like Lord Lytton I kissed every pretty woman," complained George from Simla.[114] He consoled himself at the end of March with a Nepal tiger-shoot, but the first tiger he bagged was "very fat and old and a poor colour (a pale drab)." George complained to Mary that the tiger "showed no pluck and was so stately in his movements that he might almost have been drugged."[115] Fit symbol of the dispirited Indian princes beyond the Viceregal court.

Mary did her best, as she flitted from one London drawing-room to the next, to defend the Viceroy's grand style of living, his autocratic rule and even his frontier policies. But it was hard work; no one in England, including its Sovereign, cared about India any more. "Neither King or Queen know anything about India," Mary complained to George.[116] If, in India, the Late Raj was all pageant and formalism, in England it was all too boring to pay attention to. Britain was focused instead on "King Edward the Caresser's" antics with Mrs Keppel. Only the Viceroy himself, it seemed, was still dancing to Empire ideals. "How few are there who know anything or care anything about the British dominion in India, though it is the miracle of the world," he observed that September.[117] He had achieved his ambition, but too late, and paid, perhaps, too high a price. "Grind, grind, grind, with never a word of encouragement," George wrote to Mary, sinking into a warm bath of self-pity, "on on on till the collar breaks and the poor beast stumbles and dies…. Sometimes when I think of myself spending my heart's blood here, and no one caring one little damn, the spirit goes out of me…. I am crying now so that I can scarcely see the page."[118] "I feel fearfully adrift away off here in England alone," Mary reciprocated, in the True-Woman vein which she knew George loved to hear. "There is no one I can depend on or get any help from … and all the thousand things that have to be done I must do unaided."[119] "A man can know a woman well," she told him,

> because her life – consequently the interests which mould her mind and conceive her thought – are more or less simple. A man's life is so complex, and much of it lies outside the woman's sphere…. But what is within her grasp has the power of making her truly happy. But take her away from it all and give her a blank six months in search of health, and she must feel that she has nearly lost her anchorage.[120]

With rare understatement, George admitted, in one letter to Mary, that his ambitions involved "considerable self-sacrifice and some subordination" on the part of anyone allied to him.[121] "You are a ruler and an achiever and you are the only man living who is writing *choses faites* on the slate of time," Mary encouraged him.[122]

When they weren't congratulating each other during that 1901 separation, the Curzons were criticizing the rest of the world, themselves united in a smug little twosome. "Harris is quite incompetent as Steward," George told Mary, "can't spell, can't keep accounts, and generally has no idea what to do beyond drop his h's and be in the wrong place."[123] Mary told George that Lady Roberts, wife of the famous "Bobs," was a "vulgar old snob," that George Hamilton, Secretary of State for India, was a "hopeless dotard" and "a small-minded, ferret-faced roving-eyed mediocrity." "I buttered the grim idiot," Mary continued, "by saying you appreciated his capital letters. He was delighted."[124] She recorded Henry Asquith's reckless consumption of champagne and his reckless midnight foray, down the hall in the country house where they were both staying, to pretty Pamela Plowden's room.[125] Mary's claws came out farthest, however, on the subject of George's old flame, Pearl Craigie. They met at Jennie Cornwallis-West's one night – Jennie had divorced Churchill and remarried – and Mary was shocked to see how Pearl had altered, with a "face so broad that it takes your eye several seconds to get across it – especially as a heavy moustache arrests your vision.... She was robed in a white gown without shape, which hung from the shoulder to ankle in a straight line and made her look like a caterpillar, her head was wreathed with white and cloth *ivy* leaves, so the whole effect was awful."[126] Mary's own superb taste in clothes had been recognized by Queen Alexandra herself, who had, Mary proudly told George, commissioned her to have the Queenly Coronation gown and several others made and embroidered in India. Mary also informed George in a rare burst of independence that she couldn't return in August as planned; the weather would be still too hot and her health would suffer. Instead, she went off to misty Scotland, and rented Braemar Castle. George replied in September that he was "exhausted and rather run down ... I have had serious pains all down my right leg, particularly between the knee and ankle. Just now they are paining me greatly, and I cannot stand for more than about two minutes at a time.... It all means over-strain."[127] Her consort needed her; Mary and her daughters left England on September 26th, and on October 15th, she was reunited with her beloved husband at Simla.

The autumn tour that year took them to Burma. Mary loved

the golden cone-shaped pagodas, and the ceremonial barge on the Irrawaddy river shaped like a giant swan, but her health was strained. "The heat takes it out of me terribly, but I keep up, though India saps every ounce of strength," she wrote.[128] More and more, she was feeling that physical lethargy which had conquered Emily Eden.

In March 1902, Mary accompanied George to Hyderabad, whose Nizam, a far cry from his splendid ancestors, was "a very small, shy little man, who seldom speaks" and who wore a simple black frock-coat "without any of the gorgeous ornaments usually inseparable from Oriental majesty."[129] George liked to have Mary always at his side on these tours, so she was there when he went on a tiger-shoot organized by the Nizam. The temperature went up to 100°; Mary protected herself with "black glasses, a huge helmet ... a thick wadded curtain over my head, and a thick umbrella and ice in my mouth."[130] One day she had to walk with George in that heat two miles through thick jungle, scorching her shoes. There would be no moment of elation for Mary as there had been for Fanny Eden on her Rajmahal tiger-hunt. Quite the contrary. After a tiger had appeared then disappeared, several of the *shikaris* (native hunters) "boldly descended from the elephants to direct the beat." Suddenly the tiger leapt out upon a *shikari*, and Mary saw "the great jaws close on the back of the man's head.

> I said to George, "the tiger has killed a man", but he had not seen it and said "I think you are mistaken". In the meantime four seconds were passing while both man and beast were in sickening silence behind a rock. Then back came the tiger, slowly trotting, again Captain Wigram shot, and although the shot killed, the tiger got back to his cave.... Slowly we lurched forward round the rocks, and there lay a man stone dead, his head half gone.[131]

That image of death haunted Mary long after she'd returned to Simla's luxury. According to Sir Walter Lawrence, Cassandra-like prophet, all was not well at Simla. "Baker-Carr [an ADC] and Jenn

[Viceregal physician] dismally reiterate Lady Curzon's unpopularity and her sins of omission and commission," Lawrence wrote in his diary. "I do not encourage nor repel these confidences but they are horrible and useless for I cannot tell either the Viceroy or Lady Curzon."[132] What these "sins" were is not known.

By the summer of 1902, Mary was sinking farther into lethargy. "No one knows how I loathe Simla and its cruel climate," she told her mother. "I never feel well here."[133] To her father she confided: "George never does any social functions of any sort and they all devolve on me. I do them all. He has not gone out once since he came back, so I go through all the endlessly long list, bravely making his excuses and telling no one how he suffers and works. Duty is a wonderful incentive.... So I go out to races, parties, concerts, weddings, prize-givings, polo-matches and the Lord knows what. It is all work and very little pleasure."[134] The note of self-pity was growing louder.

In August, Mary accompanied George to Kashmir whose Maharajah "is about 4 feet high and addicted to opium, which he takes at one o'clock and is under its influence until about 7. As he came to meet me at 5," Mary noted in her journal, "he was in a very torpid condition."[135] India's rajahs were now as sad a lot as India's "drugged" old tigers. The Rana of Dholpur had died the previous year of acute pneumonia and alcoholism. "One more of the disastrous consequences of English tastes, habits and sports upon an undisciplined native mind," wrote George in didactic vein.[136] As soon as the Rana was dead, the Maharani of Dholpur had gone straight to her room, taken poison and died one-and-a-half hours later; she was twenty-five, her husband thirty-nine. The Maharajah of Patiala, whose proud ancestor Emily Eden had sketched on his elephant, also died in 1902, "after a short life of debauchery," of "racing and drinking, polo and debts. It is to be hoped," Mary continued sanctimoniously, "that the new Raja, only ten, will grow up a greater credit to British training than his father did."[137] Some of the depressed, dislocated rajahs tried to forget their loss of power and prestige by running off to Europe's naughty playgrounds, until

Lord Curzon passed an edict saying they had to have his permission to do so. "For what are they but a set of unruly and ignorant and rather undisciplined schoolboys?" demanded the Viceroy, defending his new rule.[138] "Curzon treated these Princes as dogs" was the verdict of one British visitor who stayed with the Maharaja of Bikaner. "He irritated them, annoyed them, interfered with their domestic affairs and ground them down."[139] The myth of the British Raj had changed now. In the Early Raj period, the Edens' time, the inspiring myth was the pull of the exotic East's splendour and spices, of its imaginative and commercial potential. The British wanted what the Rajahs possessed: wealth and power. In the Late Raj period, the myth was the Might and Majesty of the British Raj itself, which had to be maintained and which, to some observers at least, seemed to be fraying at the edges.

Not that Lord Curzon thought so. He had been very busy ever since August 1901, making plans for a grand Delhi Durbar to be held in January 1903, ostensibly to celebrate King Edward VII's coronation. British India quickly dubbed it "the Curzonation," knowing full well who would be in the Durbar's centre spotlight. King Edward obliged by sending word he couldn't come but would dispatch the Duke of Connaught to represent him. Lord Curzon determined to make *his* Durbar the greatest show of Might and Majesty India had ever seen. In those remaining months of 1902, Mary felt especially neglected as George spent even longer hours than usual at his desk detailing his Durbar plans in seventy-seven pages of print. "He supervised everything for that Durbar," his daughter Irene would later write, "the design of a railing, the width of a road, the pattern of a carving, the colour of a plaster, the planting of a flower bed, the decoration of a pole."[140] If everything was to be done properly, His Excellency would have to do it all himself. Nor would he make any of Lord Lytton's blunders. Lord Curzon's Durbar would be all very dignified indeed with no elements of farce. The amphitheatre built for the Proclamation ceremonies would be a simple, tasteful structure in white and gold with

faint leanings to Moghul design. "I do not propose," Lord Curzon
wrote, "to make any presentation of banners to the Chiefs";[141] he
himself had seen too many of Lytton's silly banners gathering dust
in native Treasuries around the country.

While George was organizing everything in his peremptory
way, Mary planned her costumes. Then, suddenly on the very eve
of the Durbar she fell ill. On December 17th, she wrote in self-
dramatizing tone to George from Dehra Dun where she was resting:

> Every bit of my vitality has gone, and I am iller than I have
> ever been, and simply can't get back to life somehow. I hope
> the poison has not killed my spirit. My hand weighs a ton,
> and I cannot write or think but do think of a miraculous cure
> before you come: it *must* come! I *know* it will! I believe abso-
> lutely in my power of "coming up to time" or answering my
> ring, as an actor does. Some day though, the bell will go and
> I shall not appear, as India, I know, slowly but surely murders
> women. But I suppose many humble and inconsequent lives
> must always go into the foundations of all great works and
> great buildings and great achievements. Bring back a magic
> cure for poor broken Kinkie![142]

Subtly, slowly, insidiously, Mary's concept of her role was
changing. First, she had been the princess who finds her prince and
lives happily ever after in their beautiful English castle. Then, she
had been Sweetheart to a Sun-King and an Empire, serving and
serene. Now her inspiring myth had changed again. Mary saw
herself as another Charlotte Canning, as the Empire heroine who
makes the supreme sacrifice, thereby securing forever the love of
one neglectful, workaholic husband and one attentive, admiring
nation. Mary was caught now, irrevocably, in the meshes of the
Raj myth. Since Charlotte's example, the Raj myth had centred
clearly on self-sacrifice, and sentimentalized it to extremes. A flood
of memoirs and autobiographies written by prominent Indian Civil

Service officials appeared every year now, and all of them were full of bombastic self-advertisement and cloying self-pity. These memoirs didn't just give the facts; they manufactured a legend, turned all their subjects into heroes and heroines, ready to suffer and die for Empire ideals. Mary had read many of them, and she who had as a child scribbled of knights-errant got caught up in their crusade. Later, her husband would add his epic to the pile: two weighty quarto volumes entitled *British Government in India*. His treatise would, Lord Curzon declared therein, be written in vain "if it does not disclose to the British public how their principal servants in India have endured as well as wrought, have suffered as well as served."[143] "Over the Viceregal throne," wrote his Lordship, pulling out his handkerchief, "there hangs not only a canopy of broidered gold but a mist of human tears." The task of government was "not a pageant alone, but as often a pain."[144]

Mary Curzon had tripped eagerly into her prominent place in that pageant; now she was caught up in the pain, proceeding slowly, like a Hindu widow bent on *suttee*, towards the sacrificial funeral pyre which British India's myth and native India's fatalism and her own romanticism had prepared for her. "India, I know, slowly but surely murders women," Mary wrote. It had murdered Charlotte Canning and it would murder her. From now on, that thought circled in her head.

George, too, seemed bent on self-destruction, though of a milder sort. His disagreements and tussles with London's Indian Council and Secretary of State for India were accelerating as he grew ever more despotic. One current argument centred on who should pay, England's government or India's, for the Delhi Durbar's invited Indian guests. Lord Curzon won that round, but when the Cabinet rejected his proposal to announce a tax reduction at the Durbar, he hysterically threatened to resign, went sulking off to Delhi declaring that he did so "without the slightest ray of pleasurable anticipation, and with a feeling of indifference."[145] So off they went to the Durbar festivities, the Superior Viceroy, cross and apathetic, the Superior Vicereine, weary and ill, both of them not so much ready to enjoy the pageant and suffer the pain, as to suffer the pageant and enjoy the pain.

From England, on the *SS Arabia*, came eighty distinguished British guests, bringing with them forty-seven tons of dresses and uniforms for Durbar galas. Among them were the Duke and Duchess of Marlborough, the Duke and Duchess of Portland, Lord and Lady Derby, Lord and Lady Crewe, and other members of the Curzon's set. *And* Pearl Craigie, whom Henry James had just immortalized as Milly Theale in *The Wings of the Dove*. Pearl had stepped on board swathed in furs with Lord Stanley in her train bearing huge bunches of violets. Pearl was to write a series of articles on the Durbar for London's *Daily Graphic* and New York's *Collier's Weekly*. These would later appear in book form under the title *Imperial India*, and Pearl's usual pseudonym of "John Oliver Hobbes."

The Durbar's first event, on December 29th, was the State Entry into Delhi, a splendid procession of gaily painted elephants with flowered trunks, all of them drugged to keep them docile in the crowds. (The drugged elephants were, however, luckier than their dead fellows. The British had now taken to having elephant feet made into umbrella-stands and elephant penises into golf-bags.) There were in all fifty-five Ruling Chiefs in the procession. Pearl thought them

> a horrible medley of the infernal and the grotesque, the ancient barbaric and the modern vulgar, the superb and the squalid, the manifestation of power without glory, and rank without graces, of riches without beauty, of pomp without philosophy, and pride without strength.[146]

One Maharajah, drugged with opium, had, according to Pearl "a loyal, beneficent smirk, which could neither fade nor falter."[147] Some rajahs wore tiaras they had bought in Paris rather than native jewels. Sitting above everyone, on the biggest elephant in the procession, the old giant who had carried Robert and Edith Lytton through Delhi's streets in 1877 was Mary Curzon. She was less critical than Pearl, feeling only the rush and flush of her own essential drug: the crowd's adulation. Her illness and lassitude forgotten, suddenly she felt buoyed up, brilliant as a diamond, ready to sparkle to perfection. There she was, poised and beautiful as always, seated beside George in the same silver-gilt *howdah* Lord Lytton had used, although George had had Ceres and Minerva melted down and replaced by "fresh, more artistic figures."[148] The saddle-cloth on their elephant was crimson velvet, so stiff with rampant lions embroidered in gold that hardly any of the background cloth was visible.[149] (Fitting Late Raj artefact, that: more symbol than substance!) Mary knew that she drew all eyes, "smiling and radiant," wearing "a white dress with a lace fichu, caught on either side with bunches of real violets" and holding "a parasol of white, with bunches of violets painted on the panels."[150] On the steps of the Jama Masjid, India's largest mosque, little Irene and Cynthia Curzon stood; in a carefully calculated theatrical gesture, Mary kissed her hand to them as she passed.[151]

The procession ended at the Viceregal camp grounds, all very splendid with electric lights and tramways and coolies to flick the dust off all the flowers with red-feather dusters. A memento still extant, a red-leather, gold-trimmed account-book, gives us some idea of the luxurious standard insisted upon by Lord and Lady Curzon. It lists the prices paid for seventy-two satin toilet covers, fifty damask teapot covers, eighty-four dozen pastry doilies, two hundred white damask tray cloths, fifty satin counterpanes.[152]

On January 1, 1903 came the great Durbar itself, held exactly where Lord Lytton's circus had performed. The multitude gathered at eleven A.M., twenty-six thousand in all, everyone clicking cameras, with massed bands and choirs to keep them amused until the stars arrived on stage. It *was* rather crass, Pearl Craigie decided, that the Rajahs wearing the most jewels got the loudest applause as they took their seats. Finally, as a hush came over the crowd, Lord and Lady Curzon drove into the arena in a four-horse carriage with outriders in scarlet and gold. Mary wore pale blue chiffon heavily embroidered in Indian gold-work. Everyone rose and cheered

49 "The Royal Salute: The Viceroy and Duke of Connaught
Acknowledging the Unfurling of the Royal Standard at the Delhi
Durbar" (drawing by Melton Prior for Illustrated London News)

as they slowly ascended the central dais, while the massed bands played the National Anthem. Mary sat down next to the Duchess of Connaught; the Viceroy bowed regally to the Duchess and to the audience, then regally took *his* seat on a throne upholstered in red velvet and ornamented with golden crown and silver lotus leaves. All very grand; all very tasteful. Drums rolled, bugles sounded, bands and choirs thumped and trumpeted and sang. Lord Kitchener, the Army's Commander-in-Chief, had thought "Onward Christian Soldiers" would be apt, but Lord Curzon had vetoed that quickly enough. It would never do to have the words: "Crowns and Thrones may perish / Kingdoms rise and wane" falling *fortissimo* on native ears.[153] After the singing, a gold-embroidered herald rode up on a black charger with scarlet-and-gold drummer and twelve trumpeters behind him, and read the Proclamation declaring King Edward VII King of England and Emperor of India. Then came a pæan of trumpets, another go at "God Save the King" and an imperial salute. Then the Viceroy stood up, rested his shorter leg on a silver footstool, and rolled forth his usual rodomontade prose. Mary sat happily mute and marvelling, conscious of twenty-six thousand pairs of eyes upon her. What a show the British could mount! It almost made her wish Americans had never left the fold! And certainly it was all "at least five or six times as great as Lord Lytton's Durbar" as the *Daily Telegraph* had predicted.[154]

The festivities went on for two weeks – polo, cricket and hockey matches, receptions, garden parties, dinners, balls, fireworks – until everyone became "simply gorged with gaiety. There was too much of it."[155] The fireworks, on January 2nd, set off with the Jama Masjid mosque as background, were particularly splendid. A large program had been printed in red and black on thick, creamy paper for the guests. It announced that "Special Colossal Fire Portraits of His Excellency the Right Honourable the Lord Curzon of Kedleston and of the Right Honourable the Lady Curzon" were to be "carried out in lines of brilliant fire," so that His and Her Excellencies had the rare privilege of seeing themselves go up in flames: a vicarious kind of *suttee* which perhaps had its own *frisson* for self-sacrificing Empire idealists.

For two glorious weeks, Mary floated about the tents and grounds, always beautiful, always perfectly dressed, always smiling, always calm. Even her mother and sisters were awed by this queenly being, and certainly Mortimer Menpes, despatched from England to paint the usual durbar portraits, came under her spell:

> Lady Curzon swept into the room, a vision of beauty in the palest of lilac gowns. She ... by her ready tact and sympathy soon dispelled my nervousness and made the way smooth. What an ideal wife for a Viceroy, I thought! She was looking extremely well, not in the least fatigued; and when I asked her if she did not feel the effects of the Durbar she said that work was meat and drink to her.[156]

Pearl Craigie approved of Mary's wardrobe – "Lady Curzon always wears elaborately woven or embroidered materials," she noted – [157] but criticized her behaviour. Pearl wrote to her close friend the Rev. W.F. Brown that Mary was flirting outrageously with Captain Armstrong, a handsome young Army doctor who had come out on the SS *Arabia* with Pearl. Captain Armstrong had confided to Pearl that Mary "had the coarsest mind and *ways* of any woman he had ever known of *any* class. Curious. She looks so flower-like," concluded Pearl.[158] The refined *grande dame*, it seems, was not quite perfect in her role.

For Mary, the climax of the Delhi Durbar, indeed, the climax of her Indian reign, was the State Ball, held on the evening of January 6th. She thought the setting for her performance perfect: Delhi's Moghul Palace, the Emperor Shah Jehan's supreme creation, a many-pillared pleasure-house, with polished white marble walls inlaid with amethyst, agate, onyx, cornelian and jasper. And if the Peacock Throne was long gone, there was, instead, Mary Victoria Leiter, Lady Curzon, Vicereine of India, making a grand entrance

50 *"The Viceroy's Durbar Ball in the Delhi Palace. Dancing the State*

Lancers" (drawing by Melton Prior for Illustrated London News)

in her peacock dress, while four thousand guests gasped in admiration, and ladies stood on their chairs to see. Lady Curzon, with her Lord in white satin knee-breeches, arrived at ten P.M. to the strains of the National anthem, while guests parted to form a lane down the centre of the room, and the Viceregal party proceeded to the marble podium. They led off the dancing, the State Lancers, with the Viceroy dancing with the Duchess of Connaught, and the Vicereine with the Duke.

"You cannot conceive what a dream she looked," wrote one guest describing Mary. "Such beauty is not given to one woman in a million," exclaimed another.[159] The journalist Perceval Landon wrote to Mary afterwards: "The Diwan-i-Khas (or Hall of Audience), at the moment when your peacock feather dress moved across it, was the zenith of the sheer beauty of the whole time."[160] Even Pearl Craigie was impressed: "Among the many charming beings to be seen in the vast crowd, the woman who presented the most romantic appearance and embodied the romantic ideal was Lady Curzon herself," she wrote.[161] This was Mary Leiter Curzon's big scene. Above her coroneted head, as she danced around the room, were Persian words engraved in gold: "If there be a paradise on earth, it is this, it is this, it is this."

Like the setting, Mary Curzon's costume was perfect too. She had spent weeks designing, supervising the work, and having fittings on her gown. Her peacock dress was the supreme creation of her Vice-Reign and of her life. It was made of cloth-of-gold, embroidered by Delhi's superb craftsmen, with metal threads and real emeralds in an all-over pattern of peacock feathers so that the cloth beneath had virtually disappeared. The bodice was trimmed with lace, the hem with white roses. Once the dress was finished to her satisfaction, Mary posed for a series of photographs. She also commissioned a large portrait in oils; it shows her standing with her heavy train furled regally around her feet.

Earlier that evening, as she had dressed for her grandest entrance, Mary had looked into the mirror and seen a Queen: crowned in diamonds, covered in emeralds. She saw reflected there the public

51 Portrait of Lady Curzon in her peacock dress (by William Logsdail)

figure, for the public figure was now, after four years in India, almost all there was to see; Mary Victoria had never had much inner core to call her own, and the Vicereine's role had overlaid it like a pearl's nacre round a grain of sand. On that evening of January 6, 1903, much as the whole British Raj had fallen victim to its public image, Mary Curzon fell victim to hers. One cause, as stated, was her own absorption in the Vicereine's role, but another was the Viceroy's absorption in his. Despotic George had, particularly since they came to India, ground his heel so often and so firmly into Mary's delicate ego, that now it was permanently flattened. He had stamped on her initiative and independence as he had on that of the Raj bureaucracy serving under him, and the result was the same: nothing remained but ritual and resignation. As in the case of Edith Lytton, Raj and Ruler had conspired together to change the personality of their Vicereine for the worse. Edith's ego had grown iron-clad and inflexible; Mary's had almost disappeared.

The Durbar had cost £180,000, a modest cost, maintained the Viceroy, considering its splendour. But British and American newspapers accused Curzon of staging the Durbar for his own glory, not the King's. The *New York Journal* leapt to the defence of "the starving Indians who had asked for bread and been given a durbar. Such extravagance is a shameful manifestation of the cruelty of Lord Curzon's craze for imperialistic display."[162] Lord Curzon stood his ground: "The sound of the trumpets has already died away. The Captains and the Kings have departed. But the effect produced by this overwhelming display of unity and patriotism is still alive and will not perish," he intoned solemnly.[163] Privately, George and Mary patted each other on the back. "Every civilian in India knows to whom the credit is due, and your position today in India is stronger than any man's has ever been," Mary told him. "As you say," George replied, "it was a great success, and if ever the policy of doing everything oneself down to the smallest detail was justified, it was here. But after all," he continued generously, throwing a bouquet her way, "for the splendid triumph on the social side,

LADY'S PICTORIAL

A NEWSPAPER FOR THE HOME.

SATURDAY, JANUARY 10, 1903.

THE IMPERIAL DURBAR.—THE LATEST PORTRAIT OF LADY CURZON, TAKEN AT DELHI, BY BARON A. DE MEYER.

yours is the credit. Your beauty, your charm, your absolute un-
selfishness in looking after others, and your sure and unfailing
tact – these it was that carried through the whole camp life."[164]
Beyond the Curzon's complacent little duo, however, the grumbling continued. "Our friends are now beginning to return from
the Durbar," wrote the Prime Minister, Arthur Balfour. "They
seem unanimous on two things 1) that the show was the best show
that ever was shown 2) that George is the most unpopular Viceroy
ever seen."[165]

Pearl Craigie scribbled her criticisms, packed up her notes, and
went to stay, at the Viceroy's invitation, at Calcutta's Government
House till February 7th. "The Viceroy has had me next to him
three times at dinner and twice at lunch this week – which is considered a compliment," Pearl told her father.[166] To the Rev. W.F.
Brown, she confided her belief that George was desperately unhappy, that his marriage to Mary had proved to be "loveless" and
"tragic." "He is bored to death by her," Pearl declared.[167] A grand
costume ball at Government House on January 26th duplicated the
one given a hundred years before by Lord Wellesley. The Viceroy
was dressed in exact imitation of Wellesley's portrait hanging in
the Council Chamber, and 1,500 guests bowed solemnly to that
sham figure.

As soon as Mary got to Simla, the fever-pitch of durbars and
balls was followed by total collapse. "I do not see a living soul day
in, day out, and have now been flat on my back in bed or on a sofa
for one whole month," she told her mother. "I sometimes wonder
if I am the same person who lived through the gaieties of Delhi as
I lie here in the silence."[168] George was growing ever more irritable
and insomniac, flying into rages over Whitehall's interference with
his plans. Mary hated to see him like that; the sooner he left India
the better. They were slated to leave at the end of 1903, when their
five-year term would be finished. In April, George wrote to the
Prime Minister asking to be allowed to stay for a further two years
to complete his reforms. But not until June did the Prime Minister
tell Lord Curzon that he would extend his term as Viceroy. Staying

53 Lord and Lady Curzon with their staff, in the Persian Gulf, 1903

on, George told a friend, "is a prospect, not of exhilaration, but of duty; for people will have become tired of being kept up to the mark long before then, and I shall probably have broken down."[169] The irresistible Raj myth: pulling the Peacock King and Queen together towards the funeral pyre.

Their duty-rounds continued. In November and December 1903, Lord and Lady Curzon toured the Persian Gulf to plump up British prestige there. Mary was five months pregnant, so lay all day in a lounge chair aboard the *Hardinge*, either in her cabin or on deck. Her cabin was twenty-four feet long, "hung with the most lovely pink brocade – and pink furniture – writing table, long mirror, beautiful bed and pink satin sofa." But this pink cocoon didn't really help; Mary knew how despairing George would be if she didn't produce a son.

On January 10, 1904, Mary left India to await her March confinement in England. George would join her for a four-month furlough beginning in May, returning with her in September for his second term. "I watched your carriage lights as far as I could see them flitting between the Botanical trees," Mary wrote on board the boat taking her down the Hooghly river and away from George. "And then despair settled down on me with the evening mist and there was nothing to do but to put my wet face to bed."[170] "I pray in these words every day," George wrote to Mary, "may she bear a child to Thy honour and glory and to the good of Thy kingdom, and may it be a male child."[171] On March 20th, Mary was safely delivered of her third baby: another girl.

When George reached England as planned in mid-May, he was shocked by Mary's appearance, for she looked "thin, yellow, frail."[172] Away from his work, George was miserable. "What am I to do? What am I to do?" he muttered frantically, over and over, as he paced up and down.[173] He cheered up when the King made him Warden of the Cinque Ports. He accepted the post – there was no salary attached – because of his vanity, for it had been held by such famous men as the younger Pitt and the Duke of Wellington. As usual, Mary had no say in George's decision, but liked the idea of living in Walmer Castle, the Warden's residence, and went at once to inspect it. "I spent such a happy afternoon in the darling old castle," she told George's brother. "I simply loved it. I never dreamed it was so pretty and fascinating. How George and I will adore it … and we shall be happy there," she decided, resurrecting, for the moment, the princess's first myth.[174] On Saturday, July 2nd, following the ceremony, luncheon and speeches at Dover, whereby George took office, the Curzons hosted a dinner party at Walmer Castle. To make his day complete, Mary told George that she was already pregnant again, even though Alexandra – "Baba" they called her – was only three months old. Mary was doing her best to give George a son.

Mary was busy supervising improvements to Walmer Castle before they moved in, when she heard of her father's death on June

9th, at Bar Harbour, Maine. Her dearly beloved father; she hadn't seen him for nearly six years. He left a million dollars in his will for his favourite daughter; Mary would have the annual interest from that, plus an additional seventy-five thousand dollars yearly.[175] There would be even more when her mother died. Lord Curzon now had a very rich wife indeed.

On July 20th, Lord Curzon was given another honour, freedom of the City of London, and stressed in his acceptance speech that the Empire was "not a moribund organism." "Let no man admit the craven fear that those who have won India cannot hold it," he proclaimed. "That is not the true reading of history. That is not my forecast of the future."[176]

Mary was ill throughout the summer, complaining of great weariness and weakness and spent many days confined to her Walmer Castle bedroom. On the day on which the Curzon's luggage was dispatched to Marseilles to be loaded onto the liner taking them back to India, on that afternoon of September 21st, Mary went for a drive along the Kentish coast, feeling chilled and unwell. Suddenly she started hæmorrhaging, and in the early hours of September 22nd, she had a miscarriage. She called George to her bedside and told him she was dying. Her extremities were icy cold, her pulse weak, her voice no more than a whisper. George resorted at once to the written word. He grabbed paper and pencil and wrote down every syllable of Mary's last wishes. He covered thirty-four sheets. In the end, as in the beginning, would be the Word. The children, Mary murmured, were not to return to India. "Ask Mama as my last wish to come and take them to some warm place and look after them," Mary told George. She gave detailed instructions for the disposal of her jewels. "I have suffered so much, so much. I must surely go to Heaven," she added. "Keep the feathers [peacock dress] picture of me – that is the best," she told him, her voice growing a little stronger.[177]

For ten days, Mary's life hung in the balance. She contracted peritonitis, possibly from the effluvia flowing from an old, filthy drain beneath her bedroom window. Walmer Castle had been built by Henry VIII; its history was romantic but its plumbing was rank. In addition to peritonitis, Mary developed severe phlebitis in one leg. Surgeons performed two operations, but she didn't improve. More doctors were called in but none of them had either explanation or prescription for her failure to mend. Then pneumonia set in. "I am worn out with anguish and suspense," wrote George.[178] "Lord Curzon bears his anxiety with great fortitude," the London *Standard* had reported on September 26th, "and finds time to attend personally to Government Despatches, several of which have been received by him during the past week." Daily bulletins on Lady Curzon's progress were printed in all the British and Indian newspapers, just as if she were royalty. Telegrams and letters poured into Walmer Castle. Lady Curzon's popularity reached a new zenith. King Edward himself sent a medical health officer down from London to examine Walmer's drains. He found them shocking, and pronounced, with the certainty only men of science can command, that Walmer's drains alone offered "explanation of the relapses which Lady Curzon suffered."[179] Pale but convalescent against her satin pillows, Lady Curzon pronounced herself "the last victim of Walmer Castle."[180]

Everyone in England would have understood if Lord Curzon had decided not to return to India due to his wife's severe illness. But George's will could not be deflected. "It was almost as if he saw the great disaster ahead of him and, in his misery, was determined to charge bull-headed towards it," comments one of his biographers.[181] George prepared to leave for India on November 23rd.

On November 22nd, he accompanied Mary, still very weak and thin, to the castle that she had rented for her recuperation. The sensible thing would have been to convalesce in a suite at Claridges, or at least in some modern dwelling with central heating. Castles had cold stone floors, icy corridors, rattling, draughty old windows. But Mary Victoria had always been drawn to castles: Beldorney Castle, Braemar Castle, Walmer. And the particular castle which she had chosen now was a curious, and significant, choice. She moved into Highcliffe Castle on the Hampshire coast, the castle where Charlotte Canning had spent her youth, her honeymoon and many of her sad, disillusioned adult days.

George wrote to Mary from Marseilles on November 24th: "All the way through I have thought of Kinkie only – Kinkie through all the phases of her fearful illness, ... her resignation, her patience, her combat with all the foes of evil and death.... I go on existing in order to come back and try to make you happy."[182] That done, he climbed on board the India-bound ship and steamed rapidly away from his darling. Next day, he wrote again, pulling out the worn old organ-stops of self-pity: "It is with a sad and miserable heart that I go leaving all that makes life worth living behind me," he told Mary "and going out to toil and isolation and often worse. But it seems to be destiny."[183] He knew *his* health wouldn't stand the strain of India again – his doctors had told him so – knew he was close to complete breakdown both physically and emotionally, but valiantly, selflessly, the Viceroy went off to serve his country and his God. "I could not make him give up his job for me," wrote his equally selfless wife from her Highcliffe bed. "I must go out to him and join him in the summer."[184]

Day after colourless day, Mary lay in her ground-floor room at Highcliffe looking out across the garden Charlotte Canning had helped her father plan, sere and November-sad now. Mary's mother, who had darted across the Atlantic when Mary first became ill, worried about her all alone in that cold castle, but had to return to Washington to marry off Daisy and Nancy to two of Curzon's ADC's, only one of them, alas, a peer.[185] Now Mary had only Charlotte Canning's ghost for company. She shivered through December: the temperature in her bedroom stayed at forty-six degrees; its chimney smoked so that she could never have a fire when there was a wind. Two Noble Lives ... Charlotte Canning's ... and Mary Curzon's. Mary huddled into her furs, looked at the grey sea, and felt the Raj myth pulling her back to India. She was still weak and convalescent, but she decided not to wait for summer. She would return to India at the beginning of February to receive her final rounds of applause. She sent off a telegram to George. "Was not yesterday the happiest day for years?" he rejoiced, when he received the "amazing telegram to say that you were actually coming."[186]

Yes, she had made the right decision. "George's happiness is quite touching now that I am coming back," Mary wrote to her mother from Port Said on February 24, 1905, "and he is coming to meet me in Bombay. The reason he has had to stay is that there may be trouble in Afghanistan (this is private)."[187] When Mary landed in Bombay, there was her beloved consort beaming his welcome. When the Viceregal train broke down en route to Calcutta, the Viceroy and Vicereine, knowing the welcome awaiting them, and not wanting to disappoint their public, rushed ahead at sixty miles an hour, with a single carriage and engine. The Calcutta Corporation met them at the railway station and presented Lady Curzon "with a valuable jewel." The whole way to Government House was packed with cheering crowds. No Englishwoman in India had ever had such a welcome. One local newspaper called it "a spontaneous outburst of enthusiasm on the part of the population of Calcutta, such as we never remember to have witnessed before." India's most beautiful Vicereine had come back from the brink of the grave determined, though still wan and weak, to do her duty and serve the Empire. Hundreds of Calcutta ladies awaited Mary in the Throne Room and presented her with a "costly carved ivory casket."[188] Mary was enchanted; her smile had never been so radiant. And it was all for *her*; none of it was for George!

It was cold in Calcutta. "Yesterday, 8th of March, I drove out in my *chinchilla cloak*. George's care of me is simply touching and I am so relieved to be back to help and comfort him," Mary told her mother.[189] But by the time she got to Simla, the honeymoon was over, and George was as self-engrossed and neglectful as ever. Mary enlarged on her suffering to her mother:

> We had a garden party last week, and as George's foot was bad I had to do all the receiving and after shaking hands with

500 people I nearly cried with fatigue. I sometimes feel overwhelmed at having to do all the social part weak as I am....[190]

Lord Curzon had now locked horns with the Army's Commander-in-Chief, Lord Kitchener, who was quite as strong-willed
as George and who now demanded that entire control of the Army
be in his hands, rather than shared with the Military Member of
the Viceroy's Council, as it always had been. Lord Curzon insisted
that the Military Member continue to have control of administration; Lord Kitchener insisted that he alone take complete command.
George got more querulous, more insomniac, more crippled by leg
pains. Mary tried to placate them both; Kitchener, she knew, adored
her. The Home Government realized how popular Kitchener was,
a national hero in fact, who had to be placated. They granted him
most of the powers he wanted, and informed Lord Curzon of their
decision on May 31st. From his Olympian heights at Simla, George's
wrath fell like lightning bolts on those around him. He accused
Kitchener of "unblushing lying and intrigue."[191] "We have had a
week of darkness as George has been ill and Irene has been ill with
a temperature of 103° and I have had the most cruel cough," Mary
told her mother. That was in July. In August she wrote that "George
is ill in bed with anxiety and prolonged diarrhoea and the children
are all isolated in different parts of the house on account of
measles – and I have more than I can bear."[192] Surprised Simla
residents met Mary walking about the hills, "sometimes in pelting
rain without an umbrella, in order that the rain might beat on her
face."[193]

In August, having antagonized absolutely everyone in the Home
Government and still spluttering over Kitchener's victory, Lord
Curzon resigned as Viceroy, ostensibly over the silly issue that his
choice for Military Member of Council was not appointed, even
though such appointments had always been in the hands of the
Home Government. It was, to be sure, rather a farcical fall from
the heights. The Viceroy and Vicereine, who had landed at Bombay

in 1898 to such trumpet fanfares, were going home disgraced, defeated and downcast. And the Vicereine had revealed that she, too, not just his Lordship, had a fatal flaw. She could never point out to him his errors of judgment, even though she saw them clearly. She gave him nothing but smiles when what the plodding "poor beast" needed, from time to time, was a good, swift kick. The Queen only made the King's *hubris* worse.

"George's resignation has come – and now the Home Government are bent upon kicking him out with as little delay as possible but we cannot leave India in this great heat, which is terribly trying," Mary told her mother on August 24th. "The strain of all this has been terrible and my solitude has been cruel," wrote Mary. "I feel sometimes that I shall go out of my mind if I have to bear much more stress and worry."[194] Mary's health was now declining very rapidly. On October 18th she told her mother: "I went out shooting with George and fell down and hurt my back…. My cough and breathing are very troublesome, and I get upstairs with infinite difficulty … the perpetual breathlessness is a terrible nuisance."[195] George refused to face the truth and six days later, on October 24th, wrote to his mother-in-law: "You will be pleased to see Mary looking quite a different person from the last time when you saw her, stouter but in splendid looks. What she wants is exercise."[196]

On November 18th, Lord Minto arrived in Bombay to take up his duties as Viceroy. ("Isn't that the gentleman who only jumps hedges?" Curzon sniffed when told of his successor.[197]) Lord Curzon gave orders that no one was to be at the quayside to receive Lord Minto; no red carpet, no massed bands, no cheering crowds, nothing. When he got to Bombay's Government House, Minto found only Lady Curzon awaiting him at the top of the steps. Lord Curzon was nowhere in sight. "We all went into the drawing room," reported Dunlop Smith, Minto's Private Secretary, "and after we had been there for a few minutes Lord C. walked in. It was really terrible [he was wearing a shooting jacket and slippers], I cannot conceive what led him to take up this curious line."[198]

Lord Minto was understandably angry: the order of ceremony for the arrival of a new Viceroy was, like every detail of Raj protocol, properly spelled out in printed regulations and George, more than any other Viceroy, was a protocol fanatic. Nevertheless, "the observance of these customs and courtesies," fumed Minto, "was entirely and inexcusably absent."[199] The deposed "King" was making his exit not only on a farcical note, but with a rude gesture as well.

Next day, Lord and Lady Curzon left their disenchanted kingdom. His Lordship saw to it that he did so with proper Viceregal escort, but Minto noted in his diary "the marked coldness with which he was allowed to leave both by the people in the streets and the people on the pier."[200] And so the perfect Viceroy and Vicereine, with no cheers to comfort them, left India for good.

*T*HEIR HOMECOMING was equally doleful. When the Curzons reached London's Charing Cross station on December 3rd, not a single member of the government was there to greet them. Back in England, George had good reason to mutter, "What am I to do? What am I to do?" Prime Minister Balfour refused to recommend him for an English Earldom so that he could sit in the House of Lords. When Curzon had gone out to India, Queen Victoria had given him only an Irish peerage so that, on his return, he could, if he wished, return to the House of Commons. Now King Edward decided, ironically, that it was unseemly for a former Viceroy to face the hustings. George Nathaniel found himself without any work at all, and Mary Victoria found herself with a first-class fidget on her hands.

"I have had to see the doctor here about my heart," Mary told her mother, "as I nearly suffocate from breathlessness at the least exertion.... I still have the cough, the white leg and the heart! What a heritage from Walmer."[201] On July 18, 1906, seven months after leaving India, at Carlton House Terrace, Mary Curzon died from a heart attack, at the age of thirty-six. Lord Curzon refused to view the corpse, and gave orders that Mary was to be placed in her coffin with his photograph in her hand and a single flower on her breast. Next day he wrote to Mary's mother: "There has gone from me the truest, the most devoted, most unselfish, most beautiful and brilliant wife a man has ever had, and I am left with three little motherless children and a broken life."[202] "Every man's hand," he wrote, "has long been against me, and now God's hand has turned against me too."[203] A private funeral for family only was held at Kedleston on July 23rd; a memorial service for the public was held at the same hour in St Margaret's, Westminster. At both services the hymn "Fight the Good Fight" was sung.[204]

Less than a month later, on August 13th, Pearl Craigie, aged thirty-eight, also died of a heart attack. George Moore circulated the wicked rumour that she had taken an overdose of sleeping pills, disappointed that Lord Curzon had not come running with offers of marriage. When a memorial to Pearl Craigie was unveiled at London's University College, it was Lord Curzon who made the obligatory speech, quoting an epigram from one of her books: "The great thing is to love, not to be loved."[205]

Meanwhile, the golden myth, much as it had in Charlotte Canning's case, began to take shape round Mary, Lady Curzon, she who had died serving an adoring husband and an adopted Empire. "No wife ever entered more wholeheartedly into her husband's work," declared the *Westminster Gazette* on July 19th. Perceval Landon commended "that intense and single-souled loyalty to her husband which was the golden thread running through every action of her life."[206] "Out of the pageantry and splendour of her public life," declared a Bombay newspaper on July 22nd, "as the consort of the representative of the King-Emperor, she set a noble example in the virtues of chastity, fidelity and all those feminine attributes that make for domestic bliss." "Lady Curzon possessed talents which would have enabled her to mark out and pursue with distinction a career of her own," decided the *Times of India* on July 20th. Instead, "she was content to devote them entirely to the consummation of Lord Curzon's high Imperial purpose." Preaching the Sunday after Mary's death at an English parish church, the Rev. W.M. Magrath

54 *"The late Lady Curzon" (Illustrated London News,
July 28, 1906)*

asked, "Among the countless women, who in every age, have sacrificed their lives for love and duty may we not mention that talented and beautiful woman whose soul last Wednesday evening passed to the Paradise Land?"[207] Mary's death inspired the Rev. E.S. Lang-Buckland to address the Bridgeward Liberal Association on "The Imperial Ideal," declaring that "British citizens would ever, through all history, revere her work and memory.... In the Imperial Ideal the inspiring spell and influence of pure and noble women will be reverently recognized."[208] Mary Curzon's death turned the still-glowing embers of Empire idealism into one last, leaping incandescence, and it was the despairing widower, as one could have predicted, who pumped the bellows hardest. "We have seen the bowed form of Canning," Lord Curzon wrote in *British Government in India*,

> following his beautiful wife to her grave by the bamboos that quiver above the tranquil river-reaches of Barrackpore. A later Viceroy lost the partner and main author of his happiness in India a few months after they had left the shores of that country, to whose climate the recurrence of the illness which terminated her life was largely due.[209]

Lord Curzon shrugged on his self-pity like a great-coat, and pulled it snugly round him.

An Earldom finally came his way in 1911, to be followed later by a Marquessate. In 1916, on his father's death, he inherited Kedleston. In 1917 he married another American heiress, Grace Duggan; this one was twenty years his junior. At thirty-six, she was still young enough to give him a son, but didn't. Marquess Curzon of Kedleston went on antagonizing everyone in his path; servants came and went at an alarming rate. When a butler finally quit, having lasted longer than most, his Lordship asked him to suggest a successor. "There are only two people," the butler fumed, "who could take my place. One is Jesus Christ. I am the other."[210]

Curzon was having alterations done to Kedleston when he

became ill there in 1925. He retired to bed in the State Bedroom, and wrote an elaborate will, doing it all himself with no help from secretary or lawyer, in a "style reminiscent of a Caesar."[211] He also sorted, bundled and labelled all his letters according to period and subject. The sum total, "in boxes, tin trunks, wicker boxes and packing-cases" filled two whole rooms.[212] Lord Curzon died on March 20, 1925, aged sixty-six, and was buried at Kedleston, in the chapel which he had built, and beautified through the years, for Mary.

The chapel was his final homage to his beloved first wife, not, of course, to himself. He designed it all, including the wrought-iron grilles, the light fittings, everything. He scoured the world for suitable candelabra and crucifixes and paintings. He commissioned stained-glass windows to depict the figures of the nine Marys of the Christian church – and another window to show the most illustrious George of them all: St George fighting his dragon. The sidelights "hold the shields or flags" denoting Lord Curzon's connections "with Eton College; Balliol College, Oxford; All Souls College, Oxford (Fellow); India (Viceroy); the Cinque Ports (Lord Warden) and Oxford University (Chancellor)."[213] The chapel floor is made of green quartz, chosen to show off the central show-piece: a large white Italian marble monument of Lord Curzon recumbent in his Viceregal robes, with Lady Curzon stretched out beside him. The marble monument took six years to complete; the Viceroy's and Vicereine's hands are clasped; over them bend two angels holding out a celestial crown of love. The inscription to Mary Curzon written by his desolate Lordship reads:

Mary Victoria
Lady Curzon of Kedleston
Born May 27 1870. Died July 18 1906.
Perfect in love and loveliness
Beauty was the least of her rare gifts
God had endowed with like Graces
Her mind and soul

From illness all but unto death
Restored, only to die.
She was mourned in three continents,
And by her dearest will be
For ever unforgotten.

Lord Curzon had the final word.

Elsewhere now, in one of Kedleston's lofty rooms, Mary Victoria, resplendent in peacock dress, coronet and a Rajah's ransom of diamonds, looks down with queenly mien from the ancient panelled wall. There she stands, transfixed, transported, in her finest hour. For the peacock, symbol of royalty for the Moghuls, object of worship for the Hindus, that was the final indignity: to find itself seamed and darted between frothing lace at one extreme, and fake white roses at the other.

W E'VE COME A LONG WAY since Emily Eden held in her hand an emerald peacock fanned to mythic splendour, and the British Raj, fired with ambition, fanned out across India in search of other treasures. Its early servants could not have known that their inspired quest would lead eventually to a banal ball-gown covered with emeralds, one in every blind, bogus peacock-feather eye. Between Emily's emeralds and Mary's came sixty-six years of Raj rule. We have followed its red-carpeted route in the train of four very different First Ladies: Emily Eden, growing old and sad and weary in India's dusty world; Charlotte Canning, holding a Mutiny at arm's length with a watercolour brush; Edith Lytton, marching reluctantly into the doll-house of Raj formalism with her feelings left outside; Mary Curzon following the Vicereine's script all the way to the big death-bed scene.

After these four had come and gone, the Raj shuffled forward, growing old and tremulous, until 1947. Then, at midnight on August 14th, the Raj's last Viceroy, Earl Mountbatten, with commendable dispatch, ended its guardianship and granted India the double-edged sword of independence and division. The civilian British packed up first; the military took longer to depart, but finally, on February 28, 1948, the last British troops, the 1st Battalion of the Somerset Light Infantry, marched aboard a transport ship in Bombay's harbour, and India was henceforth left to her own devices. "Kingdoms rise and wane...."

What remains from those three-hundred-odd years of Raj rule? In India: a legacy of democratic and legal institutions, a neat grid of train tracks and canals, and some larger-than-life statues, crumbling round the edges, of its august Viceroys. In England: memoirs and diaries, both printed and hand-written, great stacks of official papers, such imperial plunder as Ranjit Singh's golden armchair, and a few hundred Indian words taken permanently into the English language. Verandah, bungalow, bangle, chutney, khaki, calico, seersucker, chintz, shawl and loot are among them. The British ended as they had begun in India: with the Word.

Most precious, perhaps, of all those Raj words are the ones penned by its First Ladies and *memsahibs*, revealing, as they do, what a crucial role they played in the Raj pageant. British menfolk provided the iron of rigid rule and railroad. Their wives and sisters supplied the irony: the double view granted only to those who stood always slightly to one side, able to picture themselves both inside the regime and outside it. It was the British women in India who humanized the Raj, who *civilized* it. They didn't just add some lace around the edges; they gave the Raj its heart. Bright women like Emily Eden provided satiric wit and much wisdom; gentle ladies like Charlotte Canning contributed devotion to duty and calm under fire; feeling ones like Edith Lytton supplied the balm of empathy and ardour; beautiful ones like Mary Curzon added grace and drama. Diaries and letters and novels written by British women in India bear witness to the scope and value of their contribution to the Raj.

Let the ladies have the last word.

NOTES

INTRODUCTION

1 Flora Annie Steel, *Miss Stuart's Legacy*, I, 7
2 "A School Song," *Rudyard Kipling's Verse*, p. 557
3 I, 55
4 *The Discovery of India*, p. 485
5 *The Englishwoman in India*, p. 23
6 "The other day we were riding by the river; we saw a dying man carried past in his *palanquin* and they put him down to die, exactly opposite to the tent where the Calcutta world was assembled to eat ice. For a certain time his friends were to sit and watch him; if he did not die then, they would either stuff his mouth with mud or leave him to the tender mercy of the alligators and nobody can interfere to prevent that kind of murder." Letter from Fanny Eden to Elizabeth Copley, June 19, 1836. Photostat Eur. 10, India Office Library manuscripts. Originals held by Department of Palaeography and Diplomatic, University of Durham.
7 Augustus Hare, *The Story of Two Noble Lives*, III, 97
8 Visiting Calcutta in the 1830s, Fanny Parkes writes of "large birds, called adjutants" and adds: "On the heads of the lions that crown the entrance arches of the Government House, you are sure to see this bird (the hargilla or gigantic crane)." *Wanderings of a Pilgrim in Search of the Picturesque*, I, 23. The adjutants disappeared once the open drains of Calcutta were replaced by a modern sewage system in the 1870s.

I EMILY EDEN

1 *Letters from India*, I, 7, hereafter cited as *LI*, with page references given in brackets following the quotation. In the collections of Emily Eden's letters, in many instances, as here, the name of her correspondent is not given.

2 *Miss Eden's Letters*, pp. 107 – 08, hereafter cited as MEL with page references given in brackets following the quotation.
3 *The Whole Duty of Woman*, pp. 27 – 28
4 *Sermons To Young Women*, p. 117
5 *A Father's Legacy to His Daughters*, p. 30
6 *The Greville Memoirs* (Second Part), ed. Henry Reed, II, 254
7 George Villiers, *A Vanished Victorian*, p. 292
8 Sir Herbert Maxwell, *The Life and Letters of George William Frederick, Fourth Earl of Clarendon*, I, 81
9 *Ibid.* I, 81 – 82
10 *Ibid.* I, 79
11 *The Lieven-Palmerston Correspondence*, ed. Lord Sudley, p. 94
12 Janet Dunbar, *Golden Interlude. The Edens in India 1836 – 42*, p. 13
13 Hon. Emily Eden, *Up the Country*, hereafter cited as UC, with page references given in brackets following the quotation.
14 Marquess Curzon of Kedleston, *British Government in India*, II, 196
15 *The Garden of Fidelity: Being the Autobiography of Flora Annie Steel*, p. 123
16 Mary Frances Billington, *Woman in India*, pp. 290 – 91
17 *The Englishwoman in India*, pp. 51, 48 – 49
18 George W. Johnson, *The Stranger in India*, I, 261 ff
19 *Ibid.* I, 5
20 Curzon, II, 197
21 Postans, II, 209
22 John Clive, *Thomas Babington Macaulay, The Shaping of the Historian*, p. 300
23 Geoffrey Moorhouse, *India Brittanica*, p. 44
24 *The History of Women from Earliest Antiquity to the Present Time*, II, 41 – 42
25 Gregory, pp. 50 – 51
26 *The Englishwoman in India*, p. 129
27 J.K. Stanford, *Ladies in the Sun: The Memsahib's India*, p. 73
28 From Volume I of Fanny Eden's Journal which covers her Rajmahal adventure, from Feb. 13, 1837 to April 1, 1837. Volume II dates from Oct. 21, 1837 to Dec. 24, 1837. Volume III, from Jan. 1, 1838 to March 18, 1838 and Volume IV from Nov. 9, 1838 to Dec. 31, 1838. All four volumes are in the India Office Library Manuscripts collection, Eur C 130.
29 *The Garden of Fidelity: Being the Autobiography of Flora Annie Steel*, p. 141
30 *Indian Daily News*, Jan. 8, 1896
31 J.K. Stanford, *Ladies in the Sun: The Memsahib's India*, p. 62
32 Particularly rhapsodic were S.T. Coleridge's *Kubla Khan* (1800) here quoted, Robert Southey's *The Curse of Kehama* (1810) and Sir Walter Scott's *The Surgeon's Daughter* (1827).
33 II, 241

34 Mrs Colin Mackenzie, *Life in the Mission, the Camp and the Zenana*, I, 35 and I, 38

35 G.B. Burgin, "A Chat with Sara Jeannette Duncan," *Idler*, August 1895, p. 115

36 pp. 60 – 61

37 Mackenzie, I, 227 – 28 and II, 19

38 Parkes, I, 321 – 47

39 Curzon, I, 225 – 26

40 For a full account of this mission, see Hon. W.G. Osborne, *The Court and Camp of Runjeet Sing* [sic].

41 Moorhouse, pp. 136 – 37

42 [Fanny Parkes], *Wanderings of a Pilgrim in Search of the Picturesque*, II, 299

43 For details of Ranjit Singh's life and character see H.E. Fane, *Five Years in India* and Sir Lepal Griffin *Ranjit Singh*.

44 Fane, I, 322

45 *Ibid*. I, 126

46 p. 317

47 Letter from Emily to Elizabeth Copley, Simla, March 28, 1839. Photostat Eur. 10, India Office Library Manuscripts. Originals held by Department of Palaeography and Diplomatic, University of Durham.

48 Fane, II, 173 – 74. H.E. Fane was nephew and aide-de-camp to Sir Henry Fane, who had been Commander-in-Chief in India since 1835.

49 *Ibid*. II, 171 – 72

50 *Ibid*, II, 184 – 85

51 Diver, p. 6

52 Sara Jeannette Duncan [Mrs Everard Cotes], *The Simple Adventures of a Memsahib*, p. 379

53 Sara Jeannette Duncan, *His Honour and a Lady*, p. 97

54 p. 146

55 Letter of May 30, 1841, to Maria, Countess of Grey. Papers of Maria, Countess of Grey, Department of Palaeography and Diplomatic, University of Durham.

56 *Ibid*

57 Fane, II, 193

58 Higginbotham, *Men Whom India Has Known*, p. 270

59 *Ibid*. p. 272. *Ghazees* were Muslim fanatics who believed that murdering unbelievers would get them into paradise.

60 Maxwell, I, 237

61 Stanford, p. 84

62 Higginbotham, p. 8

63 Philip Woodruff, *The Men Who Ruled India*, Vol. I. *The Founders 1600 –*

1857, p. 277
64 *The Greville Memoirs*, II, 89
65 Johnson, I, 222 – 23
66 *Life and Letters of Lady Dorothy Nevill*, ed. Ralph Nevill, p. 148
67 Johnson, II, 196 – 97
68 *The Greville Memoirs*, II, 150
69 Villiers, p. 71
70 *The Greville Memoirs*, III, 254
71 Obituary, *Gentleman's Magazine*, February, 1849, p. 203
72 *Ibid.* p. 203
73 "DIED. On the 26th Inst. at Eden Lodge, Frances Harriett Eden, youngest sister of the late Earl of Auckland." (*The Times*, April 28, 1849.)
74 Letter of Sept. 7, 1859. Nancy Mitford, *The Stanleys of Alderley*, p. 224
75 Maxwell, II, 224

II CHARLOTTE CANNING

1 Augustus J.C. Hare, *The Story of Two Noble Lives*. Being Memorials of Charlotte, Countess Canning and Louisa, Marchioness of Waterford, I, 61, hereafter cited as Hare, with page references given in brackets following the quotation.
2 Hon. Mrs Edward Stuart-Wortley, *Highcliffe and the Stuarts*. p. 262
3 Lady Canning papers, Harewood Collection, Leeds District Archives
4 Stuart-Wortley, p. 262. Letter from Lady Granville
5 *Letters of Harriet, Countess Granville*, II, 78
6 *Records of Later Life*, III, 348 – 49
7 *The Letters of Lady Palmerston*, ed. Tresham Lever, p. 109
8 Journal entry for December 20, 1842, quoted by Virginia Surtees, *Charlotte Canning*, p. 71.
9 *Ibid.* p. 73
10 *Ibid.* p. 148
11 Lady Canning papers, Harewood Collection, Leeds District Archives. Unless otherwise noted, all references to Lady Canning's diaries, journal-letters and letters come from this source.
12 "Oct. 5 (1847). A friend of mine in Madrid ... went to another bullfight, and there he saw Lord Canning enjoying the sport amazingly." Francis W.H. Cavendish, *Society Politics and Diplomacy, 1820 – 1864*, pp. 135 – 36
13 Lord Edmond Fitzmaurice, *The Life of Granville, George Leveson-Gower* I, 409
14 Private information. For descriptions of the other woman in Canning's

life, see Hare, I, 190, Surtees, p. 167 and Mark Bence-Jones, *The Viceroys of India*, pp. 21 – 22.

15 Cavendish, pp. 180 – 81
16 Roger Fulford, *The Prince Consort*, p. 92
17 Memorial volume of photographs, newscuttings, letters and souvenirs relating to Charlotte Canning compiled by Emily Anne Theophila Bayley, wife of Sir Edward Clive Bayley, Eur D 661, India Office Library manuscripts.
18 p. 220
19 Michael Maclagan, *Clemency Canning*, p. 23
20 Surtees, p. 196
21 Lord Canning's Indian Papers, Harewood Collection, Leeds District Archives. Unless otherwise noted, all references to Canning's private diaries come from this source.
22 Lady Canning's watercolours and drawings, bound now in eighteen large folio volumes, are part of the library collection at Harewood House, Leeds.
23 Dinah Maria Mulock (Mrs Craik), *A Woman's Thoughts about Women*, p. 295
24 Marquess Curzon of Kedleston, *British Government in India*, I, 227
25 *The Letters of Queen Victoria 1837 – 61*, ed. Arthur C. Benson and Viscount Esher, III, 228
26 Curzon, II, 222. Lord Dalhousie died on December 19, 1860.
27 p. 221
28 p. 39
29 *Sesame and Lilies*, pp. 98 – 99
30 Lady Canning papers
31 Curzon, II, 125 – 26
32 Surtees, p. 209
33 *Ibid.* pp. 219 – 20
34 G.F. Train, *Young America Abroad in Europe, Asia and Australia* (1857), pp. 182 – 83, quoted by Surtees, pp. 216 – 17.
35 *Woman in Her Social and Domestic Character*, p. 40
36 Mrs Colin Mackenzie, *Life in the Mission, the Camp and the Zenana*, II, 240
37 *Ibid.* I, 185
38 *Ibid.* I, 230 – 31
39 George D. Bearce, *British Attitudes Towards India 1784 – 1858*, p. 82
40 Michael Edwardes, *Raj: The Story of British India 1772 – 1947*, p. 348.
41 Mackenzie, II, 285
42 Christopher Hibbert, *The Great Mutiny*, p. 60
43 Letter to Lord Granville, Maclagan, p. 69

44 Eur. D 661
45 Hibbert, p. 85
46 *Ibid.*, p. 91
47 Maclagan, p. 86
48 *Ibid.* p. 106
49 Hibbert, p. 168
50 *Ibid.* p. 180 and p. 186
51 Surtees, p. 245
52 Hibbert, p. 206
53 Surtees, p. 235
54 Hibbert, p. 209
55 Eur. D 661
56 Surtees, p. 235
57 Hibbert, p. 217
58 *Ibid.* p. 247
59 *Ibid.* p. 250
60 Surtees, p. 234
61 *The Letters of Queen Victoria*, III, p. 301
62 Sir Henry S. Cunningham, *Earl Canning*, pp. 116 – 17
63 *Ibid.* p. 125
64 Hibbert, p. 211
65 *Ibid.* p. 354
66 *Ibid.* p. 214
67 October 1857, p. 593
68 Cavendish, p. 314
69 Major-General Sir Owen Tudor Burne, *Memories*, p. 30
70 Hibbert, p. 340
71 *The Stanleys of Alderley*, ed. Nancy Mitford, p. 171
72 *Ibid.* pp. x – xi
73 *Ibid.* p. 25 and p. 113
74 *Ibid.* p. 181
75 Lady Canning papers
76 Surtees, p. 257
77 *The Stanleys*, p. 178 and p. 181
78 *Ibid.* pp. 181 – 82
79 *Ibid.* pp. 181 – 82
80 Bence-Jones, p. 31
81 *The Stanleys*, p. 183
82 Surtees, pp. 263 – 64
83 *The Stanleys*, p. 220 and p. 189
84 *The Letters of Queen Victoria*, III, p. 389

85 Surtees, p. 265
86 Major-General Sir W.H. Sleeman, *Rambles and Recollections of an Indian Official*, footnote to I, 352
87 *The Stanleys*, p. 195
88 Michael Edwardes, *Raj*, p. 207
89 Michael Edwardes, *Bound to Exile*, p. 132
90 *The Stanleys*, pp. 190 – 91
91 Bence-Jones, p. 39
92 Eur. D 661
93 *The Stanleys*, p. 204
94 *Ibid.* p. 207
95 Surtees, p. 270
96 Lady Canning papers.
97 *The Stanleys*, pp. 180 – 81
98 *Ibid.* p. 263
99 Surtees, p. 294
100 *The Englishman*, Nov. 18, 1861
101 Surtees, p. 294
102 *The Letters of Queen Victoria*, III, 608
103 Curzon, II, 228
104 Lord Canning's Indian papers
105 Maclagan, p. 309

III   EDITH LYTTON

1 Born Edward Bulwer in 1803, son of General William Bulwer and Elizabeth Lytton, heiress of Knebworth House, Edward upon inheriting Knebworth in 1844 added the additional surname of Lytton. When he was created a baron in 1866, he dropped the Bulwer and became simply Lord Lytton. For consistency's sake and to differentiate him from his son Robert, second Lord Lytton, he is here called Bulwer-Lytton throughout.
2 E. Lutyens, *The Birth of Rowland*, p. 20
3 *Ibid.* p. 30
4 *Ibid.* p. 27
5 *Personal and Literary Letters of Robert, First Earl of Lytton*, ed. Lady Betty Balfour, hereafter cited as Balfour. I, 174.
6 Walburga, Lady Paget. *Embassies of Other Days and Further Recollections*, I, 186
7 Aurelia Brooks Harlan, *Owen Meredith*, pp. 26 – 27

8 E. Lutyens, *The Birth of Rowland*, p. 35
9 Balfour, II, 191
10 Mrs C.W. Earle, *Memoirs and Memories*, p. 345
11 p. 345
12 p. 137
13 E. Lutyens, *The Birth of Rowland*, p. 219
14 Mrs Sarah Ellis, *The Wives of England*, p. 59
15 E. Lutyens, *The Birth of Rowland*, p. 150
16 Balfour, I, 186
17 E. Lutyens, *The Birth of Rowland*, p. 223
18 *Ibid.* p. 110
19 *Ibid.* p. 220
20 *Ibid.* p. 175
21 Balfour, I, 226
22 Walburga, Lady Paget, *The Linings of Life*, II, 525
23 *The Wives of England*, p. 76
24 Balfour, I, 340
25 Mary Lutyens, *The Lyttons in India*, p. 11. Hereafter cited as M. Lutyens.
26 Balfour, I, 313
27 [Edith, Countess of Lytton] India 1876 – 1880. Privately printed at the Chiswick Press, London, 1899. The book is a chronological account of her Indian years, based on her diary-letters to her mother, her journals and various other letters written to her or by her. Unless otherwise noted, further quotations come from this source.
28 Earle, p. 299
29 Paget, *Embassies*, II, 306
30 Pat Barr and Ray Desmond, *Simla. A Hill Station in British India*, p. 27
31 M. Lutyens, p. 30
32 Balfour, II, 12 – 13
33 *Ibid.* II, 11
34 Lady Betty Balfour, *History of Lord Lytton's Indian Administration 1876 – 80*, p. 50
35 Christopher Hussey, *Life of Sir Edwin Lutyens*, p. 254
36 Val C. Prinsep, *Imperial India. An Artist's Journals*, p. 261
37 p. 23
38 *The Englishwoman in India*, p. 22
39 p. 271
40 M. Lutyens, p. 41
41 *The Garden of Fidelity: Being the Autobiography of Flora Annie Steel*, p. 105
42 *Ibid.* p. 105
43 Wilfrid Blunt, *Ideas About India*, p. xvii

44 Letter to Sir James Fitzjames Stephen, Balfour, II, 23
45 quoted by Barr, p. 171
46 Sir Mortimer Durand, *Life of the Right Honourable Sir Alfred Comyn Lyall*, p. 215
47 Barr, p. 27
48 Elizabeth Longford, *A Pilgrimage of Passion. The Life of Wilfrid Scawen Blunt*, p. 77
49 Balfour, II, 23 – 24
50 Paget, *Embassies*, II, 307
51 M. Lutyens, p. 98
52 *Ibid*. pp. 50 – 51
53 Balfour, I, 16
54 M. Lutyens, p. 50
55 *Ibid*. p. 63
56 *Ibid*. p. 70
57 M. Lutyens, p. 41
58 Mark Bence-Jones, *The Viceroys of India*, p. 98
59 Letter of Aug. 20, 1876, Raymond, p. 147
60 Letter of Sept. 3, 1876, *Ibid*. p. 150
61 Bence-Jones, p. 100
62 Major-General Sir Owen Tudor Burne, *Memories*, p. 219
63 Prinsep, p. 32
64 March 24th, 1877
65 Prinsep, p. 20
66 *Ibid*. p. 29
67 *The History of the Imperial Assemblage at Delhi*, pp. 71 – 72
68 *Ibid*. p. 73
69 Prinsep, p. 36
70 M. Lutyens, p. 85
71 Balfour, II, 21
72 Michael Edwardes, *Bound to Exile: The Victorians in India*, p. 143
73 Burne, p. 42
74 M. Lutyens, p. 81
75 Prinsep, p. 29
76 Wheeler, p. 103
77 Prinsep, p. 38
78 Bence-Jones, p. 100
79 Jan. 6, 1877
80 M. Lutyens, p. 90
81 Letter from Sir Alfred Lyall to his sister Barbara. April 12, 1877. Eur. F 132 – 7, Lyall Collection, India Office Library Manuscripts.

82 "Lord Lytton," March 10, 1877, p. 145

83 George Aberigh-Mackay, *Twenty-One Days in India*, pp. 1 – 2

84 M. Lutyens, p. 97

85 *Memories*, p. 212

86 Balfour, II, 25

87 E. Lutyens, *A Blessed Girl*, pp. 281 – 82

88 Prinsep, p. 218

89 *Ibid.* p. 257

90 Balfour, II, 74

91 Letter of Sept. 3, 1877, from Ajmere, Rajputana, Eur. F 132 – 7

92 Balfour, II, 80 – 81

93 Geoffrey Moorhouse, *India Brittanica*, pp. 111 – 12

94 Prinsep, p. 347

95 The former Governor was Sir Bartle Frere. J.K. Stanford, *Ladies in the Sun. The Memsahib's India*, p. 127

96 Bence-Jones, p. 102

97 Longford, p. 72 and pp. 294 – 95

98 *Ibid.* p. 96 and p. 293

99 M. Lutyens, p. 153

100 M. Lutyens, p. 155

101 Longford, p. 152

102 *Ideas About India*, p. xv

103 *Ibid.* pp. 9 – 10

104 *Ibid.* pp. xvi – xvii

105 *Ibid.* pp. 28 – 29

106 *Ibid.* p. 47

107 *Ibid.* p. 48

108 Sir Henry Cotton, *Indian and Home Memories*, p. 171

109 Lieut-Gen. Sir W.F. Butler, *Life of Sir George Pomeroy-Colley*, p. 239

110 Letter of Sept. 8, 1879, to Mrs Holland, Eur. F 132 – 7

111 Balfour, II, 171

112 E. Neill Raymond, *Victorian Viceroy*, p. 210

113 Letter of Oct. 27, 1879, Eur. F 127 – 362, Strachey Collection, India Office Library Manuscripts

114 Cotton, p. 172

115 Eur. F 127 – 362

116 Letter of Nov. 18, 1879, Eur. E 218 – 45, Lytton Collection, India Office Library Manuscripts

117 Letter to Lady Holland, Nov. 29, 1879, Balfour, II, 184 – 85

118 M. Lutyens, p. 174

119 Letter of April 16, 1880, Eur. F 127 – 362

120 M. Lutyens, p. 175
121 *Ibid.* p. 177
122 Letters to Lord Cranbrook of April 20 and April 27, 1880, Balfour, II, 201, 203
123 Raymond, p. 229
124 Edith Finch, *Wilfrid Scawen Blunt*, p. 124
125 4th Earl of Lytton, *Wilfrid Scawen Blunt*, p. 84
126 Paget, *Embassies*, II, 356
127 E. Lutyens, *A Blessed Girl*, p. 14
128 *Ibid.* pp. 41 – 42 and p. 17
129 Raymond, pp. 266 – 67
130 Letter of Aug. 3, 1887, *Ibid.* p. 262
131 Marquess Curzon of Kedleston, *British Government in India*, II, 240
132 Letter of Jan. 23, 1888, Balfour, II, 337
133 Raymond, p. 283
134 Paget, *Embassies*, II, 520
135 E. Lutyens, *A Blessed Girl*, pp. 45 – 46 and p. 43
136 Balfour, II, 430 – 31
137 M. Lutyens, p. 186
138 E. Lutyens, *A Blessed Girl*, p. 81
139 *Ibid.* p. 247
140 *Lady Lytton's Court Diary 1895 – 1899*, ed. Mary Lutyens, p. 38
141 *Ibid.* p. 37 and p. 87

IV MARY CURZON

1 Margot Asquith, *The Autobiography of Margot Asquith*, I, 174
2 Sir Malcolm Darling, *Apprentice to Power*, p. 33
3 Quoted by Nigel Nicolson, *Mary Curzon*, p. 112
4 *Westminster Gazette*, July 19, 1906
5 Mary Curzon's obituary, July 19, 1906
6 Nicolson, p. 9. For many of the biographical details on Mary Leiter and her family, I am grateful to Mr Nicolson.
7 *Ibid.* p. 18
8 Kenneth Rose, *Superior Person*, p. 19
9 Harold Nicolson, *Curzon: The Last Phase 1919 – 1925*, p. 9
10 Baroness Ravensdale [Mary Irene Curzon], *In Many Rhythms*, p. 10
11 Rose, p. 49
12 *Ibid.* p. 77
13 *Ibid.* p. 190

14 *Ibid.* p. 74
15 Earl of Ronaldshay, *The Life of Lord Curzon*, I, 103 – 04
16 Nicolson, p. 39
17 L. Mosley, *Curzon. The End of an Epoch*, p. 46
18 Nicolson, p. 93
19 Mosley, p. 46
20 Nicolson, p. 40
21 Mosley, p. 47
22 Nicolson, p. 53
23 Mosley, p. 48
24 Nicolson, p. 55
25 Margaret Maison, *John Oliver Hobbes, Her Life and Work*, p. 3
26 Letter of Jan. 13, 1900 to Rev. W.F. Brown, *Ibid.* p. 19
27 Nicolson, p. 62
28 *Ibid.* p. 60
29 *Ibid.* p. 34
30 Rose, pp. 280 – 81
31 Ronaldshay, I, 225
32 *Lady Curzon's India*, ed. John Bradley, pp. 5 – 6
33 Letters from Mary to George of Aug. 12, 1894 and Dec. 15, 1894.
   Ronaldshay, I, 224
34 Letter to Mary of Feb. 22, 1895. Mosley, p. 58
35 *Woman in Her Social and Domestic Character*, p. 14
36 *A Woman's Thoughts about Women*, pp. 23 – 24
37 *The Girl of the Period*, II, 148 – 49
38 *Advocate of India*, July 20, 1906
39 Rose, p. 283
40 *Ibid.* pp. 282 – 83
41 Nicolson, p. 92
42 Consuelo Vanderbilt Balsan, *The Glitter and the Gold*, p. 174
43 Rose, p. 18
44 *A Woman's Thoughts about Women*, p. 150
45 *The Wives of England*, p. 121
46 Nicolson, p. 93
47 Balsan, p. 174
48 Nicolson, p. 91
49 Rose, p. 324
50 Bradley, p. vii
51 Nicolson, p. 103
52 *Ibid.* p. 104
53 Rose, p. 149

54 Bradley, p. 15
55 *Ibid.* p. 19
56 *Ibid.* p. 20
57 *Ibid.* p. 20
58 Marquess Curzon of Kedleston, *British Government in India*, I, 87
59 Bradley, p. 20
60 Bradley, p. 25
61 *Ibid.* p. 57
62 Letter of April 12, 1899, to St John Brodrick. David Dilks, *Curzon in India*, I, 73
63 Mary Frances Billington, *Woman in India*, p. 274
64 *Ibid.* p. 274
65 Bradley, p. 22
66 *Ibid.* p. 25
67 *Ibid.* p. 25
68 *Ibid.* p. 27
69 July 19, 1906
70 Bradley, p. 23
71 Curzon, I, 235
72 Bradley, p. 23
73 Ronaldshay, II, 28
74 *The India We Served*, p. 223
75 Rose, p. 392
76 Lawrence, p. 237
77 Dilks, I, 94
78 *Ibid.* I, 72
79 Rose, p. 345
80 Quoted by Nicolson, p. 193
81 Mark Bence-Jones, *The Viceroys of India*, p. 178
82 Nicolson, p. 119
83 Bradley, p. 37
84 Nicolson, p. 118
85 Ronaldshay, II, 51
86 *Ibid.* II, 51 – 52
87 Quoted from an Indian newspaper, Nicolson, pp. 124 – 25
88 Philip Woodruff (pseud. for Philip Mason), *The Men Who Ruled India*. Vol. II, *The Guardians*, p. 196
89 Bradley, p. 39
90 Eur. F 143, Walter Lawrence Collection, India Office Library Manuscripts
91 Bradley, p. 38
92 Maison, p. 51

93 Nicolson, pp. 130 – 31
94 Bradley, p. 50
95 Ronaldshay, III, 390
96 The friend was Margot Asquith. Rose, p. 236
97 Bradley, pp. 60 – 61
98 Ronaldshay, II, 146
99 *Ibid.* II, 148
100 Mosley, p. 85
101 Eur. F 143
102 Lawrence, p. 241
103 Curzon, I, 177
104 Lovat Fraser, *India Under Curzon and After*, pp. 261 – 62
105 p. 282
106 *The Englishwoman in India*, p. 46
107 *Ibid.* pp. 38 – 39
108 Mosley, p. 89
109 Ronaldshay, II, 165
110 Bradley, p. 92
111 *Ibid.* p. 111
112 Mosley, p. 116
113 Bradley, p. 106
114 Arthur Edmund Sandbach (1859 – 1928) served as Curzon's Military Secretary 1898 – 99. *Ibid.* p. 114
115 *Ibid.* p. 77
116 *Ibid.* p. 101
117 Ronaldshay, II, 422
118 Bradley, p. 114
119 *Ibid.* p. 104
120 Ronaldshay, II, 177
121 *Ibid.* II, 177
122 *Ibid.* II, 172
123 Bradley, p. 86
124 *Ibid.* p. 99
125 *Ibid.* pp. 122 – 23
126 *Ibid.* p. 105
127 Ronaldshay, II, 191
128 Nicolson, p. 157
129 *Ibid.* p. 133
130 *Ibid.* p. 133
131 Bradley, pp. 141 – 42

NOTES

132 Diary entry for May 10, 1902, Eur. F 143
133 Nicolson, p. 159
134 *Ibid*. p. 134
135 *Ibid*. p. 134
136 Bradley, p. 113
137 *Ibid*. p. 145
138 Dilks, I, 75
139 Diary entry for Jan. 7, 1913. S.D. Waley, *Edwin Montagu*, p. 321
140 Ravensdale, p. 18
141 Ronaldshay, II, 228
142 *Ibid*. II, 359 – 60
143 I, viii
144 II, 414
145 Bence-Jones, p. 184
146 John Oliver Hobbes [Pearl Craigie] *Imperial India*, pp. 15 – 16
147 *Ibid*. p. 15
148 Curzon, II, 28
149 Lovat Fraser, *At Delhi*, p. 73
150 *Times of India*, Dec. 30, 1902
151 *The Empress* (Calcutta monthly magazine), January, 1903
152 "Accounts of Viceroy's Camp, Delhi Durbar, 1903," Eur. F 112 – 467,
   Curzon Collection, India Office Library Manuscripts.
153 Marquess Curzon of Kedleston, *A Viceroy's India*, ed. Peter King, p. 31
154 Dec. 22, 1902
155 Mortimer Menpes, *The Durbar*, pp. 26 – 27
156 *Ibid*. p. 185
157 Hobbes, p. 46
158 Maison, p. 53
159 Nicolson, p. 167
160 Ravensdale, p. 18
161 Hobbes, p. 45
162 Nicolson, p. 161
163 Ronaldshay, II, 233
164 Nicolson, pp. 167 – 68
165 Dilks, I, 264
166 *The Life of John Oliver Hobbes told in her Correspondence with Numerous Friends*, p. 230
167 Maison, p. 53
168 Nicolson, p. 168
169 Ronaldshay, II, 278

170 Ronaldshay, II, 320
171 Nicolson, p. 172
172 Mosley, p. 113
173 Nicolson, p. 172
174 Ronaldshay, II, 340
175 "Notes on Will of Levi Leiter," Eur. F 112 – 789, Curzon Collection
176 Fraser, *India Under Curzon and After*, p. 488
177 For a complete transcription of Curzon's notes, see Nicolson, pp. 176 – 80
178 Dilks, II, 141
179 *Daily Mirror*, Nov. 3, 1904
180 *Daily Express*, July 19, 1906
181 Mosley, p. 118
182 Nicolson, p. 181
183 Ronaldshay, II, 360
184 Ravensdale, p. 20
185 On Nov. 29, 1904, Nancy married Colin Powys Campbell and on Dec.
    26, 1904, Daisy married Henry Molyneux Paget Howard, 19th Earl
    of Suffolk and Berkshire.
186 Ronaldshay, II, 31 – 32
187 Bradley, pp. 155 – 56
188 Fraser, *India Under Curzon and After*, p. 463
189 Bradley, p. 156
190 *Ibid.* pp. 159 – 60
191 James Pope-Hennessy, *Lord Crewe 1858 – 1945*, p. 164
192 Bradley, pp. 160 – 61
193 *Daily Mail*, July 19, 1906
194 Bradley, p. 162
195 *Ibid.* p. 164
196 *Ibid.* p. 165
197 *Ibid.* p. 162
198 *Servant of India … Sir James Dunlop Smith*, ed. Gilbert Martin, p. 29
199 Michael Edwardes, *High Noon of Empire. India Under Curzon*, p. 243
200 *Ibid.* p. 244
201 Bradley, pp. 168 – 69
202 Nicolson, p. 211
203 Dilks, II, 249
204 *The Times*, July 26, 1906
205 *Life of John Oliver Hobbes*, p. 365
206 "Memories of the Late Lady Curzon," *Daily Telegraph*, July 21, 1906
207 *Cheltenham Newspaper*, July 22, 1906

208 *Daily Express*, July 22, 1906
209 II, 254
210 Rose, p. 286
211 Viscount D'Abernon, *Portraits and Appreciations*, p. 30
212 Mosley, p. xiii
213 Ravensdale, p. 23

BIBLIOGRAPHY

I MANUSCRIPT SOURCES

India Office Library, London:
CANNING, CHARLOTTE. Memorial volume of photographs, newspaper cuttings, letters and souvenirs compiled by Emily Anne Theophila Bayley. Eur. D 661
CURZON COLLECTION. Eur. F 111 and Eur. F 112
EDEN, FRANCES. Four letters dated 1836 – 41 from Frances Eden, and one from Emily Eden, to Elizabeth Copley. Photostat Eur. 10. Originals held by Department of Palaeography and Diplomatic, University of Durham.
EDEN, FRANCES. Private letter-books written from India 1837 – 38. 4 vols. Eur. C 130
LAWRENCE COLLECTION. Eur. F 143
LYALL COLLECTION. Eur. F 132
LYTTON COLLECTION. Eur. F 218
STRACHEY COLLECTION. Eur. F 127

Leeds District Archives, Sheepscar, Leeds:
HAREWOOD COLLECTION, including Charlotte, Countess Canning's letters and journals and miscellaneous items, Lord Canning's papers and diaries and Clanricarde family correspondence.

University of Durham, Department of Palaeography and Diplomatic:
PAPERS OF MARIA, COUNTESS OF GREY

II BOOKS

The following is a selection of all published works consulted, and includes all those cited in the footnotes. Periodicals consulted are listed in the footnotes only.

ABERIGH-MACKAY, GEORGE *Twenty-One Days in India*, 3rd ed., London, 1881

AIRLIE, MABELL, COUNTESS OF *Lady Palmerston and Her Times*. 2 vols. London, 1922

ALEXANDER, WILLIAM *The History of Women from Earliest Antiquity to the Present Time*. London, 1779

ASQUITH, MARGOT *The Autobiography of Margot Asquith*. 2 vols. London, 1920 and 1922

ATKINSON, GEORGE FRANCKLIN *Curry and Rice on Forty Plates* or *The Ingredients of Social Life at "Our Station" in India*, 2nd ed., London, 1859

AUSTEN, JANE *Sense and Sensibility*, 3rd ed, London, 1933

BALFOUR, LADY BETTY *History of Lord Lytton's Indian Administration, 1876 – 80*. London, 1899

BALFOUR, LADY BETTY, ed. *Personal and Literary Letters of Robert, 1st Earl of Lytton*, 2 vols. London, 1906

BALL, CHARLES *The History of the Indian Mutiny*. 2 vols. London, n.d.

BALSAN, CONSUELO VANDERBILT *The Glitter and the Gold*. New York, 1952

BARR, PAT *The Memsahibs. The Women of Victorian India*. London, [1976]

BARR, PAT and RAY DESMOND *Simla. A Hill Station in British India*. London, 1978

[BARTRUM, KATHERINE] *A Widow's Reminiscences of the Siege of Lucknow*. London, 1858

BEARCE, G.D. *British Attitudes Towards India 1784 – 1858*. London, 1961

BENCE-JONES, MARK *The Viceroys of India*. London, 1982

BENSON, A.C. and VISCOUNT ESHER, eds. *The Letters of Queen Victoria 1837 – 61*. 3 vols. London, 1907

BILLINGTON, MARY FRANCES *Woman in India*. London, 1895

BLOOMFIELD, GEORGIANA, BARONESS *Reminiscences of Court and Diplomatic Life*. 2nd ed. 2 vols. London, 1883

BLUNT, WILFRID SCAWEN *Ideas about India*. London, 1885

BLUNT, WILFRID SCAWEN *My Diaries*. Being a Personal Narrative of Events 1888 – 1914. Part One. 1888 – 1900. London, 1921

BRADLEY, JOHN, ed. *Lady Curzon's India*. Letters of a Vicereine. London, 1985

BUCK, EDWARD J. *Simla, Past and Present*. Bombay, 1925

BUCKLE, G.E., ed. *The Letters of Queen Victoria*. 3 vols. London, 1930

BURNE, MAJOR-GENERAL SIR OWEN TUDOR *Memories*. London, 1907

BUTLER, LIEUTENANT-GENERAL SIR W.F. *Life of Sir George Pomeroy-Colley*. London, 1899

CAVENDISH, F.W.H. *Society, Politics and Diplomacy 1820 – 1862*. London, 1913

CECIL, DAVID *Melbourne*. London, 1965

CLIVE, JOHN *Thomas Babington Macaulay. The Shaping of the Historian*. London, 1973

COTTON, SIR HENRY *Indian and Home Memories*. London, 1911

[CUNNINGHAM, SIR HENRY S.] *Chronicles of Dustypore*. London, 1875

CUNNINGHAM, SIR HENRY S. *Earl Canning*. Oxford, 1891

CURZON OF KEDLESTON, MARQUESS *British Government in India*. 2 vols. London, 1925

CURZON OF KEDLESTON, MARCHIONESS [GRACE ELVINA] *Reminiscences*. London, 1955

D'ABERNON, VISCOUNT *Portraits and Appreciations*. London, [1931]

DARLING, SIR MALCOLM *Apprentice to Power. India 1904 – 1908* London, 1966

DICKINSON, VIOLET ed. *Miss Eden's Letters*. London, 1919

DILKS, DAVID *Curzon in India*. 2 vols. London, 1969 and 1970

DIVER, MAUD *Ships of Youth*. London, 1931

DIVER, MAUD *The Englishwoman in India*. Edinburgh, 1909

DUFFERIN, LADY *Our Viceregal Life in India*. 2 vols. London, 1889

DUGDALE, BLANCHE E.C. *Arthur James Balfour*. 2 vols. London, [1936]

DUNBAR, JANET *Golden Interlude. The Edens in India 1836 – 1842*. London, 1955

DUNCAN, SARA JEANNETTE [MRS EVERARD COTES] *The Simple Adventures of a Memsahib* London, 1893

DUNCAN, SARA JEANNETTE *His Honour and a Lady*. Toronto, 1896

DUNCAN, SARA JEANNETTE *The Pool in the Desert*. New York, 1903

DURAND, SIR MORTIMER *Life of the Right Honourable Sir Alfred Comyn Lyall*. London, 1913

EARLE, MRS C.W. [THERESA] *Memoirs and Memories*. London, 1911

EDEN, THE HON. EMILY *Letters from India*. Edited by her niece. 2 vols. London, 1872

EDEN, EMILY *The Semi-Attached Couple and the Semi-Detached House*. Reprinted. London, 1983

EDEN, EMILY *Portraits of the Princes and People of India*. London, 1844

EDEN, EMILY *Up the Country*. Letters Written to Her Sister from the Upper

Provinces of India [1866]. Reprinted. London, 1983

EDWARDES, MICHAEL *Bound to Exile. The Victorians in India.* London, 1969

EDWARDES, MICHAEL *Glorious Sahibs* The Romantic as Empire-Builder 1799 – 1838. London, 1968

EDWARDES, MICHAEL *High Noon of Empire: India Under Curzon.* London, [1965]

EDWARDES, MICHAEL *A History of India.* From the Earliest Times to the Present Day. London, 1961

EDWARDES, MICHAEL *Raj: The Story of British India 1772 – 1947.* London, 1969

[ELLIS, MRS SARAH] *The Wives of England.* London, 1843

[ELLIS, MRS SARAH] *The Women of England.* 12 ed. London, 1839

FANE, H.E. *Five Years in India.* 2 vols. London, 1842

FINCH, EDITH *Wilfrid Scawen Blunt* London, 1938

FITZMAURICE, LORD EDMOND *The Life of Granville George Leveson-Gower, Second Earl Granville.* 2 vols. London, 1905

FORDYCE, REV. JAMES *Sermons to Young Women,* 4th ed. London, 1767

FORSTER, E.M. *A Passage to India.* Harmondsworth, 1985

FRASER, LOVAT *At Delhi.* Bombay, [1903]

FRASER, LOVAT *India Under Curzon and After.* London, 1912

FULFORD, ROGER *The Prince Consort.* London, 1949

FULFORD, ROGER and LYTTON STRACHEY, eds. *The Greville Memoirs.* 8 vols. London, 1938

GILBERT, MARTIN, ed. *Servant of India.* A Study of Imperial Rule from 1905 to 1910 as told through the Correspondence and Diaries of Sir James Dunlop Smith, London, 1966

GOLANT, WILLIAM *The Long Afternoon.* British India 1601 – 1947. London, 1975

GREGORY, DR JOHN *A Father's Legacy to His Daughters.* 2nd ed. London, 1775

GRIFFIN, SIR LEPAL *Ranjit Singh and the Sikh Barrier Between Our Growing Empire and Central Asia.* Oxford, 1905

GWYNN, STEPHEN, ed. *The Letters and Friendships of Sir Cecil Spring Rice.* A Record. 2 vols. London, 1929

HAMILTON, LORD FREDERIC *The Days Before Yesterday.* London, n.d.

HARE, AUGUSTUS J.C. *The Story of Two Noble Lives.* Being Memorials of Charlotte, Countess Canning and Louisa, Marchioness of Waterford. 3 vols. London, 1893

HARLAN, AURELIA BROOKS *Owen Meredith.* A Critical Biography of Robert,

First Earl of Lytton. New York, 1946

HETT, FRANCIS PAGET, ed. *The Memoirs of Susan Sibbald*. London, 1926

HIBBERT, CHRISTOPHER *The Great Mutiny*. London, 1978

HIGGINBOTHAM, J.J. *Men Whom India Has Known*. Biographies of Eminent Indian Characters. 2nd ed., Madras, 1874

HOBBES, JOHN OLIVER [PEARL CRAIGIE] *Imperial India*. Letters from the East. London, 1903

HOBBES, JOHN OLIVER [PEARL CRAIGIE] *The Life of John Oliver Hobbes Told in her Correspondence with Numerous Friends*. London, 1911

HUSSEY, CHRISTOPHER *Life of Sir Edwin Lutyens*. London, 1950

JOHNSON, GEORGE W *The Stranger in India* or *Three Years in Calcutta*. 2 vols. London, 1843

KEMBLE, FRANCES ANNE *Records of Later Life*. 3 vols. London, 1882

KENRICK, WILLIAM *The Whole Duty of Woman*. Philadelphia, 1788

KINCAID, DENNIS *British Social Life in India 1608 – 1937* 2nd ed., London, 1973

KING, PETER, ed. *A Viceroy's India*. Leaves from Lord Curzon's Note-Book. London, 1984

KIPLING, RUDYARD *Rudyard Kipling's Verse*. Definitive Edition. London, 1940

LAWRENCE, SIR WALTER ROPER *The India We Served*. London, 1928

LEVER, TRESHAM, ed. *The Letters of Lady Palmerston*. London, 1957

LEVESON-GOWER, THE HON. F., ed. *Letters of Harriet, Countess of Granville*. 2 vols. London, 1894

LEWIS, LADY THERESA, ed. *Extracts of the Journals and Correspondence of Miss Berry*. 3 vols. London, 1865

LINTON, ELIZA LYNN *The Girl of the Period and Other Social Essays*. London, 1883

LONGFORD, ELIZABETH. *A Pilgrimage of Passion. The Life of Wilfrid Scawen Blunt* London, 1979

LUTYENS, LADY EMILY *The Birth of Rowland*. An Exchange of Letters in 1865 between Robert Lytton and His Wife. London, 1956

LUTYENS, LADY EMILY *A Blessed Girl*. London, 1953

LUTYENS, MARY, ed. *Lady Lytton's Court Diary 1895 – 1899*. London, 1961

LUTYENS, MARY *The Lyttons in India*. An Account of Lord Lytton's Viceroyalty 1876 – 1880. London, 1979

[LYTTON, EDITH, LADY] *India 1876 – 1880*. Privately printed. London, 1899

[LYTTON, EARL OF] *Poems of Owen Meredith*. Selected, with an introd. by M. Betham-Edwards. London, n.d.

LYTTON, EARL OF (OWEN MEREDITH) *Selected Poems*. Selected and with an introd. by Betty Balfour. London, 1894

LYTTON, 4TH EARL OF *Wilfrid Scawen Blunt*. A Memoir by his grandson. London, 1961

MACKENZIE, MRS COLIN *Life in the Mission, the Camp and the Zenana*. 3 vols. London, 1853

MACLAGAN, MICHAEL *'Clemency' Canning*. London, 1962

MACONACHIE, [SIR] EVAN *Life in the Indian Civil Service*. London, 1926

MAISON, MARGARET *John Oliver Hobbes. Her Life and Work*. London, 1976

[MAITLAND, JULIA CHARLOTTE] *Letters from Madras During the Years 1836 – 1839*. By a Lady. London, 1846

MAXWELL, THE RIGHT HON. SIR HERBERT *The Life and Letters of George William Frederick, Fourth Earl of Clarendon*. 2 vols. London, 1913

MENPES, MORTIMER *The Durbar*. London, 1903

MERSEY, VISCOUNT *The Viceroys and Governors-General of India 1757 – 1947*. London, 1949

MIDLETON, EARL OF [ST JOHN BRODRICK] *Records and Reactions 1856 – 1939*. London, 1939

MITFORD, NANCY, ed. *The Stanleys of Alderley*. London, 1939

MOORHOUSE, GEOFFREY *India Britannica*. London, 1984

MORE, HANNAH *Strictures on the Modern System of Female Education*. 11th ed., London, 1811

MORE, HANNAH *Hints Toward Forming the Character of a Young Princess*. London, 1805

MORLEY, VISCOUNT [JOHN] *Recollections*. 2 vols. London, 1917

MULOCK, DINAH MARIA (MRS CRAIK) *A Woman's Thoughts About Women* London, 1891

MOSLEY, L. *Curzon. The End of an Epoch*. London, 1960

NEHRU, JAWAHARLAL *The Discovery of India*. New York, 1946

NEVILL, RALPH, ed. *Life and Letters of Lady Dorothy Nevill*. London, 1919

NICOLSON, HAROLD *Curzon: The Last Phase 1919 – 1925*. London, 1934

NICOLSON, NIGEL *Mary Curzon*. London, 1977

NORTH, MARIANNE *Recollections of a Happy Life*. 2 vols. London, 1892

OSBORNE, HON. W.G. *The Court and Camp of Runjeet Sing*. London, 1840

PAGET, WALBURGA, LADY *Embassies of Other Days and Further Recollections*. 2 vols. London, 1923

PAGET, WALBURGA, LADY *The Linings of Life*. London, 1928

PAGET, WALBURGA, LADY *Scenes and Memories*. London, 1912

[PARKES, FANNY] *Wanderings of a Pilgrim in search of the picturesque, during four-and-twenty years in the east; with revelations of Life in the Zenana*. 2 vols. London, 1850

PARRY, BENITA *Delusions and Discoveries*. Studies on India in the British Imagination 1880 – 1930. London, 1972

PINNEY, THOMAS, ed. *The Letters of Thomas Babington Macaulay*. Vol. IV. Cambridge, 1977

POPE-HENNESSY, JAMES *Lord Crewe*. 1858 – 1945. The Likeness of a Liberal. London, 1955

POSTANS, MRS *Western India in 1838*. 2 vols. London, 1839

PRINSEP, VAL CÅ *Imperial India. An Artist's Journals*. London, 1879

REED, HENRY, ed. *The Greville Memoirs*. A Journal of the Reign of Queen Victoria from 1837 to 1852. By the Late Charles C.F. Greville. 3 vols. London, 1885

REED, SIR STANLEY *The India I Knew 1897 – 1947*. London, 1952

RAVENSDALE, BARONESS [MARY IRENE CURZON] *In Many Rhythms*. An Autobiography. London, 1953

RAYMOND, E. NEILL *Victorian Viceroy*. The Life of Robert, First Earl of Lytton. London, 1980

ROBERTS, FIELD-MARSHAL LORD *Forty-One Years in India*. 2 vols. London, 1897

ROBERTS, FRED [afterwards FIELD-MARSHAL EARL ROBERTS] *Letters Written During the Indian Mutiny*. London, 1924

RONALDSHAY, EARL OF *The Life of Lord Curzon*. 3 vols. London, 1928

ROSE, KENNETH *Superior Person*. A Portrait of Curzon and His Circle in late Victorian England. London, 1969

RUSKIN, JOHN *The Works of John Ruskin: Sesame and Lilies. The Ethics of the Dust*. London, 1907

SALE, LADY [FLORENTIA] *A Journal of the Disasters in Afghanistan, 1841 – 2*. London, 1843

SANDFORD, MRS ELIZABETH *Woman in Her Social and Domestic Character*. 6th ed. London, 1839

SLEEMAN, MAJOR-GENERAL SIR W.H. *Rambles and Recollections of an Indian Official*. 2 vols. London, 1893

SMITH, NOWELL C., ed. *The Letters of Sydney Smith*. 2 vols. Oxford, 1953

STANFORD, J.K. *Ladies in the Sun: The Memsahib's India. 1790 – 1860*. London, 1962

STEEL, FLORA ANNIE *The Garden of Fidelity: Being the Autobiography of Flora*

Annie Steel, 1847 – 1929. London, 1929

STEEL, FLORA ANNIE *The Hosts of the Lord*. London, 1900

STEEL, FLORA ANNIE *Miss Stuart's Legacy*. 3 vols. London, 1893

STEEVENS, G.W. *In India*. London, n.d.

STEPHEN, LESLIE *The Life of Sir James Fitzjames Stephen*. London, 1895

STIRLING, MRS A.M.W. *Victorian Sidelights*. From the Papers of the late Mrs Adams-Acton. London, 1954

STRAFFORD, ALICE, COUNTESS OF *Leaves from the Diary of Henry Greville*. 4 vols. London, 1905

STUART-WORTLEY, HON. MRS EDWARD *Highcliffe and the Stuarts*. London, 1927

SUDELEY, LORD, ed. *The Lieven-Palmerston Correspondence, 1828 – 56*. London, 1943

SURTEES, VIRGINIA *Charlotte Canning*. London, 1975

TEMPLE, SIR RICHARD *Men and Events of my Time in India*. London, 1882

TEMPLE, SIR RICHARD *The Story of My Life*. 2 vols. London, 1896

THACKERAY, WILLIAM MAKEPEACE *The Newcomes*. 2 vols. London, 1965

TROTTER, CAPTAIN L.J. *The Earl of Auckland*. Oxford, 1893

VILLIERS, GEORGE *A Vanished Victorian*. Being the Life of George Villiers, Fourth Earl of Clarendon 1800 – 1870. London, 1938

WALEY, S.D. *Edwin Montagu. A Memoir and an Account of his Visits to India*. Bombay, 1964

WARWICK, FRANCES, COUNTESS OF *Afterthoughts*. London, 1931

WHEELER, J. TALBOYS *The History of the Imperial Assemblage at Delhi*. London, [1877]

WILSON, LADY [ANNE] *Letters from India* [1911] London, 1984

WINGFIELD-STRATFORD, BARBARA *India and the English*. London, 1922

WOODRUFF, PHILIP (pseudonym for PHILIP MASON) *The Men Who Ruled India*. I. *The Founders*. II. *The Guardians*. London, 1953 and 1954

PICTURE CREDITS

The following captions apply to the chapter opening photographs:

I, 1   Portrait of Emily Eden, with Chance (by F. Rochard, 1835)
II, 17   Lady Canning, Calcutta, 1861
III, 31   Portrait of Edith Villiers, afterwards Lady Lytton. (by G.F. Watts, 1862)
IV, 42   Photo of Lady Curzon in her peacock dress, 1903